CORRUPTI$N,
GOOD GOVERNANCE
and
ECONOMIC DEVELOPMENT
Contemporary Analysis and Case Studies

CORRUPTI$N, GOOD GOVERNANCE and ECONOMIC DEVELOPMENT

Contemporary Analysis and Case Studies

Editors

R. N. Ghosh & M. A. B. Siddique

University of Western Australia Business School, Australia

World Scientific

NEW JERSEY · LONDON · SINGAPORE · BEIJING · SHANGHAI · HONG KONG · TAIPEI · CHENNAI

Published by

World Scientific Publishing Co. Pte. Ltd.
5 Toh Tuck Link, Singapore 596224
USA office: 27 Warren Street, Suite 401-402, Hackensack, NJ 07601
UK office: 57 Shelton Street, Covent Garden, London WC2H 9HE

Library of Congress Cataloging-in-Publication Data
Corruption, good governance and economic development : contemporary analysis and case studies /
[edited] by R.N. Ghosh (University of Western Australia Business School, Australia), Md Abu Bakar
Siddique (University of Western Australia Business School, Australia).
   pages cm
   Papers presented in two major international conferences, one held at the University of Western
Australia in Perth (Australia) in June, 2009, and the other that followed in Kolkata (India) in
December, 2009.
   Includes bibliographical references and index.
   ISBN 978-9814612586 (alk. paper)
   1. Political corruption--Developing countries--Congresses. 2. Sustainable development--
Developing countries--Congresses. 3. Economic development--Developing countries--Congresses.
I. Ghosh, R. N. (Robin N.) II. Siddique, Md. Abu Bakar.
   JF1525.C66C6753 2015
   338.9009172'4--dc23

                 2014035256

British Library Cataloguing-in-Publication Data
A catalogue record for this book is available from the British Library.

In-house Editors: Sutha Surenddar/Rajni Gamage

Typeset by Stallion Press
Email: enquiries@stallionpress.com

Printed in Singapore

Acknowledgments

In preparing this volume of the papers from the two international conferences, held in Perth and in Kolkata in 2009, we received support and encouragement from a wide range of people. We wish to record our deepest debt of gratitude to all. In particular, we wish to mention the names of Ken Clements and Michael McLure, Reginald Appleyard and Rony Gabbay from the Business School at UWA, who offered unqualified support from the beginning of the project. Gautam Chakrabarti, who was Commissioner of Police in Kolkata, Surajit Kar Purkayastha (then Inspector General of Police in Kolkata) and Professor Amit Chatterjee (then the Principal at MM College in Kolkata), worked tirelessly to organize the Kolkata Conference in December, 2009.

The preparation of the final manuscript was delayed because of various other professional commitments of the two editors. But in the preparation of the final typescript we received total support of the Administrative Team of Economics, UWA Business School including Ms. Ha Le, Ms. Anna Wiechecki, Ms. Aya Kelly and Ms. Isabela Banea; and Ms. Rebecca Doran-Wu, Research Assistant, Economics, UWA Business School. Special thanks are also extended to Ms. Danielle Figg, Team Manager, Economics, UWA Business School for her assistance in finalizing the manuscript in collaboration with her efficient team members.

We acknowledge our debt of gratitude to all our colleagues in the Economics Discipline at the Business School at UWA.

Finally, a word of thanks to our publishers who were able to publish the Volume in a very short time after receiving the final typescript.

Business School   R. N. Ghosh and M. A. B. Siddique
The University of Western Australia,   Editors
   Crawley, WA, 6009   December, 2014
Australia

List of Figures

List of Tables

List of Contributors

Aldcroft, Derek H.
Department of Economics and Social History,
The University of Leicester, UK

Chakrabarti, Gautam M.
Formerly, Commissioner of Police, Kolkata, India

Ghosh, Robin N.
Senior Honorary Research Fellow, Economics,
Business School,
The University of Western Australia, Australia

Hossain, Amzad
Honorary Research Fellow,
School of Sustainability, Murdoch University, Western Australia,
Australia

Marinova, Dora
Professor and Associate Director,
Curtin University, Sustainability Policy Institute, Western Australia,
Australia

Purkayastha, Surajit Kar
Commissioner of Kolkata Police, India
State of West Bengal, India

Pradiptyo, Rimawan
Lecturer, Department of Economics, Faculty of Economics and Business,
Universitas Gadjah Mada, Indonesia

Setiyono, Budi
Department of Government, Faculty of Social and Political Science,
Diponegoro University,
Indonesia

Siddique, M. A. B.
Associate Professor,
Business School,
The University of Western Australia, Australia

Torodov, Vladislav
Vice Dean of the Faculty of Business Management,
University of Forestry, Bulgaria

Willams, Andrew
Assistant Professor, Economics,
The University of Western Australia Business School,
The University of Western Australia, Australia

Contents

Part 1

Corruption, Crime and Economic Growth

Chapter 1

Introduction

R. N. Ghosh and M. A. B. Siddique

I

The question may be asked, why is it important to discuss good governance as a prerequisite for sustainable and environmentally friendly development?

The answer to the above question lies in the historical experience of failure to achieve economic growth by many countries of Africa, Asia and Latin America in the past several decades. Since the end of World War II, the economic literature on development focused attention on key economic and demographic variables that affect development. For example, it was argued, following W. A. Lewis, that low income countries did not generate sufficient domestic savings (and investment) to bring about the necessary transformation from a low to a high income economy. Hence it was argued that such low income countries needed foreign capital and know-how to overcome the savings bottle-neck. However, despite the flow of massive amounts of foreign capital to many low income countries in Asia and Africa, many of these countries failed to record any significant improvement in the standards of living of the people. Injection of foreign aid from the international financial institutions and the OECD countries had only significantly benefited minority and vested groups, who held political and economic power, in many of the low income countries. These minority and privileged groups spent their wealth on "conspicuous" consumption of imported luxury goods; and they also engineered to spend huge amounts of money on military hardware and unproductive defense services in order to project an image of major military powers; or they spent money on "monument-building" activity such as building ultra-modern towns with luxury buildings and skyscrapers for the elite class.

Demographic factors were also cited in literature to explain why low income countries were unable to develop rapidly and reach the "take off" stage. An increase in real per capita income in a country of, say, 3% every year would be completely offset by an annual population increase of 3%. Therefore, it may be argued that a strict population control policy may be the answer to overturn the process of a very slow rate of economic growth in the less developed countries. Indeed, these countries were faced with "population explosion", not so much due to an increase in the birth rate but due to a dramatic decline in the death rate in the post-colonial period of the 1950s and 1960s.

However, the general theory of the demographic transition states that economic development itself, in its initial stage, causes a spurt in population growth, and that the birth rate would tend to decline, — along with the decline in the mortality rate, — as the process of development would reach from an initial to its final stage. While population control policy is an essential requirement for sustainable development, it is now recognized that such policy in itself, however effective it is, would not be a sufficient condition for economic growth.

By the early 1990s, there was a consensus among economists and political scientists that the failure of economic development to take place in many countries of Africa and Asia must be explained in some other way. In 1992, the World Bank published its report on *Governance and Development* in which it focused its attention on the topic of governance as a necessary precondition for development. In that Report the World Bank explored the meaning of governance and why it was important for long-term sustainable development. The Bank defined governance to mean the manner in which power was exercised in the management of a country's economic and social resources for development. The 1992 Report of the World Bank concluded that if sustainable development was to take place, a transparent and predictable framework of rules and institutions for the conduct of public and private business must exist.

In a subsequent report entitled *Governance: The World Bank's Experience* (1994), it was stated that "Good Governance is epitomized by predictable, open, and enlightened policymaking (that is, transparent processes); a bureaucracy involved with a professional ethos; an executive arm of government accountable for its actions; and a strong civil society participating in public affairs; and all behaving under the rule of law".

Indeed, it is possible to argue that good governance would need the three arms of government, viz. the executive, the legislature and the judiciary to have separation of powers. These three arms should work independently of one another; and work in a transparent manner.

Following the lead of the World Bank, a general consensus has now emerged that good governance is an important element in a complex process of economic change. Savings and investments, and population control measures cannot sustain development without efficient management of resources through good governance. To achieve a long-term process of development it is necessary to have an open, transparent and accountable administration that is free from corruption. In other words, good governance is the key to sustainable development.

II

The papers included in this volume were presented in two major international conferences, one held at the University of Western Australia (UWA) in Perth (Australia) in June, 2009, and the other that followed in Kolkata (India) in December, 2009.

The two international conferences were able to bring together a large number of participants from many countries, mainly from South and South-East Asia. Many of the participants included high officials from Australia and Asia. Thanks to a very modest contribution made by AusAid in Canberra, it was possible for the organizers of the Perth Conference to invite some distinguished participants.

The main theme of the two conferences was whether or not corruption in public office (or, in other words, the absence of good governance) might inhibit economic growth in a country. The general theme was considered in a major paper by Robin Ghosh and Abu Siddique. Although Ghosh and Siddique were primarily interested in exploring the various quantitative measures of corruption, the conclusion emerging from their paper pointed towards the long-term evil effects of corruption but argued that a limited level of petty corruption did not necessarily have an adverse impact on economic growth, at least in the short-term. In his paper on "Corruption in Bangladesh", Abu Siddique argued that corruption could lead to misallocation of resources, or be harmful to innovation, thereby inhibiting long-term growth.

Corruption would of course adversely affect the poorer sections of a community who would be asked to pay a bribe to get essential services like water, electricity, and health and educational services. In other words, the economic burden of corruption is disproportionately high on the economically disadvantaged people.

It is not easy to define corruption easily. Basically, if a person uses his/her public office to make private gains, it would be considered as an act of corruption. The widely accepted definition of corruption was given by UNDP in 1999 to refer to "the misuse of public power, office or authority for private benefit — through bribery, extortion, influence peddling, nepotism, fraud, speed money or embezzlement". By definition, then, one cannot be corrupt if he/she did not have an authority to make private gains. Therefore, very poor people who hold no public office of any influence cannot be corrupt.

Indeed, corruption was widespread in the West, prior to full industrialization that led to very substantial improvements in the standards of living of the ordinary people. Petty corruption virtually disappeared in the developed countries of the West only after a very significant long-term rise in real incomes and standards of living. It is possible to argue that corruption cannot be weeded out by legislation and political posturing.

A negative impact of corruption is that it is inevitably linked with crime and eventually with the corruption of the judiciary. In a brilliant paper, Rimawan Pradiptyo has examined how corruption has spread widely in Indonesia. Pradiptyo has done a high level of original empirical research to establish his case with reference to his country.

A major finding of Pradiptyo is that the sentences passed by the judges in corruption cases in Indonesia are generally lenient towards defendants with particular occupations but harsher toward others. The Concluding chapter contains a more detailed summary of Pradiptyo's paper.

Derek Aldcroft's paper is the only one in the volume on Africa. He examines how what he calls negative sovereignty in many countries of Africa has impacted on good governance. He concludes that despite a very bleak picture in recent years, Africa has a great potential and that it is a rich continent both in terms of natural and human resources.

The volume includes two similar papers from two senior officials from the Police Service in West Bengal, Gautam Chakravarti (who was the Commissioner of Police in Kolkata, India) and Surajit Kar Purkayastha (who was the Inspector General of Police in West Bengal, India). In the papers they presented, they examined the regional variations in the level and impact of corruption in India. Kar Purkayastha conducts a sample survey of a cross-section of the people to find out the community's perception of the interrelations between crime and corruption. Chakrabarti also conducts a similar sample survey.

During the discussion sessions in Kolkata in December, 2009, it became apparent that the participants in the Conference had differing views on the prevalence of corruption in India. While Robin Ghosh took the position that there was a positive correlation between appalling poverty of the people and the level of corruption, especially petty corruption, other participants took the view that the poor people are generally more honest and more God-fearing than those who are supposedly in the middle class with a better exposition to education.

III

The present volume contains a total of 10 papers. All these papers were sent to independent reviewers for assessment and then selected for publication. All authors were given an opportunity to revise their own papers before the final publication of the volume.

In presenting this volume to general readers, we are aware of the wide range of topics and areas covered in it. However, the present volume must be seen as a continuation of the research work that has been carried on by a group of dedicated researchers at the Business School at the UWA. With a modest seed grant from AusAid in Canberra in the 1990s, a small group of economists at UWA began to search for the interrelations between good governance and economic development. Such research efforts led to the organization of an international seminar in Perth in 1996. The purpose of this seminar was to bring together leading experts from many disciplines and professions to discuss "Governance Issues and Sustainable Development in the Indian Ocean Rim Countries".

The Seminar in 1996 led to a major publication entitled *Good Governance Issues and Sustainable Development: The Indian Ocean Region* (Atlantic Publishers, 1999). The present volume is complementary to the research work that was done earlier and led to the publication in 1999. The conclusion emerging from the present study is that good governance is probably an essential precondition, though not a sufficient condition, for a long-term sustainable and eco-friendly economic growth in a country.

In presenting this volume to the general public, we hope that the diverse issues raised by the different authors would provide food for thought and lead to further discussions on how crime and corruption could be prevented by good governance and thereby create a suitable environment for sustainable development.

We do regret the long delay in bringing out this publication so long — nearly 5 years after the two international conferences were held, one in Perth and the other in Kolkata. Despite this delay, we hope the papers in the present volume have considerable relevance to the situation prevailing in many of the countries of Asia and Africa today.

Chapter 2

Some Quantitative Measures of Corruption

R. N. Ghosh and M. A. B. Siddique*

UWA Business School

Abstract

The word "corruption" has a moral as well as a *qualitative* connotation. Corruption is immoral and therefore it has to be stamped out. In this chapter, we discuss some of the *quantitative* measures of corruption. The Transparency International (TI) has developed several measures. The most popular measure is known as the Corruption Perceptions Index (CPI).

The TI produces another measure of corruption known as the Global Corruption Barometer (GCB). A third measure is known as the Bribe Payers Index (BPI), which assesses the supply side of corruption and ranks corruption by source country and industry sector.

The World Bank corruption index is known as the Control of Corruption Index (CCI). Yet another measure of corruption known as the International Country Risk Guide (ICRG) has been published on a monthly basis since 1980 by what is known as the PRS Group.

A final measure that is discussed in this chapter is known as the Opacity Index (OI). This index was produced for the first time in 2001, by the PricewaterhouseCoopers (PwC).

Keywords: Corruption, Transparency International, Corruption Perception Index (CPI), Global Corruption Barometer (GCB), Bribe Payers Index (BPI), World Bank, PricewaterhouseCoopers, PRS Group.

*We wish to thank Rebecca Doran-Wu, UWA Business School, for her excellent research assistance in preparing this chapter.

The Concept and Measurement of Corruption

The concept of corruption

Corruption refers to "the misuse of public power, office, or authority for private benefit — through bribery, extortion, influence peddling, nepotism, fraud, speed money or embezzlement" (United Nations Development Programme, 1999, New York, UNDP). When corruption is thus defined, it has a distinct moral and qualitative connotation. No matter what, corruption is immoral and therefore it has to be routed out.

However, in real life, we have to make a distinction between 'grand' and 'petty' corruption. While a 'grand' corruption involving rich and influential people who accept millions of dollars as bribery, or who accept enormous gifts in kind, is to be unequivocally condemned, it is not certain that a level of 'petty' corruption to get a job done, without red-tape, is to be regarded as totally unacceptable. Indeed, many of the developing countries which poorly rank in any corruption index fall behind many developed countries, not because of so much more 'grand' corruption but because of 'petty' corruption that poorly paid public officials or individuals with some authority take as 'grease money'. Such 'petty' levels of corruption have existed in many societies and cultures from time immemorial. 'Petty' corruption has the same lineage as the tradition of giving '*nazrana*' in the Indian sub-continent. For example, the practice of a supplier offering some sweets to an official who has the authority to pass the bills for payment is not totally condemned in some cultures.

Corruption is by no means confined to public officials. Individuals in private companies may also take bribes to provide goods and services if these are in short supply. Scarcity leads to rationing and rationing encourages corruption. If all services and goods were available in plenty, there would be less room for both taking and giving bribes.

Unfortunately, over the past two decades, the World Bank and the IMF have increasingly used the definition of corruption in a uniform manner in all countries, irrespective of widely different cultural practices. Again, there are many financial practices which are corrupt and immoral, but when approved by a government in power are not regarded as corrupt. Switzerland, for example, is generally regarded as a country with little corruption. Yet Switzerland's banking system, under authority from the

Swiss Government, provides a haven for massive amounts of ill-gotten and corrupt sources of funds from all over the world. It is only recently that the Swiss Government has begun to tighten controls over the flow of illegal money. A similar situation exists in Singapore.

Corruption at all levels of government — the executive, the legislature and the judiciary — are now relatively uncommon in most developed countries, although some public officials are still brought to justice for acting corruptly. But in many of the developing countries corruption exists at all levels of government, and it is sometimes very difficult to get a job done, such as procuring a license for an activity, without offering bribes, in cash or in kind, to layers of public officials.

Now, the question is: does corruption have an inhibitive impact on economic growth and development? The question has been widely examined in economic literature in the past three decades. For the first few years, opinions of the experts were divided; but in more recent years, there is a growing consensus that high levels of continuing corruption tend to be inimical to long-term growth.

However, it is possible to argue the other way round. Most developed countries seem to experience much lower levels of corruption in both government and non-government agencies than in comparable agencies in developing countries. If this is so (and we will see later that all quantitative measures of corruption confirm it), we could argue that corruption is a by-product of poverty and underdevelopment, and that development itself provides an automatic mechanism to reduce (or eliminate) corruption. It is certainly arguable that when the general population in a country becomes more and more affluent with economic growth and development, they are less tempted towards 'petty' levels of corruption.

In brief, it is difficult to define corruption in a manner that would apply to all countries. What is regarded as corruption in one country may be regarded as part of a normal transaction in another country with a different cultural heritage. However, it is possible to argue that many types of 'petty' corruption are bred in an atmosphere of poverty and economic scarcity. Therefore, economic development, which leads to an eradication of poverty and also ensures a plentiful supply of goods and services, is the likely long-term solution for the lower levels of corruption in many backward countries where corruption is sometimes a necessity for survival.

The measurement of corruption

Corruption Perceptions Index (CPI)

A Berlin-based organization known as the Transparency International (TI) developed an index in 1995 to rank the level of corruption in different countries. This index is now produced annually and is known as the Corruption Perceptions Index (CPI). In its CPI produced for the year 2008, TI ranked more than 180 countries. In preparing its annual CPI, TI receives reports from its own network of personnel and also from many independent institutions: for example, TI relies on data and statistics provided by institutions such as the Economist Intelligence Unit, Freedom House, Political and Economic Risk Consultancy and many others. TI requires at least three different sources to be available in order to rank a country in the CPI. In its early years, TI used to rely on public opinion surveys, but now only uses 'experts' to compile its data base.

As the CPI is based on polls and surveys from different institutions, the results are subjective and are, strictly speaking, not uniform. Presumably, the information given by TI is less reliable for countries with fewer independent sources. It is also important to remember that the index is based on 'perception' rather than on actual 'experience'; so, the index does not provide any information about the actual level of corruption in a country. Moreover, as the CPI is constructed by compiling information from different sources, statistics for different countries and for different years are not strictly comparable. However, despite all these limitations, CPI is a widely accepted tool to rank countries in terms of the levels of corruption.

In preparing the CPI, TI uses a scale of 1 to 10 to measure corruption. A high score means less corruption; and the lower the score, the higher the level of corruption in a country. Table 2.1 summarizes the CPI ranking of some selected countries in 2008.

It is to be noted from Table 2.1 that; (1) most developed countries have a low ranking in corruption, as compared with the poor and developing countries; (2) there are exceptions to (1), for example, Russia was ranked as No. 154, i.e., a lower rank than both Bangladesh and Pakistan in the 2010 CPI; (3) Somalia was ranked 178 in 2010, the lowest in CPI ranking; and (4) Mainland China and India — two of the fastest growing

Table 2.1   CPI ranking of selected countries in 2010
(Prepared by Transparency International)

Rank	Country	2010 (Score)
1	Denmark	9.3
1	New Zealand	9.3
1	Singapore	9.3
4	Finland	9.2
5	Sweden	9.2
8	Australia	8.7
8	Switzerland	8.7
20	UK	7.6
22	USA	7.1
78	China (People's Republic)	3.5
87	India	3.3
91	Sri Lanka	3.2
110	Indonesia	2.8
134	Bangladesh	2.4
143	Pakistan	2.3

Source: Transparency International.

countries in the world still had a comparatively low ranking in CPI — 78
and 87 respectively in 2010.

Global Corruption Barometer

TI produces another measure of corruption known as the Global
Corruption Barometer (GCB). GCB is intended to indicate how and where
the ordinary people feel the impact of corruption. This Global Corruption
Barometer is a public opinion survey based on responses to questionnaires
asked in interviews to a sample population. The Barometer has been produced annually around the world since 2003. The questionnaire that is
circulated is intended to find out, among other things, the general public's
attitudes to corruption, the extent to which the public believe that corruption pervades public institutions, their own experience (not perception)

with petty bribery in their pursuits of daily activity, and how they think that corruption could be weeded out.

Some of the questions included in the questionnaire of 2007 were as follows:

1. Do you expect the level of corruption in the next three years in this country to change?
2. How would you assess your current government's actions in the fight against corruption?
3. To what extent do you perceive the following categories in this country to be affected by corruption? (This question is followed by a list of sectors: political parties, legislature, private sector, judiciary, police, military, educational system, medical services and so on).
4. In the past 12 months have you or anyone living in your household been requested a bribe from someone in the following institution/organization? (This is followed by a list of sectors similar to under question 3).

The Global Corruption Barometer (GCB) in 2007 was based on an interview of 63,199 people in 60 countries and territories between June and September 2007.

Some of the key findings of the GCB (2007) are:

(a) The poor and economically deprived sections of the population in both developed and developing countries are the worst victims of corruption whether in public or private agencies.
(b) About 10% of the people around the world had to actually pay a bribe in the year before the interview; and corruption was reported to have increased in the Asia-Pacific region and in South East Europe.
(c) Bribery is widely prevalent in public institutions, especially in inter-actions with the police and the judiciary.
(d) Half of those interviewed believe that their government's efforts to fight corruption are not very successful.

The Global Corruption Barometer (GCB) of 2010 confirmed the view that corruption adversely affected the poorer sections of the community who had to pay a bribe to get essential services like water, electricity and

Table 2.2　Countries most affected by Bribery: GCB 2010

Percentage of respondents reporting they paid a bribe to obtain a service

Quintile	Countries and Territories
Top Quintile: more than 50%	Afghanistan, Cambodia, Cameroon, India, Iraq, Liberia, Nigeria, Palestine, Senegal, Sierra Leone, Uganda
Second Quintile: 30–49.9%	Azerbaijan, Bolivia, El Salvador, Ghana, Kenya, Lebanon, Lithuania, Mexico, Moldova, Mongolia, Pakistan, Ukraine, Vietnam, Zambia
Third Quintile: 20–29.9%	Armenia, Belarus, Bosnia & Herzegovina, Chile, Colombia, Hungary, FYR Macedonia, Papua New Guinea, Peru, Romania, Russia, Solomon Islands, Thailand, Turkey, Venezuela
Fourth Quintile: 6–19.9%	Argentina, Austria, Bulgaria, China, Czech Republic, Fiji, France, Greece, Indonesia, Italy, Japan, Kosovo, Latvia, Luxembourg, Malaysia, Poland, Philippines, Finland, Serbia, Singapore, Taiwan, Vanuatu
Bottom Quintile: Less than 6%	Australia, Brazil, Canada, Croatia, Denmark, Finland, Georgia, Germany, Hong Kong, Iceland, Ireland, Israel, Korea (South), Netherlands, New Zealand, Norway, Portugal, Slovenia, Spain, Switzerland, United Kingdom, United States

Source: Transparency International, 2010.

health and educational services. In other words, the economic burden of corruption acts as a regressive tax on the poor people in a country, whether it is developed or developing. Another significant conclusion emerging from the GCB (2010) is that the public view many of the governmental instrumentalities such as the legislature, the police and the judiciary as the most tainted by corruption around the world.

The GCB also points out the extensive prevalence of 'petty' corruption in many of the developing countries. Widespread corruption tends to undermine the legitimacy of government institutions in many countries.

What is significant is to note that the GCB (2010) gives a pessimistic view of the future. Steps taken by governments to fight corruption are generally ineffective. Moreover, the general consensus seems to be that the level of corruption, far from decreasing, will probably increase in the future.

By the end of 2007, across the world, 104 governments had ratified or acceded to the United Nations Convention against Corruption. But the public opinion still seems to be that in many countries the anti-corruption measures are more cosmetic than real in effectiveness. Hence there is an urgent need for reviewing the various anti-corruption measures world-wide. Historically, developed countries of today experienced high levels of corruption in the early years of development and industrialization. These countries were able to have control over 'petty' corruption as a by-product of the development process. However, the process of elimination of corruption is still far from over in the developed world. Developed countries continue to experience high levels of corruption both in politics and business today. 'Petty' corruption has been, more or less, weeded out, but 'grand' corruption still poisons public life in many developed countries of today. In the poorer countries, on the other hand, both 'petty' and 'grand' corruptions tend to stifle progress.

Bribe Payers Index (BPI)

Transparency International (TI) has also developed the Bribe Payers' Index (BPI), which assesses the supply side of corruption and ranks corruption by source country and industry sector.

The 2008 Bribe Payers' Survey consisted of over 2,500 interviews with senior business executives in 26 countries and territories completed in October 2008. The countries surveyed were selected on the basis of their foreign direct investment (FDI) inflows and imports, and importance in regional trade.

In any corrupt transaction, there are two sides: bribe takers and bribe suppliers. In its latest BPI for 2008, TI focused its attention on the supply side of corruption. BPI is updated on a bi-annual basis. The Index (2008) ranks 22 of the world's most economically powerful countries according to the likelihood of their companies and firms offering a bribe when doing business abroad. The main conclusion of the 2008 index is that companies based in Belgium and Canada are perceived as being least likely to bribe, whereas companies from India, China and Russia are perceived as those who are most likely to offer bribes to sign up a business contract.

Table 2.3 Bribe Payers Index (BPI) 2008

Country rank	Country/Territory	BPI score
1	Belgium	8.8
1	Canada	8.8
3	Netherlands	8.7
3	Switzerland	8.7
5	Germany	8.6
5	Japan	8.6
5	United Kingdom	8.6
8	Australia	8.5
9	France	8.1
9	Singapore	8.1
9	United States	8.1
12	Spain	7.9
13	Hong Kong	7.6
14	South Africa	7.5
14	South Korea	7.5
14	Taiwan	7.5
17	Brazil	7.4
17	Italy	7.4
19	India	6.8
20	Mexico	6.6
21	China	6.5
22	Russia	5.9

Source: Transparency International, 2010.

Furthermore, the 2008 BPI indicates that companies in public works and construction, real estate and property development, oil and gas, and heavy manufacturing and mining were most likely to bribe officials to get a deal done.

While examining the CPI to rank a country, it was noted earlier that the scarcity and shortages of goods and services would generally provide the impetus to 'petty' corruption on the part of public officials. In international trade, on the other hand, the suppliers of a product or a service get involved in 'grand' corruption as a means of overcoming stiff competition from many players from many countries. Until recently it was possible that a country would try to avoid competition in overseas markets among its own nationals by giving monopoly power of international trade to one agency, such as the Australian Wheat Board (AWB). Such exclusive monopoly rights to trade in specific products and services were also intended to improve the ability of a country to more effectively face competition from other foreign suppliers.

World Bank Corruption Index

The World Bank corruption index is known as the Control of Corruption Index (CCI). Since the 1990s, the World Bank has been taking an active interest in measuring corruption in the context of 'good governance' as a precondition for country-aid and project-aid. The World Bank views good governance and control of corruption as the main strategy for alleviation of poverty. The World Bank seeks to minimize corruption on World Bank funded projects; and it also offers all technical assistance to countries in improving governance and controlling corruption.

The World Bank has recently taken the stance that corruption, particularly widespread corruption among public officials, cannot do any good to a country in the longer-term; and that it is the duty of any civilized government to provide corruption-free 'good governance' to its subjects.

According to a recent study by the World Bank (2009), known as the Worldwide Governance Indicators Project, the world's most corrupt nations are listed as: Venezuela, Guinea, Equatorial Guinea, Cote d'Ivoire, Chad, Sudan, Congo, Angola, Democratic Republic of Congo, Zimbabwe, Somalia, Iraq, Turkmenistan, Uzbekistan, Afghanistan, Myanmar, Cambodia, Democratic People's Republic of Korea and Papua New Guinea.

Some interesting conclusions emerging from the World Bank Governance Indicators (WGI) research project, covering 212 countries and territories are given below:

(1) Some countries, which have gained notoriety for political and human rights abuses, such as Rwanda, Indonesia and Tajikistan, have achieved considerable success in controlling corruption.
(2) Some of the most developed nations have become noticeably more corrupt. This challenges the view that the world's richest countries have managed to achiever a high level of integrity among public officials.

Table 2.4 The World Bank's Control of Corruption
Index (CCI)

Some selected countries	
Country	**The World Bank's CCI (2009)**
Australia	2.03
New Zealand	2.38
China	−0.53
Indonesia	−0.71
Malaysia	0.02
Singapore	2.26
India	−0.33
Pakistan	−1.10
Bangladesh	−1.29
Sri Lanka	−0.36
Korea DPR	−1.39
Thailand	−0.23
Vietnam	−0.52
Myanmar	−1.75

N.B.: CCI values range between −2.5 and 2.5; higher values
represent greater control of corruption.
Source: World Bank (2009).

(3) Over a period of 10 years or so, a number of countries, which are
poorly ranked in terms of corruption, such as Chile, Costa Rica,
Lithuania and Uruguay, have done very well in reducing levels of corruption, as compared with democracies like Greece and the United
States of America.

ICRG (International Country Risk Guide) Corruption Score by the PRS Group (PRS)[i]

The International Country Risk Guide has been published on a monthly
basis by The PRS Group since 1980. It provides political, economic and
financial risk ratings for those countries that are deemed to be important
for international business. An index is created for each of the three

categories; the Political Risk index is based on 100 points, while the remaining two are both based on 50 points. The scores are then summed and divided by two in order to obtain the weights for inclusion in the composite country score, where 0–49.9 and 80–100 points denotes Very High Risk and Very Low Risk respectively. One and five-year forecasts are made and projections are based on "best" and "worst" case scenarios.

The Political Risk Rating is made up of several components including a corruption factor. For this component each country is given a value out of 6, where 6 denotes a low risk of corruption. It is believed by the ICRG that potential corruption in forms such as excessive patronage and secret party funding can lead to a large amount of risk for foreign business as it can lead to unrealistic and inefficient controls on the state economy as well as encouraging the growth of the black market.

Political risk information is widely used by major multinational corporations in making decisions about overseas investments. It does not give any measure of the corruption level in a country but specifically measures the risk of investments in industry (sector-wise) in politically volatile vis-à-vis politically stable countries. PRS can actually help a firm or a company to design a risk forecasting system.

The PRS Group research has become very popular over the years. It now covers 140 country reports, which are also grouped into Regional Services.

Opacity Index by PricewaterhouseCoopers (PwC)

The Opacity Index created by PwC in 2001 deals with Corruption, Legal systems, management of the Economy, Accounting transparency and Regulatory opacity (CLEAR). These 5 aspects are combined in the index to provide a measure on the overall transparency of the economic environments of particular countries in their entirety. Surveys were completed by bankers, equity analysts, chief financial officers and PwC in-country practitioners and are compiled into what is called an O-Factor (Lipsey, 2001).

Since then, the Kurtzman Group has expanded the index, rejecting the idea of using surveys to collate information due to the belief that business leaders were unable to compare international business practices with their own due to the lack of knowledge of foreign counterparts. Instead, data is collected from sources such as the Global Competitiveness Report and the Index of Economic Freedom to determine how well a country's legal

Table 2.5 ICRG corruption score (2011)

Some selected countries	
Country	**Year/2011**
Australia	5.00
New Zealand	5.50
China	2.00
Korea DPR	1.00
Malaysia	2.50
Japan	4.50
Myanmar	1.50
Singapore	4.50
Bangladesh	3.00
India	2.00
Pakistan	2.00
Sri Lanka	2.50

N.B.: ICRG values range between 0 and 6; Higher values represent low potential risk of corruption.
Source: The PRS Group Inc., 2011, 'International Country Risk Guide', Available from <http://www.prsgroup.com/icrg.aspx> [16 May 2011].

system serves its businesses and investors in terms of solving disputes and providing protection. The level of economic risks a country faces, including influence of organized crime and bureaucratic barriers, is determined by a number of sources such as the World Bank Doing Business Database and the Global Competitiveness Report (Kurtzman *et al.*, 2004).

To calculate the opacity score (1) a sub-index is calculated for each of the five CLEAR categories using simple averages and (2) the simple average of the five sub-indices is taken to determine the final score. It is then possible to assign each final score with an opacity risk premium/discount expressed as an interest rate equivalent. This interest rate equivalent is calculated by taking the difference between the opacity of the subject country and the United States and multiplying it by 0.2213. If, for example, France had an interest rate equivalent of 3.53 then a US investor wanting to invest in French assets would need to receive a return 3.53% higher than he would receive in the US to offset the risk (Kurtzman *et al.*, 2004).

Table 2.6   Opacity index rank (2009)

Some selected countries		
Rank	**Country**	**Opacity score**
2	Australia	14
3	Singapore	14
18	Japan	25
22	South Korea	29
27	Malaysia	32
37	India	41
38	China	42
38	Pakistan	42

Source: The Opacity Index, Available at http:// www.pwc.fr/the_opacity_index1.html/.

Conclusion

Despite the availability of a number of quantitative measures from different agencies; for example, (1) Transparency International, (2) the World Bank and (3) the Political Risk Services (PRS) Group, the main conclusions emerging from the various measures and studies are very similar:

(1) A corrupt country is a corrupt country, no matter what index is used. For example, North Korea, Myanmar, Somalia and Bangladesh are among the most corrupt countries according to all different popular measures. Similarly, a relatively corruption free country like Denmark, or Singapore, or New Zealand will appear at the top of ranking in all different indices, although the precise ranking may be a little different from one index to another.

(2) There does not seem to be a short-term correlation between corruption and economic growth. Indeed, two of the most successful countries with two of the highest rates of economic growth in the world, are China and India. But both China and India have a low ranking in all indices. It is however possible that in the longer-term, corruption is an evil that should be avoided and eradicated.

(3) Shortages in the supply of goods and services encourage 'rationing' and thereby increase the power and authority of petty public officials. Such increased power of public officials encourages corruption. The rule that 'power corrupts' is universal, and it applies to the whole range of government activities, such as health, education, infrastructure, the judiciary, the police and the issuing of permits and licenses. Free competition is an effective method of reducing corruption. However, as we have seen earlier, in international trade and investment, competition among foreign rivals encourages corruption and the grand scale of bribe-paying.

(4) Generally speaking, poverty and low income breeds, or at least encourages, corruption. Hence poor and underdeveloped countries are ridden with more corruption than high income and developed countries. Therefore it is possible to argue that economic development itself is likely to be an effective cure for corruption, particularly the so-called 'petty' types of corruption.

Table 2.7 shows the ranking of different countries, according to the CPI and CCI.

Table 2.7   Some popular measures of corruption (2009)

Country	CPI	CCI
Australia	8	8
New Zealand	1	1
China	79	136
Malaysia	56	89
Japan	17	27
Myanmar	178	213
Singapore	3	2
Bangladesh	139	177
India	84	114
Pakistan	139	185
Sri Lanka	97	118

N.B.: At the time this paper was written, 2009 figures were the most recent that were available for both CPI and CCI.

The number of countries included in the CPI and CCI ranking are 180 and 213, respectively.

References

Kurtzman, J., Yago, G., Phumiwasana, T. (2004). *The Opacity Index 2004*, Kurtzman Group, Available from http://www.funcionpublica.gob.mx/indices/doctos/opacity_kurtzman.pdf.

Lipsey, R. (2001). PwC's Opacity Index: A powerful new tool for global investors, *Journal of Corporate Accounting and Finance*, 12(6). Available from: WileyOnlineLibrary.

The PRS Group (2011). 'International Country Risk Guide', Available from <http://www.prsgroup.com/icrg.aspx> [16 May 2011].

Transparency International (2010). *Corruption Perceptions Index 2010*, Available from <http://www.transparency.org/policy_research/surveys_indices/cpi/2010/results [4 July 2011].

United Nations Development Programme (UNDP) (1999). Fighting Corruption to Improve Governance, New York.

World Bank (2009). *Worldwide Governance Indicators*, Available from: <http://info.worldbank.org/governance/wgi/mc_countries.asp> [4 July 2011].

Endnote

i. The authors would like to thank Patti Davis for her invaluable help with regards to this section.

Chapter 3

Using the Release of Information as an Indicator of Government Transparency

Andrew Williams*

Business School, University of Western Australia

Abstract

The release of economic and social data by a government provides many benefits to its citizens on a number of different levels. However, this willingness (or otherwise) to release information to the public may also be useful as a signal of the degree of political and institutional transparency. To that end, a new index is developed that has extensive coverage across countries (175) and time (1960–2005), and is based on the quantity of reported socio-economic data contained in the World Development Indicators and the International Finance Statistics databases. This chapter briefly outlines the construction of this index, and introduces a number of case studies and illustrations that highlight the importance of transparency in economic development.

Keywords: Transparency, institutional quality, information asymmetries.

JEL Classification: O17, O47, P14.

---

*Mail Box M251, 35 Stirling Hwy, Crawley, WA, 6009. Tel.: +61 8 6488 3859. Correspondence should be sent to Andrew Williams (E-mail: Andrew.Williams@uwa.edu.au).

Introduction

Why do governments gather and release information on economic and social issues? The answer would seem obvious — information is extremely useful, and it is useful to many different parties, for many different purposes. For example, private domestic and foreign firms can use this information to help improve their financial and physical investment decisions, or to learn more about their relevant markets. Information is also useful for policy-making decisions in the public sphere. If one wants to have an 'anti-inflation' policy, for example, it would be nice to know what the rate of inflation actually is. At a more overt political level, information is useful because it can help citizens monitor the performance of their government. A government that can prove the country is undergoing strong growth, low inflation, high investment and so forth stands a much better chance (ceteris paribus) of being re-elected in the future. Across all of these factors, the common denominator is that this data can help to reduce the problems associated with informational asymmetries between parties, a fact that has been well-known in the theoretical economic literature for many years.[i]

As many empirical economists can testify, however, there are a significant number of governments around the world that release comparatively little economic and social data for public consumption. If this information is so useful to so many people, why would they do this? At a broad level, there are a number of possibilities.

Little information may be released for the simple reason that the government does not have the *capacity or capability* to do so. This incapacity may arise from the fact that governments in poor countries may not have the resources to adequately produce statistics. Indeed, perhaps the production and release of information is just a proxy for the level of economic development. Rich countries release more information *because* they are rich. If this is the predominant factor, then although it does not diminish the importance of information itself, it does suggest that greater information flows can only occur once a country undergoes a sustained period of economic development.

Another possibility is that governments may potentially collect a lot of information, but deliberately choose not to release much of it. Again, the reasons for this may be varied. Governments may, for example, have a fear of releasing 'bad news' that could affect its future electoral chances. It may also do this for more sinister motives, such as a desire to specifically maintain informational asymmetries, which may make it easier to dole out patronage to select groups, or to collect excessive rents for their own personal gain. In other words, the release of information may be closely associated with the *political circumstances* within countries. Taken in this context, these political constraints could be associated with the transparency or accountability of governments. If a government releases a relatively large quantity of data, then that might be taken as a signal that it is willing also to accept the consequences of what that information may contain.

Although the measurement of the release of information is not without precedent, there is still a big gap between the theoretical treatment of these informational asymmetries, and its empirical measurement. For example, Islam (2006) used data on the *timeliness* of the release of certain key economic variables by governments as a proxy for the transparency and accountability of governments.[ii] Her results provided evidence that the timelier was the release of information, the better was the level of governance within countries. In other words, the clear intention was to use this 'information on information' as a proxy to explain the broader implications of government transparency, which subsequently affected the quality of countries' institutions, rather than information being important in its own right.

This paper is an attempt to examine some of the key issues that may affect the level of information a country releases. The paper proceeds as follows. Section 2 will outline a measure on the release of information that introduces a temporal dimension to this issue, first developed in Williams (2009). Section 3 introduces some descriptive statistics of this index, and anecdotally analyses the question of whether it is economic or political constraints that are driving these scores. Section 4 focuses on a more formal econometric causal analysis, with a particular focus on the relationship between the release of information and the possible causes of greater information disclosure. Section 5 offers some concluding comments.

Measuring the Release of Information (RI)

In order to measure the release of information by governments, the index developed here measures the quantity of data released by governments over a relatively long period of time. In order to capture as wide a variety of comparable data as possible, I have taken the two main international databases that are currently used extensively in economic analyses: the *World Development Indicators* (WDI) produced by the World Bank, and the *International Financial Statistics* (IFS) database, constructed by the International Monetary Fund. Although each country has in some form its own statistical agency, and there are also many other regional data collection bodies (for example, the OECD, or the Asian Development Bank), these two databases ensure a commonality in methodology across all countries.

Although the easiest approach would be to just sum up the number of observations recorded for a country in a particular year over both databases, there are several reasons why this may be overly simplistic. Firstly, categories in both databases include many instances of 'doubling up,' both across and within the respective databases. For example, GDP data is often expressed in terms of current Local Currency Units (LCUs), but is also expressed in constant LCUs, current US dollars, constant US dollars and so on. As long as a country has data recorded in current LCUs, the other transformations can be performed without any input from the domestic government, and so says nothing additional about the release of information. Therefore, where an economic or social indicator appears in a multitude of transformations, it has only been counted once (generally this was the observation recorded in current LCUs). This also extends to data that appears in *both* the WDI and IFS databases, which was counted only once as well.

It should also be pointed out that a lot of information from both databases is collected from a variety of primary sources. For example, data on the balance of payments is taken from the IMF's *Balance of Payments Statistics* database, while data on government spending and revenues are taken from the IMF's *Government Finance Statistics* (which are themselves based on data largely collected form national statistical offices and other government departments). The *World Development Indicators* also draws heavily on data from a wide variety of sources, including various UN agencies, the International Labor Organisation, World Health Organisation and so on. As much care as possible has been taken to ensure that the data ultimately used here has required some form of domestic input from the country. For example, a number of categories in the WDI come from the International Telecommunications Union

(ITU). The ITU collects their data by sending annual questionnaires to governments, which the government fills out and returns. Although this certainly does not guarantee the *quality* of the data, it does mean that it is the domestic government's responsibility to collect the data and does not, for example, rely on the data being collected in each country by the relevant NGO or agency through some form of survey (in which case the ultimate scores would be more a reflection of the capabilities of the NGO that is collecting the data, rather than the government itself).

There were also issues relating to the *International Financial Statistics* that required attention. The main data has been drawn using the topic and sub-section codes. The topics covered by the IFS are:

- Topic . (dot): Exchange rate, Fund position or international liquidity;
- Topic 1: Monetary Authorities;
- Topic 2: Deposit Money Banks;
- Topic 3: Monetary Survey;
- Topic 4: Other Banking / Non-Bank Financial Institutions;
- Topic 5: Banking / Financial Survey;
- Topic 6: Interest, Prices, Production and Labor;
- Topic 7: International Transactions;
- Topic 8: Government Finance;
- Topic 9: National Accounts and Population.

However, not all topics were used. Topic. (dot) has been excluded, as the information on exchange rates and fund position could be collected without any assistance from the domestic government. Information from Topics 1 and 2 are summarized in Topic 3, and so Topic 3 has been used. Topic 4, which looks at non-bank financial institutions, has been excluded, as data has only been included from a relatively small number of countries.[iii] This is also the reason for the exclusion of Topic 5. Topics 6–8 have been included, as this incorporates information from the IMF's *Balance of Payments* and *Government Financial Statistics* databases. Finally, Topic 9 (national accounts and population data) was excluded as this information appears in the WDI.

Having decided which categories from both databases to include, scores were then derived by taking the proportion of data coverage for each country for each individual year. Because there has been a general increase in data coverage over this time, the proportions were taken by dividing a country's raw score in time t for each database by the number of categories that had data for at least one country for that year.[iv]

A final caveat was also imposed at this stage, whereby a score was only registered for a country if it was an independent nation in that year. That is, if a country was still a colony at some point between 1960 and 2005 (or, indeed, did not exist at all), then they were omitted from the analysis for the years they were not an independent nation.

Descriptive Statistics for the Release of Information (RI) Index

Table 3.1 below presents some brief descriptive statistics for the RI index between 1960 and 2005, while Table 3.2 lists the top and bottom ten countries, averaged between 1960 and 2005. As can be seen, Canada has the highest average score over the period, while the remainder are dominated by OECD countries. The bottom of the list includes countries from Sub-Saharan Africa, the Middle East, Asia and the Pacific.

Data Quantity versus Quality

One potential criticism of this index is that this simple 'count' measure may ignore the fact that quality is likely to be an equally, if not more important, issue. For example, a government that may wish to hide or

Table 3.1 Descriptive statistics for the Release of Information Index, 1960–2005

	Release of Information
Mean	0.52
Median	0.53
Maximum	0.91
Minimum	0.02
Std. Dev.	0.19
Number of countries	175
Observations	6,874

Table 3.2 Release of Information, top and bottom ten countries, average 1960–2005

Rank	Country	Rank	Country
1	Canada	166	Samoa
2	United States	167	Liberia
3	Australia	168	Lao PDR
4	Italy	169	Equatorial Guinea
5	South Africa	170	São Tomé and Príncipe
6	United Kingdom	171	Guinea
7	Sweden	172	Bhutan
8	Japan	173	Afghanistan
9	Netherlands	174	Iraq
10	Finland	175	Micronesia, Fed. Sts.

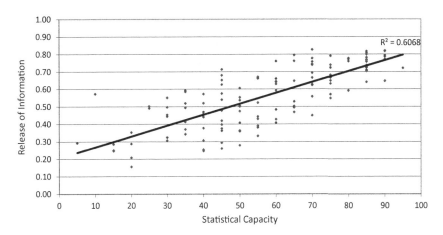

Figure 3.1 Release of Information Index and Statistical Capacity Index, 2005
Source: Author's calculations, World Bank (2004).

obfuscate its true statistics are more likely to 'fudge' the figures to say what they want, rather than omit reporting them entirely. As Figure 3.1 demonstrates, however, there is a very high correlation between the quantity of information released, and its quality, as defined in the World Bank's *Statistical Capacity Indicator*. This indicator scores developing countries on a number of issues relating to their capacity to deliver quantity and quality (with the assumption presumably that the omitted high-income developed countries would have had a score of 100). The measure below is a straight average of the sub-indices 'Data Collection,' and 'Statistical Practice,' which are a close approximation to the quality of data produced.[v] The correlation between these two indices of 0.78 suggests that countries with poor quality of statistics are also the ones that release the lowest quantity of statistics.

Factors Affecting the Release of Information

(i)   Level of development:

This first issue relates to the extent to which the release of information mirrors the level of development — rich countries produce more statistics *because* they are rich. Figure 3.2 shows that whilst there is a positive relationship between per capita incomes and this index (the correlation between per capita incomes in 2005 and data scores in 2005 is 0.39, over 169 countries), this relationship, at least superficially, does not seem to be the defining characteristic of a country's score.[vi] This is further highlighted

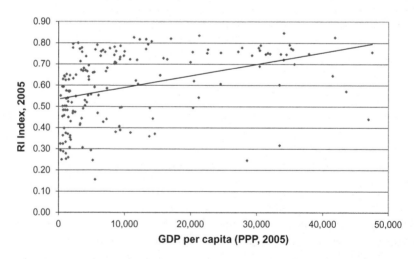

Figure 3.2   Correlation between the Release of Information Index and per capita GDP, 2005

Source: Author's calculations, World Development Indicators, World Bank (2004).

Table 3.3 Comparison of selected countries, Release of Information scores and GDP per capita, 2005

	RI score, 2005	GDP per capita in 2000 (PPP in 2005 US$)
Qatar	0.39	70,715.83
Libya	0.40	10,882.96
Oman	0.49	20,350.21
Angola	0.49	3,728.70
Saudi Arabia	0.54	21,219.71
Kenya	0.54	1,375.30
Kuwait	0.57	21,574.30
Côte d'Ivoire	0.57	1,613.61

in Table 3.3, which highlights the comparison between four Middle Eastern countries (Qatar, Oman, Saudi Arabia, and Kuwait) and four other countries that received the same or similar score as these countries in the year 2005 (Libya, Angola, Kenya and Cote d'Ivoire respectively). In each of these examples, the Middle East countries show a level of per capita income many multiples greater than their chosen counterpart. It may be argued that these Middle East countries are 'exceptional' cases because their per capita incomes are boosted due to their energy exports. But that is not the point. Irrespective of *how* they came to have higher levels of income, the fact remains that they could have chosen to spend far more resources on gathering and, importantly, releasing information if they had so chosen. The fact that they haven't, therefore, begs the question of why they have chosen not to. One possibility is that information is deliberately held back from the broader community because the lack of information helps the government to distribute patronage without overt scrutiny.

There is another compelling reason for thinking that these scores do not simply reflect the level of development by looking at some of the transition countries of Eastern Europe. Although these transition countries may prove to be the exception to the rule, they are particularly useful in this context because there is a clear distinction between their pre- and post-transition situation. Back in 1960 three of these countries

(Albania, Bulgaria, and Romania) were ranked in the bottom ten of the table, whilst Hungary was ranked 85th (out of 105 countries). By 1980 they were still ranked well into the bottom half of the rankings (albeit with more countries in the rankings by now). However, by 2005, Hungary now had proportionally the 5th highest level of data submitted to the World Bank and IMF (an amazing statistic in itself), and Romania the 15th. Albania is the only country that remains relatively low on the list (in 96th place in 2005).

The point here is that income is unlikely to be the defining issue for these countries when the scores for these countries that opened up (both politically and economically) climbed so rapidly. That is, for these transition countries, scores increased because of a move to them opening up, not because they suddenly became richer. Indeed, this is further reinforced by the fact that in the initial (often chaotic) transition to a market economy, per capita incomes actually fell, even while their scores on the release of data were rapidly climbing. Figure 3.3 clearly shows that for each of these four countries, per capita incomes fell significantly in the

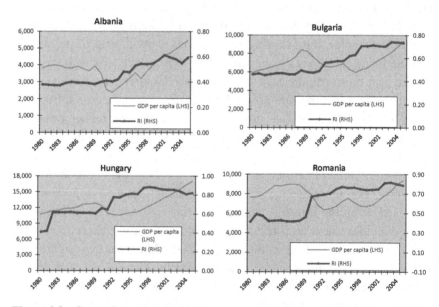

Figure 3.3   Comparison of per capita incomes and RI scores, 1980–2005 for selected Eastern European countries

Source: Author's calculations, World Development Indicators, World Bank (2005).

late 1980s and early 1990s, yet the scores on the release of data by their governments show a discernible *increase*. In this sense, the release of information by governments is clearly not based on current incomes. For these five transition countries, then, the significant increase in the release of information from the early 1990s suggests an (initial) optimistic attitude on the government's part surrounding their country's future prospects.

(ii) Political constraints:

If income does not appear to be primarily driving the release of information, then perhaps it is the prevailing political institutions that are: Figure 3.4 shows the relationship between the RI index and the degree of constraints on the executive (taken from the POLITY IV database) in 2005. As can be seen, as these constraints get larger, the release of information is also higher.[vii] Overall, the correlation between the two (in 2005) is 0.56. Of course, correlation is not causation, but this is certainly suggestive that governments tend to release more information when there is pressure on them to do so, not because they want to.

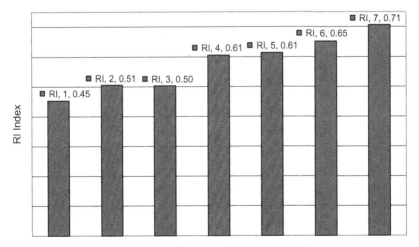

Figure 3.4   The Release of Information and degree of executive constraints, 2005
Source: Author's calculations, Marshall and Jaggers (2002).

(iii) **Other factors affecting the release of information**

The interaction between the political/institutional constraints and the release of information is not the only consideration here. There are other plausible reasons why countries may (or may not) release information.

One potentially important factor may be the **level of education** enjoyed by citizens. Education may be associated with the release of information through a number of channels. Firstly, a better educated population may demand better information from its government, and may also have a greater ability to use and evaluate the information itself, both in an economic and a political sense. For example, a better educated population would be able to see, through this information released, whether the government was doing a good job with respect to economic policies, and vote accordingly at the next available juncture. In a more practical way, a higher level of education may also improve both the quantity and quality of data. For example, the government may be able to hire qualified statisticians to process the information. In a more general sense, Rauch and Evans (2000) have shown that the quality of a country's bureaucracy depends importantly on the level of education attained by these public officials.[viii]

It has been suggested that countries with **an abundance of natural resources** (particularly energy and mineral resources) have experienced, on average, lower economic growth over the past thirty years (Sachs and Warner, 1997). One hypothesis for this slow growth is that these resources promote rent-seeking behavior on the part of public officials, which fosters poor institutions through higher **corruption**, patronage, and so forth. As Kolstad and Wiig (2008) outline, there are a number of ways that a lack of transparency can create or exacerbate the problems associated with resource-rich economies. This lack of transparency can: (i) make corruption more attractive, in that it can reduce the probability of discovery; (ii) make it easier to capture rents; (iii) create principal-agent problems (between governments and its citizens, but also between elected officials and the bureaucracy); and (iv) can undermine democracy via these resource rents by reducing the need for domestic taxation (and hence reduce demands for accountability), increasing spending on patronage, and/or increasing spending on the direct oppression of dissenting voices.

Empirical Analysis

Because it is highly likely that there are a number of factors influencing the release of information, it is therefore important to take a more rigorous statistical approach to this issue. The sample consists of 91 countries. The panel data estimation being employed is based on nine five year non-overlapping periods between 1960 and 2004 (unless otherwise stated all variables are taken as averages over each five year period). Because I am initially interested in the causal nature of the relationship between transparency and these other factors, all variables have been lagged by one period (including the lagged value of the transparency variable). Based on the theoretical considerations above, the core specification is:

$$RI_{it} = \hat{a}_1 RI_{it-1} + \hat{a}_2 LNY_{it-1} + \hat{a}_3 XCONST_{it-1} + \hat{a}_4 Z_{it-1} + \lambda_{t-1} + \eta_{it-1} + v_{it-1} \qquad (1)$$

where *RI* is the Release of Information index (proxying transparency), *LNY* is the log of per capita income, *XCONST* is the degree of executive constraints, while *Z* are additional factors that were hypothesized to be important possible determinants of transparency above (the full list of variables and their sources can be found in the Appendix).

There are two specification issues that require some initial attention. The first is that the lagged dependent variable will be endogenous to the fixed effects in the error term, which means the results will be biased. There are two possible methods to correct this. The first is to difference the data to remove these fixed effects (or equivalently to include dummy variables for each country). A second method is to instrument the lagged dependent variable and any other potentially endogenous variables in the regression with other variables uncorrelated with the fixed effects. First differencing accompanied with using the level of past values as instruments gives rise to the well-known "difference GMM" estimator from Arellano and Bond (1991). A third method is to first difference the instruments themselves in order to make them exogenous to the fixed effects. The combination of first differencing the variables and instrumenting with lagged levels of these variables, and using the levels of the variables with the first differenced instruments, gives us the 'System GMM' estimator, developed by Blundell and Bond (1998). This estimator also assumes that, whilst there will be first-order serial correlation in the error term, there should not be second-order correlation. Lastly, the validity of the instruments can be tested for using the Hansen, and Hansen-Difference tests.

Table 3.4 summarizes the initial results with the RI index as the dependent variable. Column 1 includes only the income and executive constraints variables, and both have a positive and significant effect on the index. However, the size of the coefficient for the income variable decreases substantially (and, indeed, even changes sign) once additional variables are included in Columns 2–4. Education appears to have only a marginal effect on the release of information (Column 3), however energy and mineral resource exports have a highly significant effect on the release of information. The negative coefficient on the export variable strongly suggests that countries that have a heavy reliance on energy and mineral exports subsequently also release less information.[ix] It is not altogether clear from this table, however, why this might be so. If the only reason for this lack of information is because of an increased propensity for rent-seeking or corrupt behavior, then the addition of the corruption variable in Column 4 should substantially reduce the coefficient on the resource export variable. As can be seen, however, the coefficient is virtually identical. Nevertheless, the inclusion of the ICRG corruption variable also demonstrates, for the full sample at least, that an increase in corruption leads to a decrease in the release of information.[x] Lastly, as a check to see whether these results are purely a function of the inclusion of the high-income (and largely high-transparent) OECD countries, I have removed these countries. Executive constraints and energy and mineral exports continue to have a significant causal impact on the release of information, however, it appears as though the significance of the corruption variable was due in large part to the high scores achieved by these OECD countries. Once these countries are removed, there is no evidence that corruption affects the release of information for developing countries.

Having briefly looked at what some of the determinants of the release of information are, the final step is to see what effect (if any) this has on economic growth. Column 1 of Table 3.5 includes the variables employed in the Table 3.4, as well as population growth, which, along

Table 3.4 Factors affecting the Release of Information

	Dependent variable: Release of Information (RI) index				
	1	2	3	4	NON-OECD
RI, t−1	0.6238	0.5346	0.5859	0.5826	0.6366
	0.1025***	*0.1126****	*0.1186****	*0.0937****	*0.0890****
Log of Per Capita GDP, t−1	0.0355	0.0214	0.0110	−0.0204	−0.0052
	0.0109***	*0.0155*	*0.0205*	*0.0138*	*0.0123*
Executive Constraints, t−1	0.0128	0.0111	0.0100	0.0080	0.0085
	0.0036***	*0.0033****	*0.0038****	*0.0035***	*0.0042***
Energy and Mineral resources (% GDP), t−1		−0.2119	−0.2163	−0.2034	−0.1966
		0.1042**	*0.0971***	*0.0772****	*0.0793***
Gross Secondary Enrolments, t−1			0.0304	0.0767	0.0761
			0.0599	*0.0439**	*0.0494*
Corruption (ICRG), t−1				0.0130	0.0056
				0.0063**	*0.0079*
Tests (*p*-values)					
Hansen test	0.318	0.347	0.260	0.467	0.281
Diff-Hansen	0.397	0.777	0.340	0.557	0.334
AR1	0.000	0.000	0.000	0.000	0.000
AR2	0.476	0.091	0.112	0.126	0.171
Instrument count (collapsed)	29	36	43	50	50
Countries	91	91	91	91	71
Observations	688	599	589	589	432

Note: For GMM-SYS, all variables are treated as potentially endogenous. For all regressions, the instrument count reported is based on the number of 'collapsed' instruments. Because of gaps in the panel, orthogonal deviations have been used instead of first differences. Difference-in-Hansen test reports the *p*-values based on the null hypothesis that the instruments in the levels equation are exogenous. For more details, see Roodman (2006). Coefficients based on the two-step estimation, using the Windmeijer correction. Time dummies employed but not reported. Numbers in italics are robust standard errors. *, **, *** = significant at the 10, 5, and 1% levels respectively.

Table 3.5   Regression analysis with economic growth as dependent variable

	Dependant variable: Economic growth			
	1	**2**	**3**	**NON-OECD**
Initial Per Capita GDP	0.2703	−0.7376	−1.1700	−1.0665
	1.0575	*0.9120*	*0.8819*	*0.8608*
Gross Secondary Enrolments	−3.1905	−0.8113	−0.7053	−1.3542
	2.5374	*2.1902*	*2.2353*	*2.4440*
Executive Constraints	−0.1119	−0.1670	−0.0212	−0.0835
	0.1999	*0.1691*	*0.1608*	*0.1991*
Energy and Mineral resources	2.1560	7.7085	9.9687	8.3036
(% GDP)	*5.6740*	*5.8956*	*5.7603 **	*4.8653 **
Corruption (ICRG)	0.0917	−0.1012	−0.0773 *	−0.1241
	0.3399	*0.2921*	*0.2700*	*0.3093*
Population growth	−0.6906	−0.7121	−0.6740	−0.5649
	*0.1528 ****	*0.1263 ****	*0.1346 ****	*0.1224 ****
RI		10.5806	5.2425	6.6260
		*3.5696 ****	*3.0014 **	*4.1725*
Investment			2.1933	2.0523
			*0.7552 ****	*0.8688 ***
Tests (*p*-values)				
Hansen test	0.284	0.207	0.402	0.387
Diff-Hansen	0.194	0.234	0.739	0.647
AR1	0.000	0.000	0.000	0.000
AR2	0.804	0.676	0.965	0.720
Instrument count (collapsed)	49	56	63	63
Countries	91	91	91	71
Observations	583	583	583	426

Note: For GMM-SYS, all variables are treated as potentially endogenous. For all regressions, the instrument count reported is based on the number of 'collapsed' instruments. Because of gaps in the panel, orthogonal deviations have been used instead of first differences. Difference-in-Hansen test reports the *p*-values based on the null hypothesis that the instruments in the levels equation are exogenous. For more details, see Roodman (2006). Coefficients based on the two-step estimation, using the Windmeijer correction. Time dummies employed but not reported. Numbers in italics are robust standard errors. *, **, *** = significant at the 10, 5, and 1% levels respectively.

with investment, is a commonly-used control variable in growth regressions. The dependent variable is the log change in per capita incomes over each five year period. Somewhat surprisingly, the only factor that appears to have a significant effect on growth is population growth.[xi] In Column 2 the RI index is included and, as can be seen, the coefficient is significant and positive. Countries that are more transparent have higher growth. But why? Column 3 provides one clue. As soon as investment is included as an explanatory variable, the coefficient on the RI index falls by around half, and is barely significant. In other words, one of the main transmission mechanisms through which transparency helps economic growth is by increasing the amount of information available to market participants. Although not clear from this analysis, this is likely to be either because the amount of information available is useful to them, and/or the relatively large amount of information released gives them confidence in the transparency of the prevailing economic (and legal) system. Removing the OECD countries in Column 4 does not alter these conclusions.

Concluding Comments

The relationship between the release of information by governments and economic activity is an important one, because information has value that can help reduce informational asymmetries between a number of different groups in society. The index developed here takes advantage of the amount of data sent by governments to the two major international statistical databases from the IMF and World Bank. An important initial question to address was whether this index was simply a weak proxy for incomes — rich countries provide more data because they have the resources to do so. The anecdotal evidence strongly suggests that, while incomes are undoubtedly a factor, they are not necessarily the *only* factor. A number of countries with very different levels of per capita incomes produced very different levels of data, which implies that there is *something* that leads countries to release relatively little information, even though they could easily afford to. This evidence was particularly stark for several Middle East countries, and for a number of Eastern European countries, where the sudden increase in the volume of information released occurred at the same time as they opened up, both politically and economically, and despite the fact that their per capita incomes declined considerably during this transition. In terms of what this 'something' may be, it was hypothesized that it could be due to political considerations. The anecdotal evidence was indeed suggestive of a link between the degree of political constraints placed upon the executive and the release of information, and so the next step therefore was to more formally examine whether it was the political and institutional constraints, or the prevailing resource constraints arising from low incomes, that were defining this release of information. The analysis presented here suggests that the release of information by governments does have several important institutional causes and consequences. Firstly, across each of the various regressions, constraints on the executive was a positive and highly significant determinant of the amount of information released, but once additional variables were included, per capita incomes were not. This implies that transparency only occurs once the executive is constrained in their ability to act with impunity (that is, others force them to be transparent), and is not simply a function of having a level of income that allows this information to be produced. In terms of the other possible determinants, an abundance of energy and mineral exports appear to have a negative effect on the release of information. Although this may be in part due to a greater willingness to hide or obfuscate where these resource revenues are going, higher levels of corruption only appears to explain a part of this. Finally, when looking at the impact of transparency on economic growth, it appears as though one of the main transmission mechanisms through which this operates is through investment. On average, countries with higher levels of investment are also those that release the most amount of information.

Even if one does not accept the suggestion here that this release of information index has a political or institutional dimension to it, a literal interpretation of these results is still of interest. In other words, even if this index only says that 'more information is better to less,' then this is still important, because more information is subsequently associated with higher investment and economic growth.

References

Arellano, M., Bond, S. (1991). Some tests of specification for panel data: Monte Carlo evidence and an application to employment equations, *Review of Economic Studies,* 58.

Blundell, R., Bond, S. (1998). Initial conditions and moment restrictions in dynamic panel data models, *Journal of Econometrics,* 87(1), pp. 115–143.

Bond, S., Hoeffler, A., Temple, J. (2001). "GMM Estimation of Empirical Growth Models", *CEPR Discussion Paper* 3048.

Glennerster, R., Shin, Y. (2007). "Does Transparency Pay?" *IMF Staff Papers* 55(1), pp. 183–209.

Global Development Network Growth Database (2006). Development Research Institute, New York University, Available from: <http://www.nyu.edu/fas/institute/dri/global%20development%20network%20growth%20database.htm> [December 2006].

Heston, A., Summers, R., Aten, B. (2007). *Penn World Table Version 6.2* Center for International Comparisons at the University of Pennsylvania (CICUP).

International Monetary Fund (2006). *Balance of Payments Statistics,* Washington: IMF.

International Monetary Fund (2006a). *Government Finance Statistics,* Washington: IMF.

International Monetary Fund (2006b). *International Financial Statistics,* Washington: IMF.

Islam, R. (2006). Does more transparency go along with better governance? *Economics and Politics,* 18(2), pp. 121–167.

Kolstad, I., Wiig, A. (2009). Is transparency the key to reducing corruption in resource-rich countries?, *World Development,* 37(3), pp. 521–532.

Marshall, M.G., Jaggers, K. (2002). "POLITY IV Project: Database User's Manual", Centre for International Development and Conflict Management, University of Maryland.

Persson, T., Tabellini, G. (2000). *Political Economics: Explaining Economic Policy.* MIT Press (Cambridge).

Political Risk Services (2003). *International Country Risk Guide* (PRS Group).

Rauch, J.E., Evans, P.B. (2000). Bureaucratic structure and bureaucratic performance in less developed countries, *Journal of Public Economics,* 75(1), pp. 49–71.

Roodman, D. (2006). How to do xtabond2: An introduction to 'difference' and 'system' GMM in Stata, Centre for Global Development, WP 103.

Sachs, J.D., Warner, A. (1997). "Natural Resource Abundance and Economic Growth", *National Bureau of Economic Research Working Paper* 5398.

UNCTAD (2003). *Commodity Yearbook* (United Nations Conference on Trade and Development: Geneva).

Williams, A. (2009). On the release of information by governments: Causes and consequences, *Journal of Development Economics,* 89(1), pp. 124–138.

World Bank (2004). *Measuring Results: Improving National Statistics in IDA Countries* (Washington: World Bank).

World Bank (2005). *World Development Indicators* (Washington: World Bank).

Endnotes

i. The economics of information in private markets was first brought to prominence by the Nobel Laureates George Akerlof, Michael Spence and Joseph Stiglitz. On the informational asymmetries in political markets, see Persson and Tabellini (2000), among others.

ii. This paper used data published in the World Bank's World Development Indicators and the IMF's International Financial Statistics from November 2002, while another attempt at measuring transparency from Glennerster and Shin (2007) focussed on the implementation of IMF-led reforms on data dissemination between 1999 and 2002.

iii. That is, these topics are unrepresentative not because countries are unable (or unwilling) to release data on these issues, but because many countries have alternative definitions and methods of reporting data for non-bank financial institutions.

iv. The reason for this is that not all of the data has been collected annually since 1960, and so the number of eligible categories rose steadily over the 41 year period. For example, in 1960 there were 175 eligible categories, rising to over 300 in 2005, covering a variety of economic and social statistics (categories available from the author on request). This ensures that the scores for each year are proportional to the data that could have *potentially* been collected *at that time*, not compared to the year 2005.

v. These measures include issues such as whether countries follow the IMF's accounting standards, how often they undertake a census, and the completeness of their vital registration system. For more details see *World Bank (2004) Measuring Results: Improving National Statistics in IDA Countries (Washington: World Bank).*

vi. GDP data is taken from the *World Development Indicators*, is in 2005 PPP dollars.

vii. A score of "1" in the Executive Constraints measure is defined as one where the executive has essentially unlimited authority (for example, it appoints any accountability groups itself). At the other end of the spectrum, a score of "7" is given where "accountability groups have effective authority equal to or greater than the executive in most areas of activity". For more information, see Marshall and Jaggers (2002).

viii. Specifically, the proportion of civil servants hired that have a university qualification.

ix. Furthermore, this is due to the specific type of resource, as no such significant relationship was observed for agricultural exports, nor with manufactured exports (results available upon request).

x. Following Roodman (2006), I have assumed that the ICRG scores for corruption were constant prior to 1984, the first year they appeared. This is a fairly heroic assumption. However, I separately ran three year panels between 1984 and 2001, where I have (variable) corruption data for the entire period, and I got a similar result, in that improvements in corruption led to a subsequent increase in the amount of information released.

xi. However, some of these results shouldn't surprise. Gross secondary enrolments often appear as insignificant in panel growth regressions (for example, see Bond *et al.*, 2001). The energy and mineral export variable becomes highly significant (and negative) if one takes a one-period lag, which suggests that the deleterious effects of these resources only comes into play after a period of at least five years.

Chapter 4

Deliberative Democracy, Global Green Information System and Spirituality

Dora Marinova*, Vladislav Todorov[†] and Amzad Hossain[‡]

**Curtin University Sustainability Policy (CUSP) Institute,
Curtin University, Australia
[†]University of Forestry, Sofia, Bulgaria
[‡]School of Sustainability, Murdoch University, Australia*

Abstract

Good governance is a prerequisite for a transition toward a more sustainable development. Within western democracy, governance is understood either as a management function or as a leadership role played by the government, politicians, business, academics, not-for-profit and community organizations or just particular individuals within civil society. More recently, this top–down approach has been challenged by the newly emerging methods of deliberative democracy which entrust the power of decision-making to randomly selected representatives of the public following intensive processes of deliberation. The role of experts in the process is to inform the deliberations, and the role of the traditional structures of power within society is to implement the outcomes from the deliberations.

Information availability is a serious condition for the potential of deliberative democracy to be fulfilled. Within the climate change imperatives, the focus of information delivery should be on allowing for a global picture to be created as the basis for individual localized decision-making. Based on the unprecedented power of computer and communication technology, this chapter puts forward the concept of a Global Green Information System (GGIS) which can provide the virtual space for and support on-line deliberative democracy processes. The functions that such a GGIS can provide are monitoring, information storage and transmission, facilitation of decision-making and analysis of virtual sustainability models.

Despite its enormous importance and input, the GGIS however will only be a tool in the broader deliberative processes guided by the value systems represented by society members.

Keywords: Sustainability, sustainable development, spirituality, information system, deliberative democracy, climate change.

Introduction

Liberal democracy is the Western model of good governance. In the last 10 years or so, it has been the place of deliberative democracy experiments, which aim at improving civic participation and engagement with important, often complex and new issues, such as science and technology management, health care, political governance and climate change. This deliberative "turn" in good governance (Dowding *et al.*, 2004; Edwards *et al.*, 2008) is spreading fast across the globe.

The first Australian female Prime Minister announced in her election campaign that if re-elected she would hold a Citizens' Assembly to gauge community support for climate change policies which may include price on carbon and an emissions trading scheme. Her decision has been met with a lot of criticism from industry groups and the right and left of politics,[i] but with a lot of support from academics who are familiar with the methods of deliberative democracy. According to Janette Hartz-Karp[ii]: "A randomly selected Citizens' Assembly would enable the government to understand what everyday citizens would think about the critical options available if they had the opportunity to understand the issues, and through careful deliberation, weigh the pros and cons, and determine their preferences". Lyn Carson states that: "Prime Minister Julia Gillard's announcement that the nation's response to climate change will be in the hands of such a group, demonstrates a willingness to bring people back into politics. A citizens' assembly will give the PM an insight into the considered judgment of typical Australians in a way that is impossible using opinion polls or focus groups".[iii] A year earlier, John Dryzek strongly advocated for this form of citizen participation in governance to become part of the Australian democratic processes (Dryzek, 2009). He also foreshadowed the idea for a Global Citizens' Parliament when it comes to deliberation and policy proposals around burning issues, and climate change is the most prominent example of this: "A lot of political authority is now exercised at the global level; but there is a huge democratic deficit there that a Global Citizens' Parliament could help reduce" (Dryzek, 2009: 7).

Deliberative democracy is a relatively new concept that is gaining speed around the world, including "deliberative experiments in China" (Dryzek, 2009: 7) where true democratic processes seem to have been blocked for a long time; proposals for it to become the fourth branch of government in the USA with compulsory "jury service"-like obligations for the public (Leib, 2004) and the first Citizens' Parliament in Australia examines how the country's political system can be strengthened to better the people (Hartz-Karp and Carson, 2009). The US Open Government Directive[iv] explicitly requires executive departments and agencies to solicit public input because knowledge is not only held by the experts, but is widely dispersed within society. Certain policy issues, such as biotechnologies, biomedicines and genetically modified foods have already attracted the use of deliberative techniques in the EU because of the surrounding unpredictability of impacts (Abels, 2002). Some types of deliberative tools are being used in many countries across the globe (Leighninger, 2006), from local government in Brazil to the Danish Parliament, from AmericaSpeaks discussing social security and the redevelopment of Ground Zero after September 11 to the city of Geraldton in Western Australia deciding on its transition to becoming more sustainable, in Italy (Citizens' Juries on traffic congestion in Bologna and Turin in 2006), Canada (the Citizens' Assemblies on electoral reforms in British Columbia in 2004 and Ontario in 2007) and the US (California Speaks on health care in 2007).

We have also experienced the first on-line global deliberative process in the lead to the 2009 Climate Change talks in Copenhagen.[v] Organized by Denmark, it involved 4,000 randomly selected people from 40 countries (100 from each country) helped by three panels of internationally renowned experts and its resolutions were given to the participants in Copenhagen. Despite being facilitated by the latest communication technologies, such as live videoconferencing and blog, and many results and documentary being available on the web, the participants did not have direct on-line access to information in relation to the state of the planet or modelling power that could show the implications that particular resolutions would have.

What this chapter sets to develop builds on the experiences of deliberative democracy so far and argues for the need of a global deliberation process facilitated by a global green information system (GGIS). Such a global deliberation would also reflect the values that people across the globe hold, which are rooted in their spirituality. It argues that despite the enormous advances in technologies and democratic ways of decision-making, what will determine a shift towards a more sustainable future are the common values we hold. The next section outlines briefly the potential of deliberative democracy; this is followed by the role of information and spirituality in deliberation. The final conclusions emphasize the importance of imagination and creativity to see a better world where cooperation, justice and care would prevail.

Deliberative Democracy

Deliberative democracy, "decision making by discussion among free and equal citizens" (Elster, 1998: 1), is a response to the need to change the way governments around the world engage with the community (Hartz-Karp, 2009). Its techniques and procedures, such as citizen juries, Word Cafés, 21st Century Town Meetings, deliberative polls, scenario workshops and consensus forums (Gastil and Levine, 2005) are all based around deliberation, a process that Gambetta (1998: 19) describes as a conversation during which individuals speak and listen consequentially before making a collective decision. All these tools are appearing as new ways of democratizing expertise within society when the government listens not only to what the established experts have to say but also to the experiences, concerns and knowledge that ordinary citizens hold (Görsdorf, 2006). The outcome of such deliberations is not necessarily decision-making or particular actions, but it is a process of building understanding of the various aspects of the issues (as presented by the experts), communication and reflection over the concerns, and potentially building a consensus as to what the best solutions are.

The stability and effectiveness of political systems are strongly dependent on their public acceptance and lawfulness (Jost and Major, 2001). The legitimacy of deliberative democracy, as opposed to voting or public consultation, is based on the assumption that randomly selected community representatives can freely and openly deliberate complex issues, provided they are given the relevant information from the experts, they pay respect to the pluralities of views and aims, and they are equal in the process — each one of them can put forward proposals as well as criticize or offer support to proposals by others without being bound by existing power hierarchies within society (Cohen, 1989). According to Nowothny (2003), expert knowledge is inherently transgressive because it can never address issues that can't be reduced to the purely scientific or technical aspects. Its implementation is directed not solely to the experts but also to people and institutions who have "expectations and modes of understanding [that] reflect the heterogeneous experience of mixed audiences" (Nowothny, 2003: 151). Deliberative procedures produce a different type of knowledge that is socially robust and accountable because of the involvement of an extended group of experts as well as lay people who bring different expertise, experiences and knowledges. They allow participants to be the ones setting the agenda for discussion (Hartz-Karp and Carlson, 2009), not politicians, industry, government, researchers or the media as is often the case. Most importantly, the created socially robust knowledge represents community values.

How successful a deliberative technique depends on the skills of the facilitators (Mansbridge *et al.*, 2006), the communicated knowledge from the experts and the quality of information that the deliberating citizens can access. How successful a democracy using deliberative tools would be depends on how well politicians listen to the voice of the people and what actions they take after being presented with the outcomes from deliberation. A very interesting phenomenon is that participants "are willing to revise preferences in light of discussion, new information, and claims made by fellow participants" (Chambers, 2004: 309) and shift their views, in some cases quite substantially, during the course of the deliberation process. Dryzak (2009: 4) explains this change that once engaged with the

topic of deliberation, they see it "as something that is theirs and worthwhile". The ownership of the problem that develops through deliberative
techniques continues outside the formal process and can lead to active
actions undertaken by these same participants through other channels
within society, including their place of employment, engagement with the
community and political life.

Climate change has been and will continue to be the topic of many
local and national deliberations (e.g., Edwards *et al.*, 2008) but this issue
is a stark example for the need of global deliberation. The existing body
of expert knowledge as represented, for example by the work of the IPCC
(2007), has been constantly challenged by politicians, lay people and
denialists (Diethelm and McKee, 2009). Copenhagen itself proved how
difficult it is for politicians to negotiate a fair deal for the planet as well as
for their own countries. On the other hand, computer modelling and
simulation suggest that highly competitive strategies within a situation of
limited resources (as is the case with almost anything on this planet) can
only lead to temporary competitive advantages, while the logical alternative appears to be cooperation (Todorov and Marinova, 2010). The need
for a global resolution and a global change of tactics are pressing, particularly under the existing time constraints. Governments around the world,
including those which have been democratically elected, are failing to
deliver, and a global deliberative process may be the only way to move
things forward.

Deliberation however is far from a smooth process. According to
Görsdorf (2006: 178), "dynamics of subjectivities can be expected to
emerge in deliberative procedures". On the other hand, Gambetta (1998: 22)
stresses that the "positive consequences of deliberation primarily concern
the distribution of information". These two aspects, namely information
framing and the values that people have (as represented by their subjectivities), are of particular interest to this chapter. They will be explored further
in the remainder of the text.

Global Green Information System

Access to information is crucial in raising awareness about climate change
but research shows that it has had limited influence on people's attitudes

and behaviors (Douglas *et al.*, 1998). Of central importance is not how people receive information about climate change but how they engage with its content (e.g., Hargreaves *et al.*, 2003). Deliberation is thus a highly engaging way for understanding, becoming involved and coming up with ways to reverse human impact on the health of the planet. It has the ability to capture the imagination and potentially generate a self-fulfilling image of the desired future (Olson, 1995).

Currently, despite the enormous bodies of knowledge that we have collected through research, information about the state of the planet is not directly readily available in the public domain on people's fingertips. The cloud of secrecy surrounding ownership and use of data sources is justi-fied through market-based mechanisms for paying for research, national security priorities or simply lack of funding. It has also allowed question-ing and attacks at research findings and policy measures. If climate change is a global agenda, shouldn't the information available for it to be explained and addressed, be shared?

To make things even more difficult, the reality is that the planet is never in a static state. It constantly evolves with natural and human-triggered changes. What is hence needed is a dynamic non-hierarchical GIS-based GGIS that people can access freely. Such a system can both store and transmit real live data but it could also have the capacity to model scenarios.

We have witnessed around the world the explosion of computer power and interactive software that provides unprecedented opportunities "for talking and working together through electronic media" (Gastil and Keith, 2005: 17), but we are yet to see the use of social media and e-governance penetrate the area of climate change. The GGIS should not only be inter-active but should allow for planetary citizens to contribute towards its data and content. Most importantly, GGIS could become the virtual common space for global deliberation and global deliberative democracy.[vi]

The global on-line climate change deliberation organized by Denmark in the lead to Copenhagen was the first useful step in the right direction, but what is required is a constant active process of citizens' engagement and deliberative contributions to global policy making. This is something that will need a GGIS. However the outcomes that are going to come out of such global deliberations would depend on the reasons why people who live now care about future generations, the planet, its non-human world and the future itself. The answer to this question lies in people's spirituality.

Spirituality

Deliberative democracy is based on decision-making through public deliberation by people in a democratic society following principles, such as respect, right to speak and dialogue, that affirm the need to justify decisions made by citizens and their representatives (Gutmann and Thompson, 2004: 3). Chambers (2004) points out that for each participant the deliberative process starts from a private reason, often linked to deep beliefs, and moves to a high standard of public reason. It is people's spirituality that facilitates their will to do this transition and make decisions for the common good. According to Boff (1995: 81), "(h)uman beings not only have responsibility but are connected to make the world as good as possible ... what concerns everyone should be thought about, discussed, and decided by everyone" for spirituality is a synergy between people's attitude towards themselves, society and the environment.

From a religious perspective, knowledge is holistic and represented in one book — the Gita, Torah, Bible, Qur'an, the gospel (Gambetta, 1998). Indigenous knowledge around the world, such as that of the Australian Aborigines, the American Indians, the Indigenous peoples in Africa or the Maori in New Zealand, continues to be holistic. Since the Enlightenment and the Age of Modernity however, Western knowledge has become not only partitioned but also unevenly distributed within society. What however has stayed relatively unchanged and deeply rooted in the cultures around the world is people's spirituality. In spirituality lies the potential of actualizing and exploiting the deliberative conception of democracy, for it highlights people's values for reciprocal reason-giving, discussion of public matters publicly, mutual respect, concerns about the underprivileged and weak in the society, demonstrating a good effort to find mutually acceptable terms of social cooperation.

Essential to spirituality is the strong longing and search for personal perfection (Marchetti, 1963). The case of climate change is particularly complex as it involves re-conceptualization and reconciling of the notion of justice (and global justice) in its cosmopolitan, nationalistic or individual interpretations (e.g., Tan, 2004). The current high consumption and pollution patterns of the West are not only unsustainable, they have not provided increasing happiness and satisfaction while hunger, disease and malnutrition prevail in other parts of the world (Environmental Careers Organisation, 2004). Maintaining a global deliberative dialogue will make participants engage with these problems in a deeper and more meaningful level, take ownership and initiative where possible to make the change.

By cultivating deliberative spiritual skills and virtues, such as veracity, non-violence, practical judgment, civic integrity and civic magnanimity, a democratic society treats its members as free and equal citizens (Macedo and Tamir, 2002: 25–26). As deliberative democracy affirms the need to justify decisions made by citizens (before forwarding them to their representatives such as politicians, business, academics, not-for-profit and community organizations or just particular individuals within civil society for triggering good governance), its basic presupposition is based on spirituality enabling everyone to share the common good for the satisfaction of essential needs leading towards a constant improvement of human wellbeing and maintaining the ecological capacity of the planet. Spirituality, a moral entity synergistically generated from ethics and values, intrinsically enters into the deliberative process, for people in a democratic society feel socially responsible, both from moral and practical standpoints, to find the best solutions. It is the source of the will to act morally (Smith and Standish, 1997).

Conclusion

For humanity to be able to respond to the enormity of the climate change challenge, individual people and countries "must be made to feel part of a larger collective that can successfully tackle the problem" (Moser and Dilling, 2004: 43). Deliberative democracy is a very new concept but has already been found to educate and empower people and help reconnect citizens and public officials in the search of good governance (Odugbemi and Jacobson, 2008; Gastil, 2008). It can be a way of approaching global politics on this hot issue. Whether it will become popular depends on a number of factors: the vested interests in the current political system and international organizations, the belief and supporting evidence that politicians have expert skills and abilities that cannot be found in the wisdom of the average citizen and, the under-standing of the power of cooperation when humanity faces the most urgent challenges of climate change and from other global processes. It will also depend on how people across the world want to see the future, what is possible, important, doable and right or, in Perrin's (2006) words, on their democratic imagination. In many ways this chapter also builds on the "democratic imagination" of the authors and their under-standing as to where the future lies.

According to Gambetta (1998: 22), a powerful outcome from delib-eration is that "it spurs the imagination indirectly if it reveals that, on all known options, no compromise is possible, for this provides an incentive to think of new ones." The current political deadlock on climate change requires courage, creativity and innovation to look for new solutions. A spiritually charged deliberation is crucial for finding answers, including opting for the kind of technology to address the problems. The power of communication and information technologies through a GGIS "(p)ut into the hands and minds of the global population, in continuing global disclo-sure of independent, well informed discourse and deliberated agreement on the best tradeoffs for a future that will benefit the species the most, the steep course downhill for humanity can change in a few years — a nano-second of eternity" (Becker, 2007: 6).

Acknowledgment

The first author wants to acknowledge the financial support of the Australian Research Council.

References

Abels, G. (2002). Experts, Citizens and Eurocrats — Towards a Policy Shift in the Governance of Biopolitics in the EU'. *European Integration online papers* (EIoP) 6/19. Retrieved 26 July 2010 from http://eiop.or.at/eiop/pdf/2002-019.pdf.

Becker, T. (2007). How deliberative democracy may keep pseudo-democracy, the new rule by the few, from bungling into global catastrophes, *Journal of Public Deliberation*, 3(1), Article 5, pp. 1–6.

Boff, L. (1995). Ecology and Liberation: A New Paradigm. Orbis Book, New York.

Chambers, S. (2004). Behind closed doors: Publicity, secrecy, and the quality of deliberation, *The Journal of Political Philosophy*, 12(4), pp. 389–410.

Cohen, J. (1989). Deliberative democracy and democratic legitimacy. In Hamlin, A., Pettit, P. (eds.), *The Good Polity: Normative Analysis of the State*. Blackwell, Oxford, pp. 17–34.

Dowding, K., Goodin, R.E., Pateman, C. (2004). Justice and Democracy: Essays for Brian Barry. Cambridge University Press, Cambridge.

Diethelm, P., McKee, M. (2009). Denialism: What is it and how should scientists respond? *European Journal of Public Health*, 19(1), pp. 2–4.

Douglas, M., Gasper, D., Ney, S., Thompson, M. (1998). Human needs and wants. In Rayner, S., Malone, E.L. (eds.), *Human Choice and Climate Change, Volume 1: The Societal Framework*. Battelle Memorial Institute, Columbus, pp. 195–264.

Dryzek, J. (2009). The Australian Citizens' Parliament: A World First, *Journal of Public Deliberation*, 5(1), Article 9, pp. 1–7. Also available in Republics, Citizenship and Parliament, Papers on Parliament No. 51, pp. 39–48. Retrieved 24 July 2010 from http://www.aph.gov.au/Senate/pubs/pops/index.htm.

Edwards, P.B., Hindmarsh, R., Mercer, H., Bond, M., Rowland, A. (2008). A three-stage evaluation of a deliberative event on climate change and transforming energy, *Journal of Public Deliberation*, 4(1), Article 6, pp. 1–22.

Elster, J. (ed.) (1998). *Deliberative Democracy*. Cambridge University Press, Cambridge.

Environmental Careers Organisation (2004). The Eco Guide to Careers That Make a Difference: Environmental Work for a Sustainable World. Island Press, London.

Gambetta, D. (1998). "Claro!": An essay on discursive machismo. In Elster, J. (ed.), *Deliberative Democracy*. Cambridge University Press, Cambridge, pp. 19–43.

Gastil, J. (2008). *Political Communication and Deliberation*. Sage Publication, London.

Gastil, J., Keith, W.M. (2005). A nation that (sometimes) likes to talk: A brief history of public deliberation in the United States. In Gastil, J., Levine, P. (eds.), *The Deliberative Democracy Handbook: Strategies for Effective Civic Engagement in the Twenty-First Century*. Jossey Bass, New York, pp. 3–19.

Görsdorf, A. (2006). Inside deliberative experiments: Dynamics of subjectivity in science policy, *Policy and Society*, 25(2), pp. 177–206.

Gutmann, A., Thompson, D. (2004). Why Deliberative Democracy? Princeton University Press, Princeton, NJ.

Hargreaves, I., Lewis, J., Speers, T. (2003). Towards a Better Map: Science, the Public and the Media. Economic and Social Research Council, Swindon.

Hartz-Karp, J. (2009). Climate change: The need to change community engagement paradigms and practices. International Association for Public Participation International Conference, Keynote Address, Fremantle, Western Australia.

Hartz-Karp, J., Carson, L. (2009). Putting the people into politics: The Australian Citizens' Parliament, *International Journal of Public Participation*, 3(1), pp. 9–31.

Intergovernmental Panel on Climate Change (IPCC) (2007). Climate Change 2007: The Physical Science Basis, Contribution of Working Group I to the Fourth Assessment Report of the Intergovernmental Panel on Climate Change. Cambridge: Cambridge University Press.

Jost, J.T., Major, B. (2001). The Psychology of Legitimacy: Emerging Perspectives on Ideology, Justice and Intergroup Relations. Cambridge University Press, Cambridge.

Leib, E.J. (2004). Deliberative Democracy in America: A Proposal for a Popular Branch of Government. Pennsylvania State University Press, University Park, PA.

Leighninger, M. (2006). The Next Form of Democracy: How Expert Rule Is Giving Way to Shared Governance ... and Why Politics Will Never Be the Same. Vanderbilt University Press, Nashville.

Macedo, S., Tamir, Y. (2002). Moral and Political Education. New York University Press, New York.

Mansbridge, J., Hartz-Karp, J., Amengual, M., Gastil, J. (2006). Norms of deliberation: An inductive study, *Journal of Public Deliberation*, 2(1), Article 7, pp. 1–47.

Marchetti, A. (1963). Spirituality and the State of Life. Spiritual Life Press, Milwaukee, WI.

Moser, S.C., Dilling, L. (2004). Making climate hot: Communicating the urgency and challenge of global climate change, *Environment*, 46(10), pp. 32–46.

Perrin, A.J. (2006). Citizen Speak: The Democratic Imagination in American Life. University of Chicago Press, Chicago.

Odugbemi, S., Jacobson, T. (2008). Governance Reform under Real-world Conditions: Citizens, Stakeholders, and Voice. World Bank, Washington.

Olson, R.L. (1995). Sustainability as a social vision, *Journal of Social Issues,* 51(4), pp. 15–35.

Smith, R., Standish, P. (1997). Teaching Right and Wrong: Moral Education in the Balance. Trentham Books, London.

Tan, K.-C. (2004). Justice Without Borders: Cosmopoloitanism, Nationalism and Patriotism. Cambridge University Press, Cambridge.

Todorov, V., Marinova, D. (2010). Modelling sustainability. Mathematics and Computers in Simulation (forthcoming). Retrieved 27 July 2010 from doi 10.1016/j.matcom.2010.05.022.

Endnotes

i.   See for example, The Sydney Morning Herald, 23 July 2010, http://news.smh.com.au/breaking-news-national/gillard-plan-cops-criticism-20100723-10o2j.html.

ii. http://news.curtin.edu.au/, 26 July 2010.

iii. http://pubapps.uws.edu.au/news/index.php?act=view&story_id=2750, accessed 24 July 2010.

iv. http://www.whitehouse.gov/the_press_office/TransparencyandOpen Government/, accessed 26 July 2010.

v.   http://www.wwviews.org/, accessed 26 July 2010.

vi. In this day and age, on-line deliberation is becoming essential component of advancing deliberative democracy. For example, the global network of researchers and practitioners within the Deliberative Democracy Consortium are championing global cooperation in decision-making through the use of information technologies (http://www.deliberative-democracy.net/).

Part 2

Selected Case Studies

Chapter 5

Governance, Institutions and Corruption: Negative Sovereignty in Africa*

Derek H. Aldcroft

University of Leicester

Abstract

Since the Second World War, Africa and especially Sub-Saharan Africa (SSA) has had the poorest economic performance of any region in the world. Ironically, many African countries had set out with high hopes once they had thrown off the yoke of colonial rule but it was not long before disaster struck. Against the background of an expanding world economy Africa experienced 'a chronic failure of economic growth' (Collier and Gunning, 1996), so that by the end of the 20th century incomes per capita were little better than they had been at the time of independence, and in some cases a good deal worse. The main problem was the failure to improve the efficiency of resource use; in contrast to the position in many other developing countries total factor productivity was either static or negative for much of the time (Ndulu and O'Connell, 1999; Crafts, 2000). Thus while poverty was declining elsewhere, it was increasing steadily in SSA. By the turn of the century two-thirds of the population were estimated to be living at subsistence or below the absolute poverty line, while nearly one-half the world's poor lived in Africa (United Nations, 1997).

---

*Professor Keith Snell kindly read a draft of this chapter and offered most helpful comments especially on the role of the African tribal system.

There are of course many factors which can explain this remarkable state of affairs, but the one we shall focus on this chapter is Africa's great weakness in statecraft, by which we refer to political systems, bureaucracies, administrative organizations, property and legal rights and general issues of trust and contract enforcement. In other words, it is a question of good governance as opposed to bad governance and corruption. The general argument here is that with few exceptions African countries have lacked a sound social and political base which would favor growth and development and that this base has tended to deteriorate over time.

Keywords: Corruption, governance, Sub-Saharan Africa, sovereignty, institutions, political instability democracy, Third World, nepotism, military regimes, tribal networks, social institutions, Political Elites, economic regulation, statism, government spending, Civil War, institutional structures, development agencies, multinational aid, political institutions, statecraft, social institutions.

Little else is requisite to carry a state to the highest degree of opulence from the lowest barbarism but peace, easy taxes and a tolerable administration of justice, all the rest being brought about by the natural course of things (Adam Smith)

No country has made economic progress without positive stimulus from intelligent governments (W. A. Lewis)

Since the Second World War Africa, and especially Sub-Saharan Africa (SSA) has had the poorest economic performance of any region in the world. Ironically, many African countries set out with high hopes once they had thrown off the yoke of colonial rule but it soon became apparent that freedom was not the gateway to prosperity as many of the new leaders imagined.[i] In fact it was not long before disaster struck.[ii] Against the background of an expanding world economy Africa experienced 'a chronic failure of economic growth' (Collier and Gunning, 1999b, 4), so that by the end of the 20th century incomes per capita on average were little better than they had been at the time of independence, and in some cases a good deal worse. The main problem was the failure to improve the efficiency of resource use; in contrast to the position in many other developing countries total factor productivity was either static or negative for much of the time (Ndulu and O'Connell, 1999, 45; Crafts, 2000, 17–18). Thus while poverty was declining elsewhere it was increasing steadily in SSA. By the turn of the century, two-thirds of the population were estimated to be living at subsistence or below the absolute poverty line, while nearly one half the world's poor lived in Africa (United Nations, 1997, 1–3).

There are of course many factors which can explain this remarkable state of affairs, but the one we shall focus on in this paper is Africa's great weakness in statecraft, by which we refer to political systems, bureaucracies, administrative organizations, property and legal rights and general issues of trust and contract enforcement. In other words, the question of good governance as opposed to bad governance and corruption. The general argument here is that with few exceptions African countries have lacked a sound social and political base which would favor growth and development and that this base has tended to deteriorate over time.

Government and institutions, or what Hall and Jones (1999, 84) refer to as 'social infrastructure,' have come to be regarded as important attributes for successful economic development. The relevance of institutional change to economic progress has long been recognized. A century ago Cunningham (1904), for example, touched upon many of the key issues, which were later elaborated in more detailed and rigorous form in the work of North and Thomas (1970, 1973); North (1981; 1990; 2005). In order that economic enterprise may thrive it is essential that the institutional and legal frameworks protect individual property rights, ensure trust between individuals, enforce contracts, minimize the costs of economic transactions and facilitate resource flows. In addition, social institutions should be such that they protect citizens from excessive diversion of the product of their labor, either by the state itself or by private agents through theft, protection rackets and the like. Since the state or its government is best equipped for this purpose it is important that political control does not fall into the hands of a self-chosen élite since then it may very well degenerate into what may be termed 'negative sovereignty,' states in name only, inefficient, illegitimate, corrupt and frequently unstable and which can be very harmful to development. These in Jackson's terminology are deemed to be quasi-states which have not been empowered and legitimized properly and which therefore lack the institutional features of sovereign states as defined by international law. The antithesis, 'positive sovereignty' is more likely to flourish under pluralistic democratic regimes, which have been fully legitimized by a mass electorate, producing a social infrastructure more conducive to economic development (Jackson, 1990, 1–21).

Positive sovereignty, along with modern states and appropriate infrastructures, did not happen overnight in the developed countries of the West. They evolved gradually and erratically and it was to be many centuries before they crystallized in their modern form. But when they did they provided an environment conducive to economic enterprise and personal endeavor since graft, corruption, theft, exaction and confiscatory taxation had been reduced to a minimum, while the legal framework upheld economic and commercial transactions. This of course was only true of western Europe and North America by the 19th century. Eastern Europe and much of the rest of the world still labored under negative sovereignty reminiscent of the Dark Ages in Europe.

The sad thing is that the positive sovereignty of the West was not readily transmitted to the lesser developed world in the later 20th century. Rostow believes that the greatest weakness of many developing countries, whether they are in Latin America, Africa or Asia, in the postwar decades has been their lack of a sound political base. 'The story of the developing regions since the Second World War evokes much more of the tortured and violent story of early modern Europe from, say, the 15th to the 18th centuries, than the straightforward working out of the value system of modernization' (Rostow, 1990, 403). Lal expressed similar sentiments 'Despite their trappings of modernity, many developing countries are closer in their official workings to the rapacious and inefficient nation-states of 17th- or 18th-century Europe, governed as much for the personal aggrandizement of their rulers as for the welfare of the ruled' (Lal, 1997, 108). This resulted in the persistence of institutions and value systems, which, as Lance Davis notes, unlike old machines or processes, had an amazing ability to resist the scrap heap, but which were conducive to stagnation and decline rather than growth and development (Lyons *et al.*, 2008, 36, 229).

The modern Western institutional legacy was not passed on to the ex-colonial regimes of Africa, or at least if it was, then only very briefly and in a weakened form. This is perhaps scarcely surprising since democracy and self-government had rarely featured in the bureaucratic and autocratic administrations of the colonial period, even though they were reasonably efficient and fairly incorrupt. Thus the successor states, like their counterparts in Eastern Europe after the First World War, had little experience of pluralistic democratic governance. The new regimes of the post-colonial era were anxious to claim legitimacy based on national identity and for a time to flirt with democracy and institutional systems based on western models. But, as Landes (1990, 10) pertinently observes, they tried to create the whole panoply of institutions and infrastructures in a matter of years or decades, something that had taken Europe centuries to accomplish. Very soon therefore, through the pressures of claims upon them, they degenerated into something quite different. In the words of Fieldhouse (1986, 57), "they were encumbered with layers of claimants to power and wealth whom they could not satisfy. They were saddled with promises of rapid economic and social development which were unrealizable. The common result was fundamental political instability usually concealed under monopolistic or oligopolistic authoritarian regimes".

According to Ndulu and O'Connell (1999, 47), by the mid-1970s most of the newly independent African states had cast off the trappings of democracy to be replaced by authoritarian structures of one sort or another (see also Oliver, 1999, 270). A decade or so later only a handful of countries in SSA — Botswana, Gambia, Mauritius, and Senegal — had multi-party systems with meaningful political representation. The rest could be classified as follows: 11 military oligarchies, 16 plebiscitary one-party systems, 13 competitive one-party systems and two 'settler oligarchies' (Namibia and South Africa). Tilly (1992, 209–213) reckoned that two-thirds of African states were under military control in 1986. From the late 1980s, partly as a result of pressure from the International Monetary Fund (IMF) and the World Bank, there was a trend towards greater democratization in several countries, notably Benin, Malawi, Mali, Mozambique, Niger and Zambia; by contrast, Gambia went the other way following the coup of 1994 (Barro, 1997, 84). However, one should be wary of reading too much into these positive shifts; democratic features were often cosmetic or skin deep, Zimbabwe providing the classic illustration of perverted democracy. In fact not many African countries could be classed as truly democratic in the 1990s. Most of them existed to keep in power very small political elites. When subject to pressure to introduce democratic reforms they made a showing of doing so but then proceeded to subvert the workings of the democratic process by ballot rigging, intimidation, violence and any other means that would ensure the continued rule of the elite groups (Oliver, 1999, 297).

In many Third World countries political institutions and social infrastructures have been much less conducive to economic progress than those that served the Western world in the 19th and 20th centuries. The drift to political and institutional disintegration has been deeper and more pervasive in Africa than anywhere else in the world.[iii] In fact, some African finance ministers openly admitted that by the end of the 20th century the majority of countries in SSA had a lower state capability than at the time of independence (Hawkins, 1997, 26). Many commentators have highlighted the general collapse of statecraft. The World Bank (1993, 22) described the situation in these terms: 'In many African countries the administrations, judiciaries, and educational institutions are now mere shadows of their former selves .... Equally worrying is the widespread impression of political decline. Corruption, oppression, and nepotism are increasingly evident.' Fernández Jilberto and Mommen (1996, 10), were even more forceful in their condemnation of political degeneration.

The most appalling aspect of Africa's decline is the decay of Africa's institutional capacities. Corruption, criminality, nepotism and oppression are common features of all African countries. Some regimes and their bureaucratic rulers have been extremely brutal and have regarded their dominance as an occasion for pillage. Routinely used torture and murder became their instruments when they tried to stay in power and their successor regimes have often had just as little respect for human rights and liberties. Most of these regimes have failed in their attempts to construct a nation state or to cope with the legacy of their colonial past. Military regimes have been the outcome of economic failure and most African regimes rely on ethnic support and bureaucracies in order to control the population. Growing violence and instability have accompanied and induced a process of state disintegration in many an African country.

Once this sort of situation arises the whole body politic becomes rotten and the upshot is a system of governance and administration which runs counter to best practice as far as development and human welfare are concerned. There is no longer a positive role for the state and its institutions in terms of law, order, trust, human welfare, enterprise and the protection of property and political rights of the populace at large since government, if one can call it that, is by élite groups for élite groups. The majority of the population, including the important small-scale entrepreneurial class is effectively marginalized by the political process.

In other words, the state in any real sense of the term had almost ceased to exist in many African countries. Effectively it had been captured by tiny groups of predatory leaders intent largely on perpetuating their position and enriching themselves. Questions of poverty, education, housing and the promotion of economic growth were the least of their worries. The elite groups throve by exploiting the majority (mainly the peasantry) and they were essentially a parasitical vampire class. But it was basically an unstable situation as rival groups jockeyed for position at the top and inevitably this led to strife and institutional breakdown. Thus until the state vehicle is reformed it is unlikely that African countries will move far along the development path (see Ayittey, 1998, 343).

Having said that, it should be noted that the instabilities and incongruities in the political and social structure could of course be a symptom or reflection of the stage of development, and may not therefore remain continuously a barrier to progress. After all, it took many centuries before European states resolved their inner conflicts and power struggles, and even by the 19th century eastern and southern European countries retained many of the vestiges of traditional society, including acute tribal and religious conflicts, violence, disregard of individual property rights, lack of trust and corruption. It may therefore take some time before Third World countries can adapt their state structures to those approaching western Europe in the 19th century (Rostow, 1990, 500–501).

It is sometimes argued that authoritarian governments helped to consolidate national identity given that Africa is riddled with tribal conflict as a result of its excessive ethnic fragmentation. We are somewhat skeptical of this claim for the simple reason that the extensive kinship and tribal networks in Africa and the loyalties they generate tend to transcend modern forms of government. Government leaders rely on tribal support for their power and if anything colonialism aggravated the problem by bundling together tribes which disliked each other as in the Congo, Nigeria and Rwanda. This worked to the advantage of the few educated and smart operators who saw their chance once freedom was granted to run their countries as personal fiefdoms so long as they secured the backing of the stronger tribes.[iv]

Be that as it may one thing that is certain is that elitist authoritarian regimes have done little to encourage economic development since most governments were bent on passing legislation which discouraged thrift and individual enterprise and curtailed economic freedom.[v] Most commentators believe that bad governance and poor social infrastructure have had a significant role to play in the economic degeneration of Africa. To quote Wallace '… it is not an exaggeration to argue that the failure of the state institutions is a major determinant of the limited progress in the improvement in human development indicators' (Wallace, 1999, 133). Jones (1996, 85) sees institutional failure as the main cause of Africa's economic predicament and suggests that government policies (which he refers to as macroeconomic populism) made it virtually impossible to experience agrarian-led growth following independence. Scully (1988, 652–662) stresses the importance of property rights and institutional frameworks in terms of efficiency and growth. He found that politically open societies subscribing to the rule of law, private property rights and market allocation of resources grew approximately three times as fast and were two and one half times more efficient than societies where such rights were attenuated. Hall and Jones in their wide-ranging cross-country analysis (127 countries) of differing levels of productivity conclude that differences in social infrastructure are sufficient to explain the major variations in capital intensity, human capital per worker and productivity (Hall and Jones, 1999, 110). They found a close and powerful relationship between levels of output per worker and measures of social infrastructure such that observed differences in social infrastructure between say Niger and the United States could explain most of the 35-fold difference in labour productivity between the two countries (Hall and Jones, 1999, 84–85). Freeman and Lindauer (1999) came to a similar conclusion: that given a stable political and institutional environment which enables individuals to reap the rewards of their investments, then many of the alleged barriers to growth — education, trade, inequality, the handicaps of geography and climate — will prove to be surmountable. Ayittey (1998, 343) believes that the state vehicles currently in existence in many African countries are totally unsuited to the 'development journey' of the 21st century. On the other hand, Barro (1997, 119) is a little more circumspect about the influence of regime structures, but recognizes the importance of the rule of law and an improvement in democratic rights up to a certain point.

Some authors have personalized the matter, blaming directly the unscrupulous leaders who have captured the organs of power and used them for their own purposes. Thus Collier and Gunning (1999a, 100) argue that "Africa stagnated because its governments were captured by a narrow elite that undermined markets and used public services to deliver employment patronage. These policies reduced the returns on assets and increased the already high risks private agents faced. To cope, private agents moved both financial and human capital abroad and diverted their social capital into risk-reduction and risk-bearing mechanisms". Even more forthrightly, some writers attribute the African mess largely to its leaders, who have presided over declining economies while carefully enriching themselves and their cronies, the governments of most poor countries being controlled by rich and influential people (Rotberg 2000, 47–52; Ramsay 1984, 393). We are informed that "… kleptocratic, patrimonial leaders [like Mugabe of Zimbabwe] give Africa a bad name, plunge its peoples into poverty and despair, and incite civil wars and bitter ethnic conflict. They are the ones largely responsible for declining GDP levels, food scarcities, rising infant-mortality rates, soaring budget deficits, human rights abuses, breaches of the rule of law, and prolonged serfdom for millions — even in Africa's nominal democracies" (Rotberg, 2000, 47). Another classic example is President Mobutu Sese Seko of Zaire (now Democratic Republic of Congo). While his subjects lived in abject poverty (Zaire being one of the poorest nations in the world) he amassed untold of wealth through misappropriating official funds and nefarious business contacts. It is said that he siphoned off some 18% of the national budget for his personal use and also appropriated 20% of foreign assistance that came into Zaire from 1965 when he was brought to power in a CIA-based coup. By the later 1980s, Mobutu was reputed to be one of the richest men in the world with most of his assets held abroad in hotels, mansions, luxury apartments and a fleet of Mercedes-Benz cars (Hancock, 1989, 64, 178–179).

The interesting question is how such situations arise in the first place. Did bad institutions throw up bad leaders or was it the latter that were directly responsible for the degeneration of the social infrastructure? Or was it the abject poverty of such countries that made possible the emergence of bad regimes. And in turn, how much feedback is there from poverty and slow growth to political instability and institutional degeneration? These are questions which we cannot explore here but they have been the subject of recent analysis (see Guillaumont *et al.*, 1999; Gyimah-Brempong and Traynor, 1999).

There are many ways in which states and institutions have distorted market incentives and thereby deterred enterprise and investment in African countries. Widespread economic regulation and the imposition of exacting demands on private producers seriously weakened economic incentives. The proliferation of administrative controls and licenses, bureaucratic inefficiency and red-tape, the imposition of various exactions (including taxes), the outright confiscation of property and the distortion of normal market forces by regulatory decrees, have not merely discouraged enterprise but gave rise to corruption, bribery and nepotism and set the individual against the system (McCarthy, 1990, 26; Reynolds, 1986, 129). Mauro's study of corruption and bureaucratic inefficiency suggests that there is a negative relationship between corruption and investment and growth whereas bureaucratic efficiency is conducive to growth and investment (Mauro, 1995, 705–706). Administrative control and regulation, often reminiscent of wartime conditions, have done much to increase insecurity and stifle enterprise and investment, especially among small-scale producers in both agriculture and industry. This type of climate does not favor the growth of a strong, acquisitive and market-orientated bourgeoisie, operating by and within the rule of law, which was the hallmark of 19th century western development. When the risk and reward patterns so clearly favor the politically astute and those with the right connections at the expense of individuals of enterprise and initiative, who in their right mind would risk their assets? (Landes, 1990, 10; Batou, 1990, 465). As Bruce Baker (2002, 94) observes, where people cannot easily call governments to account, they too will have recourse to clientelism, corruption, evasion of controls and regulations and legal obligations in order to assuage their own position. More than two centuries ago Adam Smith, who believed that there were some things which the state could do better than private enterprise, warned that commerce and manufactures would not flourish if proper justice and legality did not prevail:

> Commerce and manufactures can seldom flourish long in any state which does not enjoy a regular administration of justice, in which the people do not feel themselves secure in the possession of their property, in which the faith of contracts is not supported by law, and in which the authority of the state is not supposed to be regularly employed in enforcing the payment of debts from all those who are able to pay. Commerce and manufactures, in short, can seldom flourish in any state in which there is not a certain degree of confidence in the justice of government (Smith, Book V, Ch III).

In many African countries, the state has had a much higher presence in economic affairs than was the case with most European governments in the 19th century. Budgetary outlays have accounted for up to a third of national income which may be no bad thing providing budgetary systems are efficient and that revenue resources are used for the benefit of the population at large. Unfortunately, this has not generally proved to be the case. There has been a general lack of transparency in budgetary accounting, expenditure patterns are often distorted, while revenue-raising exactions have been inequitable. On balance the system favored the rich and those with power at the expense of the population as a whole.

For the majority of African countries budgets have been described as 'a figment of the imagination.' (Wallace, 1999, 32). There is a lack of direct correspondence between allocations and deliveries and only a few countries have been able to produce audited accounts within a year of the completion of the relevant fiscal period. Deviations from planned or allocated expenditure have been frequent such that funds for say school textbooks mysteriously get diverted into ministerial limousines (Wallace, 1999, 132). These aberrations apart, there are grounds for arguing that the structure of budgetary outlays is inappropriate. Something like two-thirds of budgetary expenditures on average is devoted to defense (spending on which is high by past western standards), and 'other sources'. The latter consist mainly of expenditure on general administration including employee compensation. By comparison spending on social services tends to be very modest, while the remaining outlays are devoted to economic services, the benefits from which are far from apparent.

The military budget is worth exploring in a little more detail since this is the one that has really burgeoned in the post-colonial period. On average for SSA it leapt from 0.7% of GDP in 1960 to 3.8% in 1990 and is now more than health and education spending combined (Deegan, 1996, 191). Since African countries have few major external foes, much of the expenditure is devoted to training and equipping soldiers in the art of fighting and killing domestic enemies, rather than in the skills of law enforcement and the security of resources, in order to preserve the power and privilege of military and other rulers. The problems have of course been compounded in many cases by severe internal conflicts, civil wars and border conflicts in which a regime's soldiers often end up fighting each other. Civil wars and political turmoil have been endemic in Africa — at any one time probably about one quarter to one-third of the continent is embroiled in some form of internal conflict — a situation arising more through poverty and polarization of society than from ethnic fragmentation (note however that the existence of over 2000 different tribal groups in Africa has certainly not helped matters in this respect), though no doubt sometimes instigated by rulers themselves to serve their own purposes on the divide and rule principle (Collier and Hoeffler, 1998, 563–573). Be that as it may, vulnerability to internal conflict has not only absorbed scarce resources in military spending, but civil war itself has had disastrous effects on economic performance. Collier (1999, 175–181) estimates that civil wars resulted in per capita GDP declines of over 2% a year on average, and that in a prolonged civil war of some 15 years (for example, Uganda, 1971–1986) the GDP loss could be as high as 30%. Instability and disturbance discourages inward investment and induces capital flight both of which SSA could well do without. The continent in fact has a very poor record in attracting inflows of private commercial capital compared with other underdeveloped regions of the world. Capital flight has been an endemic problem and few African states have been able to guarantee freedom from political turbulence to reassure multinational corporations, as has been the case in East Asian countries (Higgott, 1986, 294).[vi] For similar reasons there has also been a brain drain of skilled manpower from Africa because the opportunities are so limited for highly qualified labor. In 1989, some 70,000 African graduates were said to have stayed in Europe after their term of study and those remaining in North America were reckoned to be even larger (Oliver, 1999, 310).

On the revenue raising side of state accounts, tax regimes tend to be highly regressive and discriminatory and often benefit a small minority of people. This situation has been a common feature of less developed countries in the past and one from which few lessons have been learned. Agricultural producers especially are often heavily taxed (compare the situation in 19th century eastern Europe), while benefit systems tend to favor the well-paid professional classes (often government employees) with little protection afforded to the bulk of the population. In consequence, fiscal policies tend to strengthen the already unequal distribution of income and wealth, compounded in some cases by the excessive concentration of land ownership due to the absence of land reform. The result is that the majority of the population, and especially the small-scale entrepreneurial class, is marginalized by the political and economic system.

One by-product of societies with deficient social infrastructures and institutions and corrupt practices among the ruling oligarchies, is a notable lack of trust among individuals and organizations. Research by neuro-economic theorists suggest that trust or lack of it may be a significant factor in how societies develop. Where trust expectations are low and the level of deceit is high then people outwith the ruling elite will be wary about engaging in economic and financial transactions, and this in turn will react adversely on economic growth. The level of trust varies a great deal between countries but it appears to be especially low in many lesser developed nations, often falling below the critical level of 30%. Persaud (2004, 24) believes that 'countries where trust is lower than a critical level of about 30%, as with much of South America and Africa, are at risk of remaining in a suspicion-locked poverty trap.'

Allied to this are the important issues of risk control, the maintenance of law and order, the protection of property rights, the enforcement of contracts and contractual obligations, and the reduction in rent-seeking and the violence and intimidation associated with it. Only the political system/government can put in place a system of risk control and protection which is essential if economic development is to flourish and this is probably only going to take place where conditions of participatory democracy provide group trust and loyalty as opposed to the corruption and rent-seeking that prevails under rule by authoritarian elites (White, 2009, 132, 166).

We know that the politico-institutional structure has been responsible for the restrictive economic policies of many African countries which in turn have, it is argued, damaged African growth prospects. Sachs and Warner (1997) reckon that Africa is not incapable of generating fairly robust economic growth despite geographic, demographic, resource and climatic handicaps. However, they argue that African countries have been held back since independence as a result of highly distorted trade policies and non-market-orientated institutions. Had Africa followed growth policy strategies similar to those of East Asian countries, it is estimated that it could have achieved a per capita growth averaging 4.3% a year over the period 1965–1990. This appears a very optimistic scenario however. The emphasis is very much on the gains to be had from trade liberalization and trade openness and the prospects for trading on a global basis (see also Sharer, 1999, 93; Basu *et al.*, 2000, 9), but one wonders whether this would have been enough, or indeed whether it could have been realized without significant political and structural reforms first having taken place.

Sad though it is to report the western developed nations have been partly responsible for the state of poor governance in Africa and some other less developed countries. From the colonial rulers the incoming indigenous leaders inherited a comprehensive system of controls which had largely been put in place in the early postwar era prior to independence and which were accepted like manna from heaven. Thus the ex-colonies of Sub-Saharan Africa passed into the 1960s with economic power highly concentrated in the hands of the state and the local representatives of international companies (Munro, 1976, 205). Bandow reckons that it was the metropolitan rulers who taught the educated indigenous elites how to use economic controls to extract vast wealth from their populations and then how to spend the funds for their own political and personal advantage. 'The creation of a dirigiste economic structure, hand-made for the authoritarian leaders who took control in developing countries, may be the most important and destructive legacy of colonialism' (Bandow, 1998, 213–219; Bauer, 1984, 28–33). There is no doubt that many African politicians and bureaucrats aspired to the life-style of their western counterparts and were prepared to go to any lengths to achieve their ambitions.

The pernicious system was further consolidated when various development agencies, the international financial organizations (the World Bank and the International Monetary Fund), together with the many political and economic experts who arrived in their hordes to tell the new governments what they should do. By channeling billions of $ of aid to African and other underdeveloped countries through official channels these agencies helped to prop up a system which brought few benefits to the mass of the populations but enriched the chosen few. When everyone had their cut there was little left for the benefit of the ordinary population. As Hancock writes: "After the multi-billion-dollar 'financial flows' involved have been shaken through the sieve of over-priced and irrelevant goods that must be bought in the donor countries, filtered again in the deep pockets of hundreds of thousands of foreign experts and aid agency staff, skimmed off by dishonest commission agents, and stolen by corrupt Ministers and Presidents, there is really very little left to go around". (Hancock, 1989, 190). In the 1980s, the World Bank pledged some 80% of its funds through parastatels and other official organs yet there were few success stories to report (Roberts, 1998, 229–232). Even the World Bank had to admit in one of its later reports that the costs of state-led development far outweighed the benefits: 'Governments embarked on fanciful schemes. Private investors lacking confidence in public policies or in the steadfastness of lenders, held back. Powerful rulers acted arbitrarily. Corruption became endemic. Development faltered, and poverty endured' (World Bank, 1997, 1–2).

In other words, foreign multinational aid can quite easily sustain political and institutional structures and systems of economic values and property rights which are basically detrimental to growth. One might of course wonder why western governments, officials and leaders do not learn from their mistakes. The simple answer is that it is not in their interest to do so. Everyone involved in official aid stands to benefit. And in any case, it is easier and simpler to channel aid through recognized official agencies regardless of whether they are corrupt or not. But as one former Czech prime minister reflected: 'Where ... institutions emerge from the spontaneous activities of free individuals, they guarantee freedom and progress. Where they emerge from the powers of government, they bring oppression rather than freedom, corruption rather than the rule of law and decay rather than efficiency and equity.' (Klaus, 1998, p. xi).

Intrinsically Africa has great potential. There is no doubt that it is a rich continent both in terms of natural and human resources. Indeed, in the early postwar years, it was considered to have a more promising future than East Asia.[vii] It therefore deserves a better deal in terms of governance and statecraft. Maybe it is only a matter of time. After all, good governance was not something that materialized overnight in the West. It took centuries before value systems, institutions, property rights and trust were fashioned to the point where they became supportive of growth and development rather than an impediment to it (Landes, 1999, 507). As Lilian Knowles reminded us a long time ago 'When one looks back in English history and sees how civilized persons [e.g., Roman occupiers] must have regarded us about 1,900 years ago one need not despair of the tropics'. (Knowles, 1924, 509). One might also glean consolation from the fact that some late developers, for example the East Asian countries and even one or two in Africa such as Mauritius, managed to eliminate the worst aspects of negative sovereignty in good time before they had a chance to overwhelm them and condemn them to perpetual stagnation.

In this paper, we have emphasized the importance of political and social institutions which cover a wide range of issues including *inter alia,* monetary and financial institutions, cooperate governance, business-government relations, labor market practices, legal institutions and political and social institutions. Institutional reform became the buzzword in the later 20th century which was usually interpreted to mean the neo-liberal stance of the major international financial institutions such as the World Bank and the International Monetary Fund, or in short, the Washington consensus. There were two main defects to this strategy: first the notion that the neo-liberal policy fits all situations, and secondly, that reform to be effective needs to be radical and wide-ranging. In fact drastic neo-liberal reform if carried out suddenly may do more harm than good. This was demonstrated in the shock treatment in several East European countries in the 1990s. Instead the more promising scenario, where countries fall well below their potential, may be moderate and incremental reforms in the institutional structure, policies and political governance, which can produce a worthwhile pay-off. The key, according to Rodrik, is to identify the binding constraint on growth before it suffocates the country in question. This may be easier said than done, but it has happened in countries such as South Korea in 1961, China in 1978 and India in 1980 (Rodrik, 2007, 182–183, 191–192). History suggests not only that incremental reform rather than drastic upheaval has been more productive but that institutional diversity rather than institutional convergence has been the order of the day.

However, an important caveat is in order especially with reference to Africa. Changes in the institutional structure may be very difficult to implement in the absence of political consensus and social cohesion. In contrast to somewhere like South Korea, the majority of African countries have been, and still are, notorious for their limited political consensus and low level of social cohesion to bind societies together in networks of trust and loyalty which are essential for the unlocking of human potential (Moe, 2007, 22–261).

References

Ayittey, G.B.N. (1998). *Africa in Chaos*, New York: St Martin's Press.

Bandow, D. (1998), 'The first world's misbegotten economic legacy to the third world', in Dorn J.A. Hanke, S.H., Walters, A.A. (eds.), *The Revolution in Development Economics*, Washington DC: Cato Institute.

Barro, R.J. (1997). *Determinants of Economic Growth,* Cambridge, MA.: The MIT Press.

Basu, A., Calamitsis, E.A., Ghura, D. (2000). *Promoting Growth in Sub-Saharan Africa,* Washington DC: IMF.

Batou, J. (1990). Cent ans de résistance au sous-développement: l'industrialisation de l'Amérique latine et du Moyen-orient au défi européen, 1700–1870. Geneva: Droz.

Bauer, P.T. (1984). *Reality and Rhetoric: Studies in the Economics of Development,* London: Weidenfeld and Nicolson.

Collier, P. (1999). "On the economic consequences of civil war", *Oxford Economic Papers*, 51.

Collier, P. (2007). *The Bottom Billion: Why the Poorest Countries Are Failing and What Can Be Done About It*, Oxford: Oxford University Press.

Collier, P., Gunning, J.W. (1999a). Explaining African economic performance, *Journal of Economic Literature*, 37.

Collier, P., Gunning, J.W. (1999b). Why has Africa grown so slowly?, *Journal of Economic Perspectives*, 13.

Collier, P., Hoeffler, A. (1998). "On the economic causes of civil war", *Oxford Economic Papers*, 50.

Crafts, N. (2000). 'Globalization and growth in the twentieth century', in IMF, *World Economic Outlook: Supporting Studies*, Washington DC: IMF.

Cunningham, W. (1904). *An Essay on Western Civilisation in its Economic Aspects*, Cambridge: Cambridge University Press.

Deegan, H. (1996). *Third Worlds: The Politics of the Middle East and Africa*, London: Routledge.

Fernández Jilberto, A.E., Mommen, A. (1996). 'Setting the neo-liberal development agenda: structural adjustment and export-led industrialization', in Fernández Jilberto, A.E., Mommen, A. (eds.), *Liberalization in the Developing World: Institutional and Economic Changes in Latin America, Africa and Asia*, London: Routledge.

Fieldhouse, D.K. (1986). *Black Africa: Economic Decolonization and Arrested Development*, London: Allen & Unwin.

Freeman, R.B., Lindauer, D.L. (1999). 'Why not Africa', National Bureau of Economic Research Working Paper 6942, Cambridge, MA.

Guillaumont, P., Jeanneney, S., Brun, J.-F. (1999). How instability lowers African growth, *Journal of African Economies*, 8.

Gyimah-Brempong, K., Traynor, T.L. (1999). Political instability, investment and economic growth in sub-Saharan Africa, *Journal of African Economies*, 8.

Hall, R.E., Jones, C.I. (1999). Why do some countries produce so much more output per worker than others? *Quarterly Journal of Economics*, 114.

Hancock, G. (1989). *Lords of Poverty*, London: Macmillan.

Hawkins, T. (1997). 'Gloom starting to lift', *Financial Times World Economy and Finance Survey,* Part II, 19 September.

Higgott, R. (1986). 'Africa and the new international division of labour', in Ravenhill, J. (ed.), *Africa in Economic Crisis*, Basingstoke: Macmillan.

Jackson, R.M. (1990). *Quasi-states: Sovereignty, International Relations and the Third World*, Cambridge: Cambridge University Press.

Jones, S. (1996). "Macroeconomic populism and economic failure in Africa since 1960", in Aldcroft, D.H. Catterall, R.E. (eds.), *Rich Nations — Poor Nations: the Long-run Perspective*, Cheltenham: Edward Elgar.

Johnson, B.T., Sheehy, T.P. (1998). In Dorn, J.A., Hanke, S.H., Walters, A.A. (eds.), *The Revolution in Development Economics,* London: Institute of Economic Affairs.

Klaus, V. (1998), 'Foreword'. In Dorn, J.A., Hanke, S.H., Walters, A.A. (eds.), *The Revolution in Development Economics,* London: Institute of Economic Affairs.

Knowles, L.C.A. (1924). *The Economic Development of the British Overseas Empire,* London: Routledge.

Lal, D. (1997). *The Poverty of Development Economics,* London: Institute of Economic Affairs.

Landes, D.S. (1990). Why are we so rich and they so poor?, *American Economic Review, Papers and Proceedings,* 80.

Landes, D.S. (1999). *The Wealth and Poverty of Nations,* London: Abacus.

Lewis, W.A. (1955). *The Theory of Economic Growth,* London: Allen & Unwin.

Lyons, J.S., Cain, L.P., Williamson, S.H. (eds.) (2008). *Reflections on the Cliometrics Revolution: Conversations with Economic Historians,* London:. Routledge.

McCarthy, S. (1990). Development stalled: the crisis in Africa: a personal view, *European Investment Bank Papers,* 15.

Mauro, P. (1995). Corruption and growth, *Quarterly Journal of Economics,* 110.

Moe, E. (2007). *Governance, Growth and Global Leadership: The Role of the State in Technological Progress, 1750–2000,* Aldershot: Ashgate.

Monsarrat, N. (1956). *The Tribe That Lost Its Head,* London: Cassell.

Monsarrat, N. (1968). *Richer Than All His Tribe,* London: Cassell.

Munro, J.F. (1976). *Africa in the International Economy 1800–1960,* London: J.M. Dent.

Ndulu, B.J., O'Connell, S.A. (1999). Governance and growth in sub-Saharan Africa, *Journal of Economic Perspectives,* 13.

North, D.C. (1981). *Structure and Change in Economic History,* New York: Norton.

North, D.C. (1990). *Institutions, Institutional Change and Economic Performance,* New York: Cambridge University Press.

North, D.C. (2005). *Understanding the Process of Economic Change,* Princeton NJ: Princeton University Press.

North, D.C, Thomas, R.P. (1970). An economic theory of the growth of the western world, *Economic History Review,* 23.

North, D.C., Thomas, R.P. (1973). *The Rise of the Western World.* Cambridge: Cambridge University Press.

Oliver, R. (1999). The African Experience, London: Weidenfeld and Nicolson.

Persaud, R. (2004). 'The animal urge', *FT Magazine,* 28 August, 70.

Ramsey, R. (1984). UNCTAD's failures: the rich get richer', *International Organization,* 33.

Reynolds, L.G. (1986). *Economic Growth in the Third World: An Introduction,* New Haven, Conn.: Yale University Press.

Roberts, P.C. (1998). 'Shut down the architects of failed policy', in Dorn, J.A., Hanke, S.H., Walters, A.A. (eds.), *The Revolution in Development Economics,* London: Institute of Economic Affairs.

Rodrik, D. (2007). *One Economics: Many Recipes: Globalization, Institutions and Economic Growth,* Princeton: Princeton University Press.

Rotberg, R.I. (2000). Africa's mess, Mugabe's mayhem, *Foreign Affairs,* 79.

Rostow, W.W. (1990). *Theorists of Economic Growth from David Hume to the Present with a Perspective on the Next Century,* Oxford: Oxford University Press.

Sachs, J.D., Warner, A.M. (1997). Sources of slow growth in African economies, *Journal of African Economies,* 6.

Scully, G.W. (1988). The institutional framework and economic development, *Journal of Political Economy,* 96.

Sharer, R. (1999). 'Liberalizing the trade system', in Wallace, L. (ed.), *Africa: Adjusting to the Challenge of Globalization,* Washington DC: IMF.

Smith, A. (1776). An Inquiry Into the Nature and Causes of the Wealth of Nations, Modern Library, New York, 1937.

Tilly, C. (1992). *Coercion, Capital and European States, AD990–1990,* Oxford: Blackwell.

United Nations/Economic Commission for Africa (1997). *Report on the Economic and Social Situation in Africa,* Addis Ababa: United Nations.

Wallace, L. (ed.) (1999). Africa: Adjusting to the Challenge of Globalization, Washington DC: IMF.

White, C. (2009). *Understanding Economic Development: A Global Transition from Poverty to Prosperity,* Cheltenham: Edward Elgar.

World Bank (1993). *Annual Report,* Washington DC: World Bank.

World Bank (1997). *World Development Report 1997,* Oxford: Oxford University Press.

Endnotes

i. Kwama Nkrumah in 1949 stated that given independence the Gold Coast would be transformed into paradise within a decade. Needless to say paradise failed to materialize.

ii. Interestingly, Landes raises the point that no one paused to ask why the metropolitan powers relinquished the colonies with such indecent haste (Landes, 1999, 499).

iii. The degeneration of the political structure in much of Africa was brilliantly foreshadowed in Nicholas Monsarrat's gripping novel *Richer Than All His Tribe* in which he tells the story of a mythical African island following independence (Monsarrat, 1968).

iv. Again Nicholas Monsarrat outlines the sequence of events in Pharamaul in his earlier novel *The Tribe That Lost Its Head,* 1956.

v. It should be noted that political and economic freedom are not synonymous. While economic freedom and economic liberalisation are often accompanied by strong economic performance, economic freedom is not always associated with political freedom. In fact economic freedom has sometimes been the precursor to political relaxation, as in East Asia, while in Africa those countries with positive economic growth have not generally been politically free (Johnson and Sheehy 1998, 290–296).

vi. Despite being the most capital starved region in the world estimates suggest that in 1990 some 38% of Africa's private wealth was held abroad — in the case of Uganda almost two thirds — far more than any other region (Collier, 2007, 91–92).

vii. It is worth recalling that in the early 1960s there was not a great deal of difference between many Asian and African countries in terms of the level of development. Korea's per capita GDP in 1960 was about the same as that of the Sudan, while Taiwan's was similar to Zaire's, now one of the poorest countries in the world. Incomes in Ghana and Nigeria at that time were ahead of those in Korea and Indonesia. Overall Africa was the deemed then to have the edge on Asia as regards development prospects.

Chapter 6

Corruption in Bangladesh: Review and Analysis

M. A. B. Siddique*

UWA Business School

Abstract

Corruption is understood by the majority to be harmful to a country although the reason why is rarely understood. For this reason, economists have endeavored to determine the causes and consequences of corruption. Corruption is an important issue for Bangladesh since it is widely spread throughout the country and can lead to many unwanted consequences. Li *et al.* (2000) found that corruption, for example, can lead to misallocation of resources. Once bribing becomes an integrated part of the market, it will no longer be equal to bidding for scarce resources. They also found that corruption can be harmful to innovation; entrepreneurs have to get licenses and permits to start up new businesses and are often subjected to corruption. This is a consequence of corruption that could be detrimental to Bangladesh's growth. The quality of goods may also be adversely affected, with decisions about the issuing of permits and licenses being determined by the largest bribe paid rather than the highest quality of goods (Lambsdorff, 2007).

This chapter is divided into 4 parts: Part I discusses the concept and various quantitative measures of corruption. As far as this author is aware the PRS Group was the first to score countries based on corruption. Since then a multitude of indices have been produced by

* I wish to thank Rebecca Doran-Wu, UWA Business School, for her excellent research assistance in writing this chapter.

well-known institutions such as Transparency International, the World Bank and PricewaterhouseCoopers.

Part II deals with the magnitude of corruption in Bangladesh and more specifically looks at the effectiveness of anti-corruption agencies within the country. The causes of corruption in Bangladesh are also explored, with particular emphasis on banking, customs and telecommunications sectors. In addition, Part II looks at the consequences of corruption on economic growth.

Part III discusses five possible remedies for corruption in Bangladesh and Part IV provides a conclusion.

Keywords: Corruption, measurement of corruption, corruption in Bangladesh, consequences of corruption, remedies for corruption.

The Concept and Measurement of Corruption

The concept of corruption

Corruption refers to "the misuse of public power, office, or authority for private benefit — through bribery, extortion, influence peddling, nepotism, fraud, speed money or embezzlement" (United Nations Development Programme, 1999, New York, UNDP). When corruption is thus defined, it has a distinct moral and qualitative connotation. No matter what, corruption is immoral and therefore it has to be routed out.

Corruption is by no means confined to public officials. Individuals in private companies may also take bribes to provide goods and services if these are in short supply. Scarcity leads to rationing and rationing encourages corruption. If all services and goods were available in plenty, there would be less room for both taking and giving bribes.

Corruption at all levels of government — the executive, the legislature and the judiciary — are now relatively uncommon in most developed countries, although some public officials are still brought to justice for acting corruptly. But in many of the developing countries corruption exists at all levels of government, and it is sometimes very difficult to get a job done, such as procuring a license for an activity without offering bribes, in cash or in kind, to layers of public officials.

Now, the question is: does corruption have an inhibitive impact on economic growth and development? The question has been widely examined in economic literature in the past three decades. For the first few years, opinions of the experts were divided; but in more recent years, there has been a growing consensus that high levels of continuing corruption tend to be inimical to long-term growth.

However, it is possible to argue the other way round. Most developed countries seem to experience much lower levels of corruption in both government and non-government agencies than in comparable agencies in developing countries. If this is so we could argue that corruption is a by-product of poverty and underdevelopment, and that development itself provides an automatic mechanism to reduce (or eliminate) corruption. It is certainly arguable that when the general population in a country becomes more and more affluent with economic growth and development, they are less tempted towards 'petty' levels of corruption.

The measurement of corruption

There exists currently six popular measures of corruption, the; Corruption Perceptions Index (CPI); Global Corruption Barometer (GCB); Bribe Payers Index (BPI); World Bank Control of Corruption Index (CCI); International Country Risk Guide (ICRG) Corruption Score; and the Opacity Index.

The CPI was created in 1995 by a Berlin-based organization known as Transparency International (TI). Since then, the index has grown to include more than 180 countries and is produced annually. TI gathers its intelligence from its own network of personnel as well as other institutions such as the Economist Intelligence Unit, Freedom House and Political and Economic Risk Consultancy. In order to be eligible to be ranked in the CPI a total of 3 or more sources must be available for that particular country. The CPI gives participating countries a score out of 10, with 0 the highest level of corruption and 10 the lowest. TI then ranks the countries accordingly.

In more recent years TI has developed two other corruption measures: (1) the Bribe Payers' Index (BPI) which seeks to assess the supply side of corruption and ranks corruption by source country and industry sector and (2) the more recently developed is the Global Corruption Barometer

(GCB) which systematically surveys public opinion in order to assess the general public's perception and experience of corruption in more than 60 countries.

The CCI, along with other governance indicators, has been produced by the World Bank since 1996 for 213 countries. The World Bank views good governance and control of corruption as the main strategy for the alleviation of poverty. The World Bank seeks to minimize corruption on World Bank funded projects; and it also offers all technical assistance to countries in improving governance and controlling corruption.

The International Country Risk Guide has been published on a monthly basis by The PRS Group since 1980. It provides political, economic and financial risk ratings for those countries that are deemed to be important for international business. An index is created for each of the three categories; the Political Risk index is based on 100 points, while the remaining two are both based on 50 points. The scores are then summed and divided by two in order to obtain the weights for inclusion in the composite country score, where 0–49.9 and 80–100 points denotes Very High Risk and Very Low Risk respectively. One and five-year forecasts are made and projections are based on "best" and "worst" case scenarios.

PricewaterhouseCoopers created a new opacity index in 2001 which deals with five crucial pillars of the economy that affect business prospects, including corruption. While initially relying on surveys conducted by employees within the countries in question, it has since evolved into an index which is reliant on a comprehensive list of resources including the Global Competitiveness Report and the Index of Economic Freedom.

Corruption in Bangladesh

How corrupt is the country?

What becomes obvious when reading through the literature, is the extent of corruption within Bangladesh. Perhaps the most scandalous, but not surprising, is the magnitude of corruption in the Bangladesh police department. A survey conducted by Transparency International Bangladesh (TIB) discovered that the police department is the most corrupt public institution within the country; 84% of people who had dealings with police reported corruption and 75% paid bribes while seeking services (Wattad, 2003). Despite the extent of corruption within Bangladesh the number of people convicted for this crime still remains at a minimum. The number of cases actually filed, compared to those reported, is low due to lengthy bureaucratic procedures. Between 1972 and 1998, the annual proportion of cases filed with respect to the number reported was approximately 75% with only 32% of those resulting in conviction (Zafarullah and Siddiquee, 2001). The low conviction rate is the result of lack of evidence and determination of public prosecutors.

While there exists many different types of corruption, in 2003 TI found that the number one type of corruption in Bangladesh was the abuse of power, with 1336 cases, followed by bribery, 441, and asset stripping, 382 (Transparency International, 2003). Knox (2009) surveyed households and found that within the previous 12 month period 96.6% of households had experienced corruption within the law enforcement sector; 52.7% of which was in land administration while 47.7% was in judiciary sub-sectors. He also found that within the education sector 51% of corruption was due to negligence while embezzlement and bribery accounted for 21% and 20% respectively. In addition, 41.8% of households experienced corruption within the health sector with bribery and negligence accounting for 42 and 43% of total corruption within the division respectively.

Despite the lack of convictions, the extent of corruption that exists in Bangladesh cannot be disputed. Not only is it a hindrance to the operations of daily life it is also extremely costly to the Bangladeshi government; between 1999 and 2000 the government lost US$757.2 million (1.85% of GDP) due to corruption (Transparency International, 2003).

The indicators as discussed earlier allow us to draw conclusions on the level of corruption in Bangladesh based on quantitative measures. While Bangladesh is not included in the GCB, BPI or Opacity Index, it is included in the remaining 3 indices. Table 6.1 shows the 2010 percentile rank of Bangladesh in 2010 for the CPI, CCI and ICRG.

Since its introduction into the Transparency International Corruption Perception Index in 2001, Bangladesh has managed to move up the ranks

Table 6.1   Percentile rank of Bangladesh (2010)

CPI	CCI[a]	ICRG
25%	17%	42%

Source: Transparency International (2010); World Bank (2009); The PRS Group (2011).
[a] The data for CCI is taken from 2009 as at the time that this paper was written this was the most recently available data.

from 91 out of 91 countries in 2001 to 134 out of 178 in 2010 as shown in Table 6.2 which suggests that as a country it is experiencing some improvement.

What Causes Corruption in Bangladesh?

Causes of corruption can differ from country to country. Rock and Bonnett (2004) found that some of these differences can be contributed to the varying sizes of countries. They argue that for a large market with a large amount of labor, foreign investors may be more willing to accept their way of business with the inclusion of corruption. Smaller countries, however, may not have as large an influence on investors, and will have greater pressure to conform to international standards with regards to corruption. They also found that high levels of corruption are positively correlated with the amount of time managers have to spend dealing with bureaucrats.

Corruption within a country can be caused by different things. Rent-seeking behavior is one such example. The state has a responsibility to create policies that stimulate economic growth within a country. These policies depend on bureaucrats to transfer economic resources to private individuals who may obtain economic rent from these transfers. Bureaucrats are sometimes able to claim a part of this share in the form of bribes. Such rent-seeking behavior is likely to occur when a lack of government intervention leads to excess profits. Examples of this include trade restrictions, price controls and government-controlled provision of credit. Low-paid workers also have a greater incentive to accept bribes in order to survive.

Table 6.2 Ranking of top six corrupt countries based on Corruption Perception Index: 2001–2010[a]

Year/country	Bangladesh	Nigeria	Uganda	Indonesia	Kenya	Somalia	Number of countries in TI CPI	Most corrupt country and rank (in parentheses)
2001	91	90	98	88	84	N/A	91	Bangladesh (91)
2002	102	101	93	96	96	N/A	102	Bangladesh (102)
2003	133	132	113	122	122	N/A	133	Bangladesh (102)
2004	145	144	102	133	129	N/A	145	Bangladesh (145)
2005	158	152	117	137	144	N/A	158	Bangladesh (158)
2006	156	142	105	130	142	N/A	163	Haiti (163)
2007	162	147	111	143	150	179	179	Somalia (179)
2008	147	121	126	126	147	180	180	Somalia (180)
2009	139	130	130	111	146	180	180	Somalia (180)
2010	134	134	127	110	154	178	178	Somalia (178)

Source: Corruptions Perceptions Index, http://transparency.org/policy_research/surveys_indices/cpi, accessed 10 May 2011.

[a]This ranking should be interpreted with caution since it changes with the inclusion of more and more countries in the TI Corruption Perception Index.

The principal–agent model occurs when the government (principal) pays a salary to bureaucrats (agent) to provide some service to clients. Clients then reimburse the bureaucrats with a tax or tariff. Corruption occurs when the client has to pay an additional bribe to the agent in order to receive the service that the bureaucrat is already being paid for. In this case, the bureaucrat is earning more than the initial specified salary.

Corruption in Bangladesh has a long history. Pre-liberation the Pakistani government gave out large loans to financial institutions in the hopes that they would in turn pass it on to new industrialists and agriculturalists. This was done in order to promote the industrialization and modernization of agriculture. The large, but limited, amount of funds passing through these institutions gave bank officials an enormous amount of power in deciding who received loans. There were numerous reports of bribing and it was of general consensus that to be considered for the larger industrial loans political benefaction was required. After 1971, all private banks were nationalized. While the new government promoted industrialization, the methods which determined the receivers of loans largely mirrored the previous government, with many being the result of political patronage to party supporters, bureaucrats and their relatives. Those who had close relationships with the bureaucracy were able to default on loan repayments due to concessions in the forms of interest waivers, "blocked accounts" and repeated rescheduling (Transparency International Bangladesh, n.d.).

While corruption in the banking sector is widespread, it is also a large problem for the customs sector. Corruption in this sector is caused by the excess and unnecessary power given to customs officers. Current regulations give customs officers a high degree of discretionary power, allowing them to declare the value, quality or quantity of goods that enter the country. Customs officers are required to complete their assessment of incoming goods "without undue delay", which is again up to the discretion of the officer. These provide more than enough reasons for importers to pay for the misdeclaration of goods as well as "speed money" to customs officers, who have more than enough power to accept bribes (Transparency International Bangladesh, n.d.).

More recently, corruption has become prevalent in the telecommunications sector. Despite the high level of growth experienced by this sector, the revenues of the Bangladesh Telegraph and Telephone Board (BTTB) fell from 2001 to 2006. This was caused by the large growth of illegal Voice over Internet Protocol (VoIP) operations by private operators. The ability of the operators to provide such illegal services with such ease is a result of inaction by the Bangladeshi government to regulate the VoIP industry. As reported by Transparency International (2009a), 53.3% of the daily 30 million calls entering Bangladesh are controlled by illegal VoIP operators, causing the government to lose TK12 billion in revenue each year.

What becomes obvious when examining the above three sectors is that corruption in Bangladesh has arisen due to a lack of regulation. In the case of the customs sector this lack of regulation has resulted in large amounts of power being placed in the hands of customs officers allowing them to accept bribes without the consequences. In the telecommunications sector, however, a lack of regulation has allowed public companies to run illegal services, again without fear of the government and any retribution it may entail.

What are the consequences of corruption?

Existing literature has explored the empirical relationship between corruption and economic growth as well as other factors existing within a country. Husted (1999) found that the level of a country's corruption is correlated to the levels of; economic development; high uncertainty avoidance; high masculinity and; high power distance. Correlation with some of the variables may, surprisingly, show corruption to be a positive influence within certain communities. Uncertainty avoidance, for example, is "the extent to which members of a culture feel threatened by uncertainty or unknown situations" (Hofstede, 1997, cited by Husted, 1999). Corruption, as found by Husted (1999), reduces this uncertainty. In contrast, Mo (2000) found that a 1% increase in corruption levels reduces growth by 0.72%; the most effective pathway through which corruption has this effect is through political instability. In addition, he found that corruption leads to the reduction in the level of human capital and private investment. More recently, Schneider (2007) found that the extent of the shadow economy within a country also determines the extent of corruption present. To be more precise, he found that in high income countries corruption and the shadow economy are substitutes, while in low income countries they are complements.

There exist two opposing views on the impact of corruption on economic growth; some argue that it retards while others suggest that it promotes growth. Those that argue the former suggest that corruption distorts the composition of government expenditure. It is in the interest of corrupt politicians that they promote those industries in which it is easier to exact large bribes. This can cause larger spending of public resources in these areas. Corrupt politicians may therefore be more inclined to spend on large-scale investment projects than on textbooks and teachers' salaries, even though these promote greater economic growth than the former. It can be argued that corruption has a negative effect on economic growth mainly through private investment. Mauro (1996) found that a country that experiences an increase from 6 to 8% on the CPI score will also have a 4 percentage point increase in the investment rate and a 0.5 percentage point increase in its annual per capita GDP growth rate.

Li *et al.* (2009) found that corruption leads to workers moving from innovation to rent-seeking sectors, thereby decreasing growth. In addition, they found that the greater the inequality of asset distribution, the greater corruption decreases growth rates. They argue that corruption in countries with higher government spending experiences lower growth rates. This is because a large amount of spending by the government reduces investment rates which in turn discourages people from becoming entrepreneurs.

Rock and Bonnett (2004) also emphasize the effects of the organization of corruption on growth. They find that a higher level of organization corruption will have less effect on growth than if it was disorganized. This is because if there was a low level of organization then there would exist a number of people operating as individual monopolists. When this occurs, bribes have the potential to reach infinity, causing both economic growth and investments to decrease. On the other hand, if there is a high level of organization, people will monopolize corruption thereby limiting what they take as they know it will be possible to increase returns in the long run by giving them incentive to invest.

It has been argued that "corruption can, in extreme cases, be not only desirable but essential to keep the economy going" (Morgan, 1964). Mauro (1998) has reasoned that government employees who are allowed to exact bribes may work harder and corruption may help entrepreneurs

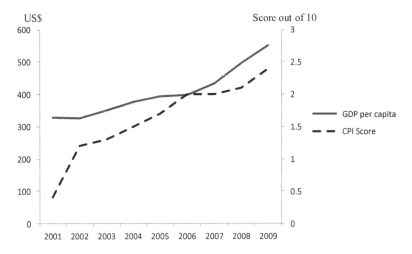

Figure 6.1 Comparison of Bangladesh's CPI score and GDP per capita (2001–2009)[i]

Source: Transparency International <http://www.transparency.org/policy_research/surveys_indices/cpi>, accessed 30 May 2011. World Bank, 2010a, <http://data.worldbank.org/indicator>, accessed 30 May 2011.

get around bureaucratic impediments. As suggested by Huntington (1968), Leff (1964) and Nye (1967) this is especially the case of cumbersome regulations, excessive bureaucracy and market restrictions. One line of research, as described by Lambsdorff (2007), argues that corruption is in fact a factor of production and so does not affect the growth of GDP.

Despite the magnitude of corruption in Bangladesh, the country has been experiencing a steady improvement in score in the Corruption Perceptions Index (CPI). As shown in Figure 6.1, the CPI score of Bangladesh has risen steadily since the country joined the index in 2001. One of the larger increases in ranking occurred in 2009 when CPI rose from 2.1 in 2008 to 2.4. This relatively large increase can be attributed to the introduction of institutional and legal reforms in the period of 2007–2008 which gives the government a greater capacity to tackle corruption (Transparency International, 2009). In the past 49 or 50 years, Bangladesh has experienced a high level of economic growth. Between 1960 and 2009 GDP increased from US$4,274,893,910 to US$89,359,767,442, that is, a growth rate of approximately 1990.34%. Exports have also experienced a drastic increase over the same period, rising from US$427,347,689.70

(approximately 10% of GDP) to US$17,360,479,651 (approximately 19.43% of GDP). Similarly, imports increased from US$397,875,424.2 to US$23,727,165,698 over the same period (World Bank, 2010a).

The similarities in trend between increases in CPI score and GDP per capita is shown in Figure 6.1. The figure shows that there is a correlation between CPI score and GDP per capita; as one rises, so does the other. As discussed earlier, Mauro (1996) found that this correlation was in fact causation. Evidence suggests, however, that if this is true for some countries, for example Bangladesh, it is definitely not true for others.

Remedies of corruption in Bangladesh

There exist a number of possible solutions for the corruption experienced by Bangladesh:

(1) Presently, both the Bureau of Anti-Corruption (BAC) and the Comptroller and Auditor General (CAG) do not have enough power and authority to carry out their responsibilities effectively. Not only has it been estimated that it takes BAC an average of three years to investigate a case it has also been accused that it is itself corrupt (Zafarullah and Siddiquee, 2001). It is suggested, therefore, that the corruption within these institutions should be eradicated and that greater authority should be given to BAC and CAG.

(2) Bangladesh does not suffer from a lack of rules against corruption, but a lack of enforcement. For example, according to Transparency International (n.d.) many assistant engineers to the Bangladesh Power Development Board (BPDB) own luxury cars which they should not be able to afford on their official salaries. In addition, Transparency International (n.d.) reported that a ledger keeper for Dhaka Electric Supply Authority (DESA) was able to purchase a house for Tk3.8 million as well as an allotment in a shopping arcade. Despite there being laws against public servants possessing money or property larger than their official salary, no action has been carried out against these obvious violations.

(3) In 1972, the Bangladesh Constitution allowed for an ombudsman that had power to investigate complaints against a ministry, an official or

a statutory public authority (Zafarullah and Siddiquee, 2001). Since then, however, Bangladesh has failed to create such a body, a lacking that needs to be corrected. Without good leadership, the government cannot expect the Bangladeshi community to change its ways.

(4) As suggested by Transparency International (n.d.) the Bangladesh Bank should have complete autonomy from the government to ensure that it is not influenced by politics. In addition, if greater transparency in political party funding sources existed it would be more difficult for them to receive contributions from bank defaulters.

(5) To minimize corruption in the customs sector a system needs to be introduced which makes officers responsible for any "misuse of power for gainful power". In addition, the amount of speed money in transactions can be reduced by removing inefficient steps from appraisals, while keeping the integrity of the assessment procedure. (Transparency International, n.d.).

Conclusion

As can be seen from Table 6.1, on a global scale Bangladesh ranks poorly with respect to corruption. The paper then explored the magnitude of corruption within the country. It found that the police department is the most corrupt public institution within the country and that the number one type of corruption in Bangladesh, with 1336 cases in 2003, was the abuse of power.

The lack of dedication of the judiciary to the cause was emphasized with approximately 24% of cases filed annually resulted in a conviction. This costs the government around 1.85% of GDP.

The main cause of corruption in Bangladesh is shown to be a lack of regulation, particularly in the banking, customs and telecommunications sectors. Public officials in both banking and customs sectors take advantage of too much power and a lack of regulation. In the telecommunications sector a lack of regulation by the government has resulted in the growth of illegal VoIP services.

The consequences of corruption are then explored. It was found that two opposite conclusions could be drawn; corruption can retard, or promote growth. The main arguments for the former is that it distorts the composition of government expenditure. Mauro (1996) found an increase in CPI score can also increase a country's investment rate and annual per capita GDP growth rate. On the other hand, it is argued that those who receive bribes may have more incentive to work harder. The impact corruption has on economic growth is then explored in the paper.

Five possible remedies were suggested including giving the BAC and CAG more power and authority so that they may carry out their responsibilities effectively. It is suggested by this author that the government needs to reflect on the impact that corruption is having on its country. Once the full extent is known it may push Bangladesh to pay more attention to its current bureaucracy and judiciary thereby increasing regulation.

References

Hofstede, G. (1997). *Cultures and organizations: Software of the mind.* New York, McGraw Hill.

Huntington, S.P. (1968). Political Order in Changing Societies. New Haven: Yale University Press.

Husted, B. (1999). Wealth, culture and corruption, *Journal of International Business Studies*, 30(2), pp. 339–359. Available from: JSTOR. [16 May 2011].

Knox, C. (2009). 'Dealing with sectorial corruption in Bangladesh: Developing citizen involvement, *Public Administration and Development*, 29, pp. 117–132. Available from <http://www.ti-bangladesh.org/about/ColinKnox-pap-Mar09.pdf> [9 May 2011].

Lambsdorff, J. (2007). 'Corruption in South Asia: Causes and consequences' in A Siddiqui (ed.), *India and South Asia: Economic Developments in the Age of Globalization*, M.E. Shapre, Inc., Armonk, pp. 360–379.

Leff, N.H. (1964). "Economic Development through Bureaucratic Corruption", American Behavioural Scientist, November 1964, pp. 8–14.

Li, H., Xu, L., Zou, H.-F. (2000). Corruption, income distribution and growth, *Economics and Politics*, 12(2), pp. 155–182.

Mauro, P. (1996). "The Effects of Corruption on Growth, Investment, and Government Expenditure," IMF Working Paper 96/98 (Washington: International Monetary Fund).

Mauro, P. (1998). "Corruption: Causes, Consequences, and Agenda for Further Research" Finance & Development, March, pp. 11–14.

Mo, P.H. (2000). Corruption and economic growth, *Journal of Comparative Economics*, 29(1), pp. 66–79. Available from: idealibrary.com. [16 May 2011].

Morgan, Theodore (1964). The theory of error in centrally-directed economic systems, *The Quarterly Journal of Economics*, 78(3), pp. 395–419.

Nye, J.S. (1967). Corruption and political development: A cost–benefit analysis, *American Political Science Review*, 61(2), pp. 417–427.

Rock, M., Bonnett, H. (2004). 'The comparative politics of corruption: Accounting for the East Asian paradox in empirical studies of corruption, growth and investment, *World Development*, 32(6), pp. 999–1017.

Schneider, F. (2007). 'Shadow Economies and Corruption all over the World: New Estimates for 145 Countries', Available from <www.lawrence.edu/fast/finklerm/shadeconomy corruption_july2007.pdf> [16 May 2011].

The PRS Group (2011). 'International Country Risk Guide', Available from <http://www.prsgroup.com/icrg.aspx> [16 May 2011].

Transparency International (2003). *Transparency International Country Study Report-Bangladesh 2003*, Available from <http://www.transparency.org/policy_research/nis/nis_reports_by_country> [9 May 2011].

Transparency International (2009). *Corruption Perceptions Index 2009, Regional Highlights: Asia-Pacific*, Available from <http://www.transparency.org.au/documents/CPI%202009%20Regional%20Highlights%20Asia%20Pacific_en.pdf> [30 May 2011].

Transparency International (2009a). *Global Corruption Report 2009*, Available from <www.transparency.org/publications/gcr/gcr2009> [4 July 2011].

Transparency International (2010). *Corruption Perceptions Index 2010*, Available from <http://www.transparency.org/policy_research/surveys_indices/cpi/2010/results> [4 July 2011].

Transparency International Bangladesh, *Corruption in Public Sector Departments Manifestations, Causes and Suggested Remedies*, Available from <http://www.tibangladesh.org/docs/misc/overview1.htm> [9 May 2011].

United Nations Development Programme (UNDP) (1999). Fighting Corruption to Improve Governance, New York.

Wattad, N. (2003). 'The Subcontinent', *The Washington Report on Middle East Affairs*, Vol. 22, p. 48. Available from: ProQuest [23 May 2011].

World Bank (2010). *Worldwide Governance Indicators,* Available from: <http://info.worldbank.org/governance/wgi/mc_countries.asp> [4 July 2011].

World Bank (2010a). *World Development Indicators*, Available from: <http://data.worldbank.org/indicator> [16 May 2011].

Zafarullah, H., Siddiquee, N. (2001). 'Dissecting public sector corruption in Bangladesh: Issues and problems of control, *Public Organization Review: A Global Journal*, 1, pp. 465–486.

Endnote

i. Bangladesh has only been included in the CPI Index since 2001, and as such previous data is not available. At the time of writing, the dtat for GDP per capita was only available up to and including 2009.

Chapter 7

Restoring Sustainable Governance in Bangladesh

Amzad Hossain and Dora Marinova

Curtin University Sustainability Policy (CUSP) Institute, Curtin University, Australia

Abstract

Since the country's birth in 1971, Bangladesh has hardly experienced good (i.e., just) governance that could potentially allow for political stability and sustainable development. In fact, many commentators consider that challenges such as the rising degradation of natural resources, water crises, the widening gap between the rich and the poor, corruption, crimes and gender issues, are largely due to persisting mal-governance. The growing scale and mutual reinforcement of these conditions appear to have been pushing the country towards social, economic and environmental vulnerability.

Against this background, the paper explores ways to address the prevalent unsustainable situations focusing on the need for just governance within the cultural and human context of the country. It outlines the importance of nurturing and strengthening the cultural beliefs and traditions, including religiosity, patriotism, family and social bondage, self-reliance and traditional happiness that can help progress Bangladesh towards achieving a better governance in terms of socio-economic and environmental justice. Depicting the inherent sustainability characteristics of Bangladesh, the paper argues that refurbishing of governance with competent, honest, responsible and patriotic politicians, civil servants, activists and other actors is of utter necessity for reversing the current trends in the country.

The chapter concludes that the cultural values of Bangladeshis, which were remarkable in the past, can help revitalize the country's governance for achieving a locally branded "sushashon", i.e., good and just governance.

Keywords: Sustainable development, sustainability, self-reliance, natural resources, corruption, traditions.

Introduction

In this chapter, the term 'sustainable governance' for riverine, agrarian, and so inherently sustainable Bangladesh denotes a governance that is just for pursuing uninterrupted water- and agro-based sustainable development in the country's geo-environmental and cultural conditions. Sustainable development for Bangladesh warrants, as Rogers *et al.* (2008: 23) emphasize, to leave everything in a pristine state, or return to its pristine state; develop not to overwhelm the carrying capacity of the ecosystem; and leave future generations with the sustainability prospects of the present. We have used 'restoring' in the title of the chapter to indicate that Bangladesh had enjoyed good governance accommodating sustainable development in the past that earned it the fame of 'Golden Bengal' (Sonar Bangla), despite the fact that no gold mines ever existed there. Sonar Bangla denotes that the country was full of gold-like precious resources to sustain its people. This legacy is still widely used: in the literature, by the politicians, village elders and the mystic Baul philosophers[i] of Bangladesh. In fact, the Bangladesh national anthem begins with the words: "*Amar Sonar Bangla, Ami Tumai Valobasi*", meaning "My Golden Bengal, I adore you."

Governance is the jugular vein of a nation. It is meant to influence social changes through its 'mechanisms' and 'instruments', steering the country in a preordained direction (Lafferty, 2004: 5) and hopefully contributing to sustainable development. Lafferty (2004: 5) also indicates that the icon of governance sits on the top rung of the development ladder in order to materialize the processing of 'social engineering for sustainable development'. A major component of governance is the use and development of resources, including human and natural, and hence it is also a crucial aspect of sustainability.

According to Roy and Prasad (2007: 3), governance is exerted through the traditions and institutions by which the authority in a country is exercised for the common good. While institutions are more representative of the current mechanism and instruments needed to allocate resources, coordinate or control social and economic activities within a society (Bell, 2002), traditions determine the way the social knowledge is passed from a generation to generation. In many countries with a long history of democracy and economic development, institutions have replaced or become representative of traditions; but in others the two co-exist and have different ways of influencing and governing social behavior. Bangladesh is typical of the latter and this is a very important consideration for the sustainable development of the country. The key to sustainability is the fostering of the human-nature interconnectedness, an area with long and well-established traditions in Bangladesh where the Baul philosophers sing: "*Manuser preme mati pai jibon, jodi thake sushashon*" or in translation: "Humans and nature can serve each other for their sustainable coexistence prosperously when 'sushashon' (good and just governance) prevails."

Sushashon, or good and just governance, is crucial for humankind to "live on renewable income and not to deplete natural capital" (Kangas, 2004: 287). There are clear limits on the exploitation of finite or depletable resources and the principle that can induce humans to adhere to these limits is good and just governance. Bangladesh is predominantly a country of agriculture, including fisheries. Sushashon, or good and just governance, for sustainable development requires traditions within the Bangladeshi society to inform government institutions in a way that compels them to make a moral, social and spiritual commitment to equitable distribution of resources at present and with a view of the future. Such a development should not degrade the natural resource base of the country and should preserve the natural capital of Golden Bengal.

The understanding and commitment to sustainability are deeply connected to people's spirituality and linked to their value system. According to Baul guru Aziz Shah Fakir,[ii] today's environmental and social problems have their roots in individual behavior and attitudes that are not encouraging people to share and care for natural resources. The disconnection between tradition and modern governance institutions in Bangladesh has allowed people to disengage themselves from their spiritual core built around the values of self-reliance. This has generated major problems in the governance of the country, including degradation of natural resources, water crises, the widening gap between rich and poor, extensive corruption, crimes and gender issues.

This chapter focuses first on the historical background and then sheds light on the essence of the above problems. Its second half establishes an argument for good and just governance in Bangladesh that, according to Shotter (1993) and Barr (2002), should be culturally appropriate for the geo-environmental and spiritual contexts of the country.

Historical Background of Governance in Bangladesh

Prior to 1971 East Pakistan (now Bangladesh) was the more populous but less developed part of Pakistan with a predominantly traditional lifestyle. The constant political, economic and social conflicts between the two physically disconnected wings of Pakistan (East and West) resulted in a nine-month bloody liberation war that led to the birth of Bangladesh in 1971 (Hasan, 2007). The new Constitution of the country incorporated many secular and democratic ideas but became a challenging task to implement through institutions and practices. According the Hasan (2007: 47), the major obstacles were the military, the under-developed economy of the country which soon triggered donor dependence, vulnerability to the winds of globalization and Islamization, and ineffective political leadership.

After the 1974 famine, foreign investors started to pour aid into the country in the name of hunger elimination and economic development tying up its new governing institutions to the Western market-based model of democracy (Sen, 1981). The new country attracted extensive foreign aid from organizations such as the World Bank, the International Monetary Fund (IMF) and the Asian Development Bank (ADB), and even today remains heavily dependent on it. Currently for every dollar in foreign aid received, the Government of Bangladesh pays back $1.5 in external debt repayments (SUPRO, 2008).

A school of thought amongst Third World economists postulates the theory that foreign aid is but a strategy of the donor countries and organizations to keep the recipient countries perpetually indebted and degrading

(Cassen, 1994). Gupta (1999: 223–224) explains that foreign aid capital has exerted significant negative effects on the recipient countries because it substitutes (rather than complements) domestic resources, helps import inappropriate technology, distorts domestic income distribution, and is biased toward a larger, inefficient and corrupt government in those countries.

Bangladesh is a prime example of these problems. Socio-moral degradation, poverty elevation, high rate of population growth with lower rate of intellectual growth, increasing foreign debt, renewable resource degradation resulting in floods, droughts, desertification, pollution and biodiversity depletion — are all on the increase. The mal-growth of population in the poor and rich communities is affecting the country most alarmingly. The highest rate of population growth is amongst the poorest who cannot afford even primary education for their children while the lowest rates are amongst the people who can provide their families with good education. Mal-governance is gradually pushing the country towards intellectual bankruptcy (Hossain and Marinova, 2005). In fact, Bangladesh has hardly experienced good and just governance that could potentially steer the country away from corruption, poverty, unrest and environmental deterioration towards sustainable development. It is making the country vulnerable and exposed to severe environmental, social and economic setbacks.

Governance Challenges

The challenges of the governance system in Bangladesh are profound in nature, scope, scale and effect. Often it is difficult to identify when one problem finishes and another begins because of their complex interwoven social, economic, environmental and political aspects and consequences. What appeared to be good intentions in some cases have generated unexpected severe damaging effects. In other cases, there have not been the right desire and will to fix the problems because of the lack of accountability. The following examples represent the fabric of the challenges. We start with the Green Revolution and the water crises as major cases of environmental mismanagement, then turn to corruption as a serious economic misconduct and crime as a socially unacceptable behavior. On the other hand, the influence of globalization processes has impacted both the social and economic makeup of the Bangladeshi traditional society bringing to the fore gender issues that never existed before. The protracted reaction of the Bangladeshi government in response to the social and economic hardship of ordinary people has triggered socio-political unrest exposing the country to the uncertainty and ambiguity of emergency measures. All this has created strong tensions within the Bangladeshi society and calls for restoring good governance.

The Green Revolution

The Green Revolution (GR) has been a major agent of mal-governance in Bangladesh effecting the politics of corrupting the natural, socio-economic and political (governance) processes of the country's development. Though the green revolution technology has increased food production, it also has created a wide range of problems, from pollution of water bodies by farm chemicals, accelerated land degradation and increased pressure on water supplies to a loss of genetic variability and enhanced vulnerability in crops, spread of pests and diseases. It has also brought a series of social and cultural problems, including widening of the economic gap between affluent and poor farmers, and politico-cultural crises due to the erosion of moral values (Shiva, 1993: 11; Basalla, 1988: 164).

According to Shiva (1993), the ecological breakdown in nature (as GR created major changes in natural ecosystems and agrarian structures) and breakdown of society (as GR replaced local labor with capital- and chemical-intensive solutions, creating debt for farmers) were consequences of a policy based on tearing apart both nature and society. She refers to this poor governance as politics of degradation. The GR program produced more food, but in the process it also increased the number of landless laborers. Many small farmers became agricultural workers for the large farmers who bought up their lands. The small farmers' choices were further limited by bad governance.

The prevailing government policies favored the large farmers when it came to providing access to better seeds, fertilizers, irrigation water, roads and communal storehouses. A good example of this type of favoritism is in the case of diesel fuel. During the GR, the government of Bangladesh imported diesel fuel, with the honest intention of selling at subsidized prices to local communities to run their irrigation pumps. It failed because the large farmers had high visibility and a voice in local politics, which the poor farmers did not have. Consequently, it became increasingly difficult for the poor farmers to modernize, and as they could not farm efficiently, the benefit–cost ratio of their lands remained the same as under rain-fed conditions. During the GR the income gap between the rich and the poor actually increased, even though the total production of food crops increased (Rogers *et al.*, 2008: 74).

Shiva (1993) points out that field records of undivided India for 10 centuries prove that the land produced fair crops year after year without failing in fertility, with a perfect balance reached between the manuring requirements of the crops harvested and the natural processes which recuperate fertility. The new GR seeds and chemicals destabilize the farm ecology and create pest outbreaks as the shift from organic to chemical fertilizers reduces the plant resistance to pest attacks. In Mulder's (2006) words, the use of agricultural chemicals had created severely pervasive problems.

Water crises

Bangladesh has hundreds of rivers and lakes including the mighty Ganges, Jamuna and Brahmaputra rivers, precipitation is about 2000 mm per annum, and most of Bangladesh remains submerged under water for weeks and months during the wet months (June–November). Despite all this, desertification and salinity intrusion are active in the western half of the country. A major cause of this is the failure of the government to negotiate with India its legitimate share of water from the Ganges that flows to mix with the salty water of the Bay of Bengal. During the dry months (December–May) India blocks the flow of the Ganges through its Farakka Barrage built in the mid-1970s and located upstream of Bangladesh. Khan[iii] observes that Bangladesh is getting drier every year due to India's unilateral withdrawal of water from the common river. Despite over 100 bilateral talks to establish provision of guarantee for Bangladesh,[iv] the quantity of water down the Farakka point has been critically declining due to taking out from the Ganges by upper riparian India through various canals by violating the water sharing agreement. This has resulted in serious adverse effects, including salinity intrusion and desertification in the south-western and western districts of Bangladesh, affecting almost 20% of the country's area.

The water crises are further aggravated by the demands of the GR-based agricultural practices. Because of unavailability of required water from the Ganges for irrigation during the dry months, farmers lift underground water intensively and extensively to irrigate the highly thirsty GR crops such as rice, wheat and potato. Consequently, the water table keeps falling in the irrigation regions as the natural seepage cannot recharge the amount of withdrawal. Desertification is activated. Thus, India's unilateral withdrawal of water from the common river Ganges flowing upstream from India and the GR crops have destabilized the water balance in the region resulting in the severe degradation of ecological balance.

The water crises have adversely affected the environment, agriculture, industries, fisheries, navigation of the river regime and salinity culminating in the surface and ground water. This prolonged environmental hardship is causing socio-economic breakdowns. The political regimes in Bangladesh however are never seen capable of addressing the water issues that are threatening the sustainability of the country.

Corruption

A recent World Bank (2004), in Roy and Prasad (2007) "study shows that corruption hurts growth, impairs capital accumulation, reduces the effectiveness of development aid and increases income inequality and poverty. There is an inverse relationship between good governance and corruption, an inverse relationship between corruption and development outcomes and a positive relationship between good governance and development outcomes; i.e., the higher the quality of governance, the lower the level of corruption and the higher the level of development outcomes" (Roy and Prasad, 2007: 3). Bangladesh is infected with mal-governance, and corruption largely hinders or damages the process of sustainable development, even when conditioned by donor agencies. Each year the Bangladesh government accepts foreign aid to initiate sustainable development projects, such as re-excavation of water bodies, mass education or family planning, but often funds are being stolen from such projects by politicians, bureaucrats, technocrats and implementing contractors. The outcomes of the projects are utterly unproductive, often counter-productive.

Corruption was widespread in the 1970s, 1980s (e.g., De Vylder, 1982) and 1990s (Hamid, 1999) but also continued in the 2000s. In fact, in 2004, Bangladesh was a champion in the field of corruption ranking 145th (i.e., last) out of 145 countries according to Transparency International's corruption perception index.[v]

"DHAKA, Sept 13, 2009 (Reuters) — Some people compare it with cancer, some with a less fatal but fast spreading virus. The government says it is under control while independent global monitors say they see marginal improvement at best. The issue is corruption in Bangladesh...".[vi]

The rampant corruption in Bangladesh includes bribery, illegal toll collection, rent-seeking, stealing funds from development or service projects, exploiting employees by private sector employers, exploiting and cheating consumers by the sellers of essential commodities such as food items and medicines. It is clear that Bangladesh is in a vicious cycle in which corruption begets corruption and creates a society where one is either a giver or taker of bribe. Very few Bangladeshis can claim to be outside this noxious embrace. Hasan (2007: 49) witnesses that corruption has become "all-pervasive, extending from petty corruption to project corruption (e.g., taking large commissions for securing large public sector contracts) and program corruption (food scandals)." Mal-governance is responsible for such a scale of corruption to persist. In particular, the integrity of the legal system is constantly compromised when law-enforcing agencies, including the police, misuse their power or are irresponsible and inefficient in carrying their duties (Khair, 2005). Siddique and Ghosh (2007: 80) observe that the efforts of the government to weed out corruption from Bangladesh have been half-hearted.

Crime

Crime has serious social implications as it relates to human insecurity and affects the economic and political life of the country. In some cases, it can also have environmental dimensions, such as the illegal occupation of land for shrimp cultivation or real estate business. The level of violent and non-violent crimes in Bangladesh is high and the long list includes extortion, tender snatching, mugging, robbery, prostitution, drug dealing, smuggling of contraband goods, money laundering and election rigging. People who are politically or administratively not powerful, but appear of becoming wealthy imperceptibly are generally the preys of crime. The victims are subject to physical injury including murdering if they resist the attack of criminals. This is a frequent phenomenon in Bangladesh, particularly in the cities.

A newspaper report reveals that citizens, especially businessmen, pass their tense days with worries and anxieties fearing extortion. An incoming call from unknown person over a cell phone can ask for a large sum of money. "Either you pay or be prepared to say goodbye to this world" is the common message now being conveyed to many from a syndicate of extortionists who are reportedly backed by a syndicate of godfathers linked with the government.[vii] The Bangladesh Development Partnership Cooperation (BDPC, 2005) also finds that the crime syndicates in the country are run by top notched godfathers.

Regular incidence of crime raises public concern of insecurity but the response from the government has been far from adequate. A relatively new occurrence is the criminalization of politics, including the "hired groups of hoodlums, popularly known as *'mastans'*, who work individually or collectively for political parties" (Khair, 2005: 4). According to BDPC (2005), the crime rate and ownership of firearms in Bangladesh have increased due to an arms race between the main political parties: "The party who has the biggest arsenal has the most power, and poor governance along with an ineffective police force do nothing to prevent the proliferation of weapons".[viii] The country's governance has failed to restore law and order in a way that helps improve people's quality of life.

Gender issues

Traditional Bangladeshi culture maintains religio–spiritual balance between men and women in order to sustain social norms in respect of gender roles (Hossain *et al.*, 2007; Hossain and Hossain-Rhaman, 2007). Modernity or modernism as provoked by outsiders has now attracted the attention to gender issues in the country. Under the post-liberation mal-governance, there is an ongoing hue and cry in Bangladesh by outsiders, including diplomatic missions, human rights groups, foreign funded NGOs and aid agencies. Among others, they see the women's socio-economic system of Bangladesh as a violation of their rights. The tension between the local and universality in human rights debates is not an easy question (An-Naim *et al.*, 1995) but this is also a sphere where governance should have a very prominent role.

Under the traditional social norms in Bangladesh, women are better respected and cared for when they maintain Purdah[ix] and pursue their socio-economic activities in the vicinity of their homes. The wide use of Burqa (a veil covering the body and the face) for maintaining Purdah was never the Islamic tradition in Bangladesh.[x] On the other hand, the covering of the body, including the hair, by a Sari was the age-long tradition to manifest modesty in dress by both Hindu and Muslim Bangladeshi women.[xi]

Modernization is impacting on women making them increasingly more physically mobile to eke out an earning. According to Rozario (2006: 368), "a significant proportion of these newly mobile women, including university students, is adopting the Burqa as a practice associated with modern Islamist movements against modernism which was previously almost non-existent in Bangladesh". The choice by women for a more overt Islamic identity goes against the traditional ways of interaction between men and women within the Bangladeshi society. Provocations against the Purdah system have attracted Islamic fundamentalism that Bangladeshi culture never respected, to grow as a means of resilience against the socially aggressive modernity. On the other hand, the Burqa seems to be a tool to degrade other women's rights in a regime of mal-governance in Bangladesh, particularly those who do not use it. The government policies indicate that: "The state is not taking any responsibility: women have to behave themselves and obey rules. As for those who are not covered (including non-Muslims), if they are assaulted or violated, it is their own fault" (Rozario, 2006: 378).

The picture of gender relations in Bangladesh is also changing from another perspective. The continuing fragmentation of land holdings (Baden *et al.*, 1994) means that the number of households constituted as extended family is fast declining. In the process, many women are being deprived from being cared for by traditional family support. Baden *et al.* (1994: viii) find that the disintegration of the joint family system is associated first, "with a loss of security for women from the family network and with reduction in the scope for sharing household tasks ... . Second, women's work possibilities outside the homestead have declined" with the application of technologies, such as harvest paddy, husking, rice pressing or powdering and other post harvest work tools.

Globalization has further put the governance of Bangladesh under tremendous stress, the worst affected being the weakest in society — women, as well as the poor and indigenous people of the country. Structural adjustment policies have taken them away from their traditional means of self-reliant livelihood. Women working in the garments sector provide an example where women are largely treated as economic slaves (Hasan, 2007: 55). This has triggered hardship and increased violence against women. Men become more aggressive and vent their frustration on women when they themselves fail to earn enough income to support the family, and women refuse to work outside the home leaving their children unattended and unsafe.

A good and just governance would build upon tradition and incorporate local features within the newly developed institutions to prevent socio-economic degradation of women rights. Sustainable development can only be achieved when there is basic human security, including social and economic stability.

Socio-political unrest

Persisting unrest comprising Hartals (general strikes), work stoppages, hunger strikes, street processions, barricades, Gherao (besieging) etc. by opposition political parties, students, industrial and transport workers, oppressed and deprived masses and other miscellaneous social unrest, such as conflicts between intra-political party and trade union groups, depict the acute mal-governance in Bangladesh. A large number of days in a year witness such unrest in the country.

As blaming and lying against each other in politics or in government on crucial issues is rampant, creating unrest is the most common and sought-after recourse against poor governance (Hasan, 2007: 68). A massive unrest in 1990 caused the fall of the Ershad government (March 1982–1990). Again, unrest through street violence in October 2006 against the massive mal-governance by the Khaleda Zia government resulted in the emergence of the army backed caretaker government on 1 November 2006 (popularly known as One-Eleven or 1/11), which also mal-governed the country for two years.[xii]

In a country such as Bangladesh where widespread poverty exists in terms of scarcity of food, shelter, health care, formal education and income generation opportunities, occurring largely due to mal-governance as well as natural reasons,[xiii] sustainable good governance is central to people's access to natural justice and improved quality of life. How can the prosperity of Golden Bengal be restored?

Remedies for Restoring Sustainable Governance

The history of Bangladesh reveals progressive struggles for democracy in order to ensure justice underpins the inherent traits of the country. Bangladesh is inherently sustainable and the following characteristics describe its potential to restore a good quality of life for its people:

- the climate of the country has six seasons — the two extra seasons, namely the rainy season and dewy season, contribute to diverse and enhanced agricultural practices;
- it experiences healthy growth of rural labor force — most rural people live self-reliantly engaging in agricultural, fishing or industrial work. Traditionally rural uneducated people are fond of more children as old-age security but with constantly dropping infant mortality rates and increasing life expectancies and educational levels, people's behavior is gradually changing towards a smaller number of children. Even with family planning programmes not so easily accessible in rural areas, particularly during the rainy season, and poor management of access to contraceptives, Bangladesh's fertility rates have been steadily falling. They are currently at 2.7 children/woman and expected to drop to about the replacement rate of 2.1 by 2025 (http://www.census.gov/ipc/www/idb/country.php). All this indicates a healthy demographic shift in the country;

- Bangladeshi people are eco-spiritual — they are not materialistic and not interested in high consumption patterns, they are happy with less, show reciprocal respectfulness in gender relations and are nature loving;
- Bangladesh maintains a culture that can be described as sustainable poverty — it encourages people to live simply in terms of moderate poverty; to support beggars or destitute people by well-off people is regarded as a religious act;
- There is political vitality at the grassroots — most people of Bangladesh are actively associated with political parties and election works; and
- People possess sustainability wisdom — this is expressed in the numerous traditional proverbs and teachings, such as 'happiness with less', 'cut your coat according to your cloth', 'eat less, live longer', 'look before you leap', and 'self-reliance is the best sustainability'. As the philosophical tradition of Bangladesh, they encourage self-reliance and development without destruction of the natural resource base.

These pro-sustainability characteristics however are not properly maintained, for most people in governing positions lack values, such as patriotism, competency, honesty, responsibility and naturalism, that can encourage good and just governance. Inculcating in these people the above values and restoring the traditional sustainability characteristics would be of utter necessity for reversing the current mal-governance trends in the country.

Roy and Prasad (2007: 3) emphasize that a sound governance system should focus on the following: transparency to the public; simplicity of procedures of all economic, political and social matters with minimum people; responsibility and accountability; and fight against corruption. These all refer to having good mechanisms and instruments in place but the underlying problem with governance in Bangladesh is the discrepancy and incongruity between people's actions (which can also be perceived as incompetence) and moral values. Hasan (2007: 50) describes this in terms of a proverb that reflects public perception: "*Jar nai kono niti, shei kore raj niti*" or translated: "The one who does not have any moral principles does politics." Political parties in Bangladesh appear to be trapped within the politics of hatred; one can call it the death of imagination and values.

Education is always called upon when there are serious problems within society. In this case, however, what is lacking is a system that allows for values education to be transmitted not only through the secular educational curriculum but also through the traditional roots within the Bangladeshi society. The attempts to build new governance institutions without properly incorporating tradition has proven the wrong way of achieving development. Conservation and revival of the traditional spiritual values of Bangladeshi people is a better way, if not the only way, to restore good governance for sustainability.

Cawsey (2002) advocates the importance of values education for changing attitudes, rather than institutions or regulations, towards consumption of the earth's natural resources. The Baul tradition supports a self-reliant way of living with family and social and environmental bondage: "The less you have, the more you are". Gandhi expanded this concept to incorporate a simple life style asserting that nature produces enough for our wants, and if only everybody took enough for him/herself and nothing more, there would be no people dying of starvation (Kripalani, 1965: 130). Lorey (2003: 44) talks about achieving satisfaction with less and with what you already have. Aspin (2002) also argues that values education is necessary for educating people to understand the past with regards to finite renewable resources and to envision sustainable common futures for the coming generations. Values education can be the mechanism by which positive attitudes toward sustainable practices and lifestyles can be fostered. It can also be the mechanism for restoring good and just governance in Bangladesh.

A change is never smooth, nor is it easy and requires politically strong champions, social determination and commitment to see through the process of transition (Eyben, 2006). Mal-governance however is a relatively new phenomenon compared with the country's traditional spiritual roots. Long before the western world focused on the implications of unsustainable human activities and ways of living, traditional communities possessed the blueprint for their sustainability in their spirituality. The Baul philosophy, the Bangladeshi religious tradition that integrates wisdom from Islam, Hinduism, Buddhism and Christianity into religious secularism and has the elements of liberalism, universalism, particularism, naturalism and mysticism, has always promoted living in harmony with nature and a sustainable self-reliant lifestyle (Hossain and Marinova, 2003). An implication from this characteristic of self-reliance is the choice of resources used and the preference for renewable resources that can be replaced in a reliable sustainable way.

Restoring governance in Bangladesh would mean to implement through values education the most powerful ways to transform the extant culture of unsustainable dependency on alien socio-economic and cultural development prescriptions into a sustainable traditional culture of self-reliant living entrenched with good and just governance.

Implications for Politics

"*Chora na shune dharmer kahini*" or translated: "The scapegrace will never listen to a moral lecture". The general public, encountering the immorality of the corrupt people in government and business, often use this rebuking Bengali proverb. It seems difficult to convince the dishonest and incompetent people in the governance of Bangladesh to restrain themselves from corruption, without improving their morality. The public perception in this regard is that no head of the state, except the late President Ziaur Rahman, can be said to be honest and competent. This perception may be true as no head of the government of Bangladesh so far has been able to proclaim that: "I am honest and competent; I run my government only with honest and competent people".

The words of Harun Baul[xiv] provide a sound political platform and goals for the Bangladeshi government and policies:

Restoration of traditional values education;
Fish and fruit tree for everyone;
Full support for the people willing to work overseas;
Facilities for small-scale industrial activities;
To minimize the lifestyle gaps between rich and poor; and
Equitable foreign policy.

This platform is easy to understand and achieve, as in traditional Bangladeshi culture people are happy and sustainable with such a lifestyle. The blueprint for sustainable (development in) Bangladesh would comprise:

"Nadi vora jol	Water in river,
math vora sashay	field full of crops,
pukur vora maas	pond full of fish,
gohal vora garu	cow in the cowshed,
bari vora gaas	homestead with trees,
pakhir kolotan	melodious tune of the birds,
shisur koahol	uproar of children,
bauler o majheer gaan	songs of Bauls and boatmen,
Rathe banya jantu O vuther voy".	ear of wild animals and ghosts at night.

The restoration of traditional values education is the first and foremost policy requirement for politics as values can contribute to holistic sustainability management, including good governance, as a panacea can contribute to heal diseases. Baul philosophers have already been discoursing on the criticality values of education[xv] in order to establish "honesty is the best policy" for good governance.

Conclusion

The cultural values of Bangladeshis, which were remarkable in the past, can help revitalize the country's governance for achieving a locally branded sushashon, i.e., good and just governance. In Bangladesh, the sense of social responsibility is strong. People share each other's joys and sorrows. The Baul philosophers teach: "One's joy is doubled when shared by another person, and sorrow is halved when shared by another person". These spiritual practices still prevail amongst the people at the grassroots, and are likely to remain vibrant in the future due to the increasing popularity of the Baul culture and spirituality.

The sustainability icon for Bangladesh has physical and non-physical components. The physical components are natural resources, population and technologies including energy supply. Culture, poverty and political performance constitute the non-physical components. While the physical elements conjointly represent a vehicle to progress toward a sustainable future for the country, the others generate 'values' that drive the vehicle. As the values required for good governance are gradually degrading because of the disconnection between tradition and institutions within the society, the physical components are not being appropriately explored and attained. This is why sustainability challenges are prevailing.

Nevertheless, the history of Bangladesh reveals progressive struggles by its general masses for good governance in order to ensure the security of people, corruption free society, the rule of law, equality and justice. Within this aspiration, cultural characteristic and framework, the emergence of just governance remains in the hands of the ruling party leaders. Maak and Pless (2006: 188) point out that when leaders are good communicators, storytellers, networkers and relationship managers, at that point they become part of the collective human capacity. These leaders will also have the task of restoring values of education not just within the Bangladeshi society but also within its governance structures.

Bangladeshi culture has a blueprint for the sustainability of rural Bangladesh. It is unlike any other place; it would not be possible to develop a Bangladesh resembling Australia or America or Europe. There is no evidence to suggest that the developed countries achieved their development by duplicating others. Each country evolved in its own way over time based on its own cultural heritage and traditions. Bangladesh is no exception. Its future shape or infrastructure need not be radically different from what they are now. If future Bangladesh can be provided with the shape of the past, it can be argued that the country will be sustained in a better condition resembling Golden Bengal. To achieve this goal, it is crucial for good and just governance to say goodbye to environmentally harmful technologies, to corruption, crime, Islamisation and socio-political unrest.

In Harun Baul's view: "*Jiboner janya pani jemon, Bangladesher janya suniti temon*" or translated: "As water is for life, so are good principles for Bangladesh". The Baul proclaims that revival of the traditional suniti (good principles) values and sushashon (good and just governance) is the most required spiritual value at the moment to reinstate Bangladesh on the track of sustainable development.

References

An-Naim, A.A., Gort, J.D., Jansen, H., Vroom, H.M. (1995). Human Rights and Religious Values: An Uneasy Relationship? William B. Eerdmans Publishing, Grand Rapids, MI.

Aspin, D. (2002). An ontology of values and the humanisation of education. In Pascoe, S. (ed.), *Values in Education*. The Australian College of Educators, Canberra, pp. 12–14.

Baden, S., Green, C., Goetz, A.M., Guhathakurta, M. (1994). Background Report on Issues in Bangladesh. Report No. 26, Institute of Development Studies, University of Sussex, Brighton, UK. Retrieved 21 July 2010 from http://www.bridge.ids.ac.uk/reports/re26c.pdf.

Bangladesh Development Partnership Cooperation (BDPC) (2005). Illegal Small Arms and Human Insecurity in Bangladesh. BDPC, Dhaka.

Barr, M.D. (2002). Cultural politics and Asian Values: The Tepid War. London: Routledge.

Basalla, G. (1988). The Evolution of Technology. Cambridge University Press, Cambridge.

Bell, S. (2002). Economic Governance and Institutional Dynamics. Oxford University Press, Melbourne, Australia.

Capwell, C. (1988). The popular expression of religious syncretism: The Bauls of Bengal as Apostles of Brotherhood. *Popular Music*, 7(2), pp. 123–132.

Cassen, R. (1994). Does Aid Work? Report to an Intergovernmental Task Force. Clarendon Press, Oxford.

Cawsey, C. (2002). Naming, measuring and modeling the values of public education. In Pascoe, S. (ed.), *Values in Education*. The Australian College of Educators, Canberra, pp. 71–84.

De Vylder, S. (1982). Agriculture in Chains. Zed Press, London.

Eyben, R. (ed.) (2006). Relationships for Aid. Earthscan, London.

Gupta, K.L. (1999). Foreign Aid: New Perspectives. Kluwer Academic Publishers, Boston.

Hamid, M.A. (1999). Governance Issues and Sustainable Development: A Critique of the Regulatory Maze in Bangladesh. In Ghosh, R.N., Gabbay, R., Siddique, A. (eds.), *Good Governance Issues and Sustainable Development: The Indian Ocean Region*. Atlantic Publishers and Distributors, New Delhi, pp. 55–66.

Hasan, Z. (2007). Democracy in Muslim Societies: The Asian Experience. Sage Publications, New Delhi.

Hossain, A. (1995). Mazar Culture in Bangladesh. PhD Thesis, Murdoch University, Perth, Australia.

Hossain, A. (2001). Renewing Self-reliance for Rural Bangladesh through Renewable Energy Technology System. PhD Thesis, Murdoch University, Perth, Australia.

Hossain, A., Marinova, D. (2005). Poverty Alleviation — a Push towards Unsustainability in Bangladesh? Presented at the International Conference on Engaging Communities 14–17 August, Brisbane. In *Proceedings of the International Conference on Engaging Communities*. Brisbane, Queensland: Queensland Department of Main Roads [E-text type]. Retrieved 18 July 2010 from www.engagingcommunities2005.org/abstracts/Hossain-Amzad-final.pdf.

Hossain, A., Marinova, D. (2003). Assessing tools for sustainability: Bangladesh context. *Proceedings of the Second Meeting of the Academic Forum of Regional Government for Sustainable Development*. Fremantle, Australia, CD ROM.

Hossain, A., Hossain-Rhaman, P. (2007). Men's Spirituality and Women in Bangladesh. *Proceedings of the 2007 International Women's Conference "Education, Employment and Everything ... the triple layers of a woman's life"*, Toowoomba, Australia, pp. 90–94. Retrieved 20 July 2010 also from http://www.shararhitu.com/index.php/survive-better/46-spiritual-articles/85-mens-spirituality-and-women-in-bangladesh-culture.html.

Hossain, A., Hossain-Rhaman, P., Islam. R., Marinova, D. (2007). Women at the Heart of Sustainability: Bangladeshi Perspective. *Proceedings of the 2007 International Women's Conference "Education, Employment and Everything ... the Triple Layers of a Woman's Life"*, Toowoomba, Australia, pp. 95–99.

Kangas, P.C. (2004). Ecological Engineering: Principles and Practice. Lewis Publishers, London.

Khair, S. (2005). Challenges to Democratisation: Perspectives of Structural Malgovernance in Bangladesh. South Asia Together — International Centre, Goa. Retrieved 21 July 2010 from http://www.internationalcentregoa.com/southasia/Malgovernance%20in%20Bangladesh%20-Sumaiya%20Khair.pdf.

Kripalani, K. (1965). All Men Are Brothers: Life and Thoughts of Mahatma Gandhi as Told in His Own Words. Columbia University Press, New York.

Lafferty, W.M. (ed.) (2004). Governance for Sustainable Development: The Challenge of Adapting Form to Function. Edward Elgar, Cheltenham, UK.

Lorey, D.E. (2003). Global Environmental Challenges of the Twenty-First Century: Resources, Consumption and Sustainable Solutions. SR Books, Delaware.

Maak, T., Pless, N. (2006). Responsible Leadership. Routledge, London.

Mulder, K. (2006). Sustainable Development for Engineers: A Handbook and Resource Guide. Greenleaf Publishing, Sheffield, UK.

Rogers, P.P., Jalal, K.F., Boyd, J.A. (2008). An Introduction to Sustainable Development. Earthscan, London.

Roy, K.C., Prasad, B.C. (2007). Governance and Development in Developing Countries. Nova Science Publishers, New York.

Rozario, S. (2006). The new burqa in Bangladesh: Empowerment or violation of women's rights? *Women's Studies International Forum*, 29(4), pp. 368–380.

Sen, A. (1981). Poverty and Famines: An Essay on Entitlement and Deprivation. Clarendon Press, Oxford.

Shiva, V. (1993). The Violence of the Green Revolution. Zed Books, London.

Shotter, J. (1993). Cultural Politics of Everyday Life: Social Constructionism, Rhetoric and Knowing of the Third Kind. Open University Press, Buckingham.

Siddique, M.A., Ghosh, R.N. (2007). Corruption and Economic Growth: The Case of Bangladesh. In Roy, K.C., Prasad, B.C. (eds), *Governance and Development in Developing Countries*. Nova Science Publishers, New York, pp. 69–87.

Solomon, C. (1991). The Cosmogonic Riddles of Lalan Fakir. In Appadurai, A., Korom, F.J., Mills, M.A. (eds.), *Gender, Genre, and Power in South Asian Expressive Traditions*. University of Pennsylvania Press, Philadelphia, pp. 267–304.

Sushasoner Jonny Procharavizan (SUPRO) (2008). External Debt, MDGs & Essential Services in Bangladesh. Retrieved 18 July 2010 from http://www.jubileenederland.nl/db/upload/documents/External_Debt_MDGs__Essential_Services_in_Bangladesh.pdf.

Endnotes

i. The Bangladeshi culture is largely dominated by the Baul philosophers — a cross-cultural tradition that was engendered with the admixture of Islamic Sufi culture of the medieval period and native Hindu–Buddhist cultures of the time (Hossain, 1995). The Bauls, both male and female, can be from Muslim or Hindu background and generally reject caste and religious dogma (Capwell, 1988). They are mostly unlettered, simple, natural and unembellished, but show a full measure of poetic, musical and philosophical talents though the songs they sing. Bauls roam from one shrine to another in Bangladeshi villages and cities along with a spouse associate. Their songs, often cast in riddles and enigmatic metaphors (see for example, Solomon, 1991 about the riddles of Lalan Fakir), are at the root of the Bengali culture.

ii. Aziz Shah Fakir (94) lives in Charaikole village of Kushtia district in Bangladesh. He has hundreds of disciples all over Bangladesh who visit the guru regularly to receive his reflective teachings on doing good deeds, supporting good people, opposing and encountering bad deeds and people, and spirituality, naturalism and longevity (sustainability) management.

iii. Khan, A.R. Bangladesh drying up as India withdrawing Ganges water. The News from Bangladesh, 28 March 2008, www.bangladesh-web.com.

iv. Hussain, M. She loves me, she loves me not. Dawn.com, 1 May 2009.

v. The corruption perception index (CPI) rank shows how one country compares to others in the perceived level of public-sector corruption; in 2009 Bangladesh improved its comparative ranking to 139th out of 180 countries, nevertheless corruption continues to be rampant in the public sector of the country (http://www.transparency.org/policy_research/surveys_indices).

vi. Ahmed. A. Bangladesh struggles to control corruption, News From Bangladesh. September 13, 2009, www.bangladesh-web.com.

vii. Khan, M.A. When crime stoppers are crime committers. The News from Bangladesh, 8 June 2009, www.bangladesh-web.com.

viii. http://www.ryerson.ca/SAFER-Net/regions/Asia/Ban_JY04.html, accessed 21 July 2010.

ix. Purdah is the practice of separating the world of the woman and the world of the man.

x. Some elderly Muslim women used the Burqa as a socio-religious dignity (Hossain, 2001).

xi. Some women from a Bangladeshi background continue with the practice of wearing saris, covering the body and the hair, also in western countries, such as in Australia.

xii. For details see http://rumiahmed.wordpress.com/2008/01/11/bangladesh-one-year-after-111/, accessed on 21 July 2010.

xiii. Uncontrollable natural phenomena such as unusual draught, flood, river erosion, cyclones etc. push frequently many people in short term poverty.

xiv. The News from Bangladesh, 29 April 2008 and 3 June 2008, www.bangladesh-web.com. Harun Baul (68) of Choraikole, Kumarkhali, Kushtia is one of the disciples of Baul guru Aziz Shah Fakir. The Baul never went to school but has learnt to read and write simple Bangla informally. Harun is a poet–philosopher–singer. Amzad Hossain publishes articles on the Baul's views on sustainability management on behalf of Harun (I'm Harun Baul Speaking) in "The News From Bangladesh" — a daily news monitoring service.

xv. See "I'm Harun Baul Speaking" (13, 14, 15 and 16), 25 May 2004, 14 April 2005, 5 July 2005 and 10 February 2006 respectively, The News from Bangladesh, www.bangladesh-web.com.

Chapter 8

Crime, Corruption and Economic Growth — A Study in Indian Perspective

Gautam M. Chakrabarti, IPS

Former Commissioner of Police, Kolkata, India

Abstract

Corruption has existed in every country in some form of the other since time immemorial and India has been no exception. But until the Second World War (1939–1945), corruption in India was confined within a few departments like police, roads and so on, but the huge amount of money pumped into the war efforts changed the entire scenario and corruption became widespread in all government sectors. On the recommendation of the Santhanam committee, formed under the noted educationist and parliamentarian Professor Santhanam, the government of India set up five-fold Anti-corruption machineries during the early 60s to fight corruption in Public life, but it appears that there is a huge gap between anti-corruption policies and practice. Although India has been achieving record growth reaching almost 9% during the last few years, its position in the Global Corruption Index is rather low. During 2008, it slipped further to a rank of 85. An estimated amount of Rs. 21,000 crores is lost every year just from petty corruption. The fight against corruption has been declared a high priority by Prime Minister Dr. Manmohan Singh and some recent measures including RTI Act, 2005 and WHISTLEBLOWER Resolution have been adopted in recent years.

India has a decentralized Federal system in which state governments possess broad regulatory powers. Several reports indicate important regional variations in the level and impact of corruption. In this study, we have attempted to study these regional variations by studying action taken by various anti-corruption agencies *vis-à-vis* the economic indicators in those states. We have also conducted a representative sample survey to study public perception of corruption in India and suggested measures to combat it effectively. An analysis of the sample survey has been made to understand the impact of corruption in those states.

Keywords: Crimes in India, corruption in India, impact of crime and corruption on economic growth in India, measures to combat corruption in India, punishment for crime and corruption in India.

Mahatma Gandhi, the father of Indian Nation once said that in this world there is enough for man's need but not for man's greed. Kautilya in his *Arthshastra* stated that "Just as it is impossible not to taste honey or poison that one may find at the tip of one's tongue, so it is also impossible for one dealing with Government funds not to taste, at least a little bit, of the King's wealth. Just as fish moving under water cannot possibly be found out either as drinking or not drinking water, so Government servants employed in the Government work cannot be found out (while) taking money (for themselves)". He further mentioned as many as forty ways of embezzlement which are equally applicable in the present time. Kautilya's forty ways of embezzlement included:

a. What was accrued first is realized afterwards, what is to be accrued later is realized first.
b. What is to be paid is not paid and what is not to be paid is paid.
c. What is paid to one is made out as paid to another.
d. What is delivered is made out as not delivered and what is not delivered is made out as delivered.

2. In fact corruption exists in every country in some form or the other since time immemorial and India is no exception. Corruption is not culture specific. As Peter Ustinov once stated "Corruption is nature's way of restoring our faith in Democracy". It is thus only natural that corruption exists in fair measure in the largest

democracy in the world. But till the Second World War, Corruption in India remained confined within a few Government Departments like Police, Roads, etc. But the huge amount of money pumped into the war efforts changed the entire scenario and corruption became widespread in most of the Government Departments. The Government of India became so alarmed with the situation that it constituted a commission under the well-known educationist Professor Santhanam to make a study on the actual state of corruption that existed in the country. The report of Professor Santhanam, which was published in 1963 revealed two very important things: that corruption was no longer confined to only a few departments but had pervaded almost all the Government Departments and that more alarmingly, it was not practised by only the lower level functionaries but even the senior Government officers were often found involved in corrupt practices.

3. Alarmed at this report Government of India decided to set up five-fold machineries to tackle the increasing corruption scenario in the country:

    a. Administrative Vigilance Division (AVD) in the Home Ministry (MHA) which is primarily responsible for formulation and implementation of Government policies in the field of Vigilance and Anti-corruption work.

    b. Vigilance units headed by a senior officer termed as CVO in every Government Department for intensive anti-corruption work in the Department.

    c. The Disciplinary authorities to take Departmental Action against corrupt Public Servants in the concerned Department.

    d. The Delhi Special Police Establishment subsequently renamed as the CBI which is the primary Investigating agency to investigate all cases of corruption involving Public Servants. and

    e. The Central Vigilance Commission (CVC), which is the apex organization for exercising general superintendence and control over vigilance matters in administration and probity in public life.

4. Government of India publishes Annual Crime Statistics every year in a compendium called "Crime in India". If we examine the crime and

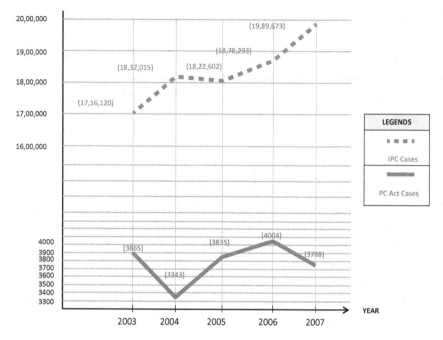

Figure 8.1   Crime and corruption cases 2003–2007

corruption cases during the period 2003–2007 the following graphical representation can be seen:

From Figure 8.1, it may be seen that while the crime figures are increasing steadily, the cases under the Prevention of Corruption Act are showing a fluctuating trend. While the total number of cases under the PC Act, 1988 decreased from 3,865 in 2003 to 3,343 in 2004, it again increased to 3,835 in 2005 and further to 4,004 in 2006. Again, surprisingly, it decreased to 3,788 in the year 2007. Our study did not reveal any specific reasons for such a fluctuating trend. In fact there could be no reason why corruption cases should have decreased in the year 2007 from the previous year 2006.

Table 8.1 shows the number of cases registered under the Prevention of Corruption Act, 1988 by the CBI and the States during 2003–2007. It may be seen that the maximum number of cases were registered in 2005 and the least in 2007. But the number of persons arrested during 2007 was the maximum which indicated that more number of corrupt

Table 8.1 PC ACT Cases by CBI and States 2003–2007: Details of cases registered and persons arrested under prevention of corruption act

Sl. No.	Year	No. of vigilance cases registered by		Persons arrested	
		CBI	States/UTs	CBI	States/UTs
1	2003	707	3,158	409	3,320
2	2004	758	2,585	292	3,209
3	2005	827	3,008	NA	3,510
4	2006	719	3,285	NA	3,425
5	2007	610	3,178	NA	4,531

Table 8.2 Major fraud cases during 2005–2007: Major frauds reported during 2005–2007

Sl. No.	Value of property lost/defrauded (in Rs. Crore)	2005		2006		2007	
		CBT	Cheating	CBT	Cheating	CBT	Cheating
1	1–10	17	86	58	285	74	147
2	10–25	4	11	0	4	3	7
3	25–50	1	3	4	1	0	21
4	50–100	1	1	0	0	1	0
5	Above 100	1	0	0	0	1	1
	Total	24	101	62	290	79	176

public servants have been working in groups or syndicates, which again is a cause for worry. Table 8.1 also highlights the details of public servants arrested in corruption cases during the relevant period by the CBI and the States/UTs. From this table, it is seen that the State Governments are taking more and more initiative to enquire into cases of corruption involving corrupt State Government officials.

Table 8.2 highlights the major frauds reported during 2005–2007. It may be noticed that number of cases of CBT has gradually been increasing while the number of high-value cheating cases decreased during 2007 as compared to previous year. The State Vigilance Bureau seized property worth Rs 29.6 crore in various seizures connected with corruption charges showing a 101.4% increase in value of seizure over the year 2006 when the figure was Rs 14.7 crore. However, a very conservative estimate of public money lost only in petty corruption cases stands at more than Rs 21,000 crore as per the study of corruption undertaken by the Transparency International in 2005. This figure does not take account of the big frauds/scams involving Ministers, Senior Politicians and Public Servants. So the percentage seizure of the misappropriated money stands at a meager 0.0014%.

If we critically examine the total number of cases under PC Act started by CBI and the State Anti-Corruption Bureau during the year, we find that Rajasthan, Maharashtra, Kerala, Punjab and Haryana started the maximum number of cases as against Arunachal Pradesh, Meghalaya, West Bengal, Tripura and Mizoram recording the minimum number of cases. On the other hand, the maximum number of IPC crimes were registered in Madhya Pradesh, Maharastra, Tamil Nadu, Andhra Pradesh and Uttar Pradesh, while minimum number of cases were registered in Sikkim, Arunachal Pradesh, Nagaland, Meghalaya and Mizoram. During the same year, the economic growth of the States are given in Table 8.4.

India has a decentralized federal system in which State Governments possess broad regulatory power. Although corruption is found to be pervasive across all states and public services, several reports indicate important regional variations in the level and impact of corruption. HP, AP and Maharashtra are perceived to experience moderate levels of corruption while states like Bihar, J&K and MP are affected with an alarming level of corruption. There are also regional differences in the sectors and institutions most affected by corruption at the state level, as illustrated in the TI's 2005 study:

a. In Gujarat, the judiciary, the police and the land administration are ranked the most corrupt services.

b. In Maharashtra, the Municipal services are perceived to be the most corrupt.

c. In Punjab, the judiciary, the police and the municipal services are perceived to be the most corrupt.

Table 8.3 Max/Min PC Act cases vis-à-vis IPC cases

	Max	Min
PC Act	Rajasthan	Arunachal Pradesh
	Maharashtra	Meghalaya
	Kerala	West Bengal
	Punjab	Tripura
	Haryana	Mizoram
IPC	Madhya Pradesh	Sikkim
	Maharashtra	Arunachal Pradesh
	Tamilnadu	Nagaland
	Andhra Pradesh	Meghalaya
	Uttar Pradesh	Mizoram

Table 8.4 State-wise economic growth

Max	Min
Himachal Pradesh	Bihar
Punjab	Jharkhand
Maharashtra	Madhya Pradesh
Gujarat	Chattisgarh
Kerala	Assam

d. In Bihar, all public services are ranked among the most corrupt in India.
e. According to Freedom House 2008, rebel groups operate extensive extortion networks in the north east of the country, compounding the impact of corruption in the various affected states.

In our study we decided to closely examine the relationship between Crime, Corruption and State Domestic Product in 5 states, viz. Kerala and Gujarat which are perceived to be "Less Corrupt States" (as may be seen in Table 8.5), Punjab and West Bengal known to be "Moderately Corrupt States", and Bihar which is at the bottom of Table 8.5 indicating the Most Corrupt State.

Table 8.5   State-wise corruption perception ranking of states

State	Composite index	Rank
Kerala	240	1
Himachal Pradesh	301	2
Gujarat	417	3
Andhra Pradesh	421	4
Maharashtra	433	5
Chattisgarh	445	6
Punjab	459	7
West Bengal	461	8
Orissa	475	9
Uttar Pradesh	491	10
Delhi	496	11
Tamil Nadu	509	12
Haryana	516	13
Jharkhand	520	14
Assam	542	15
Rajasthan	543	16
Karnataka	576	17
MP	584	18
J&K	655	19
Bihar	695	20

      Table 8.6 gives the Comparative Bar Diagram of Crime, Corruption and SDP in these 5 states. While Kerala and Gujarat expectedly had significant higher SDP as compared to West Bengal and Bihar (having the least SDP), Punjab which is ranked 7th in Table 8.5, achieved much higher SDP than Kerala(1st) and Gujarat(3rd), reasons of, which could be attributable to other factors.

9.   Slow disposal of court cases again weakens the anti-corruption efforts of the Government only 2,004 out of 15,861 cases under PC Act registered by the State Anti-corruption Bureau were disposed of during 2007. Out of these 2,004 cases only 739 cases ended in conviction. The position of trial of CBI cases gives a better picture with 744 out of 6,172

Table 8.6　Complaints received and disposed of during 2008

Complaints	Nos.	Action taken
No. of complaints received and B/F	10,330	
Anonymous/Pseudonymous	673	Filed
Vague/Unverifiable	2,343	Filed
Non-vigilance/officials not under CVC jurisdiction	6,025	For necessary action to Orgns./Depts.
Verifiable	1,147	Sent for investigation to CVO/CBI
Total disposed of	10,188	
Pendency	142	

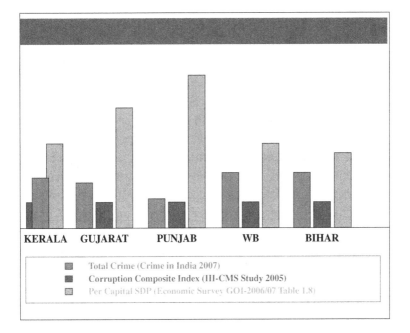

Figure 8.2　Crime, corruption and economic growth

cases in trial were disposed of by the courts. Out of these disposed of cases 492 which is 66.13% of total cases ended in conviction.

10. The fight against corruption has been declared a high priority by Prime Minister Man Mohan Singh. In the last G20 Summit in

April, Dr. Singh urged the G20 leaders to bring tax havens and non-cooperating jurisdiction under close scrutiny as part of implementing tighter global financial revelations. It may be mentioned that recent estimates of such Indian money outside India reached INR 7.5 million crore. Black money circulating inside India appears to be no less in quantity than its outside component. Corruption continues to be wide-spread in the country. India is ranked 85 out of 179 countries in Transparency International's Corruption Perception Index (CPI). There have been many instances of political and bureaucratic corruption, public fund embezzlement, fraudulent procurement practices and judicial corruption. The sectors most affected are public procurement, tax and customs administration, infrastructure, public utilities and the police.

11. The economy in India was under socialist-inspired policies for an entire generation from the 1950s until the 1980s, and was subject to extensive regulation, protectionism, and public ownership. Since 1991, economic liberalization in India has reduced red tape and bureaucracy, supported the transition towards a market economy with record growth rates of 9.2 % in 2007. However, its growth has been uneven across social and economic groups, with sections of society experiencing some of the highest levels of poverty in the world. Endemic corruption contributes to uneven distribution of wealth. The cost of corruption, perceptible in public sector inefficiencies and inadequate infrastructure, is undermining efforts to reduce poverty. According to the Global Corruption Barometer 2007, petty corruption is common practice in India with 25% of the respondents admitted paying bribes to obtain basic services. India is also perceived to export corruption outside its border. A study made by Diane Mak of TI, in 2006 ranked India at the bottom of the Bribe Payers Index (BPI) table out of 30 countries selected for study. This indicates that Indian firms are perceived by business people as very likely to engage in bribery when doing business abroad.

12. Long procedural delay in the finalization of Court cases, as mentioned earlier, is a big failure to reduce corruption. A case under PC Act usually takes 10 to 15 years to be finalized and even the same judgment and all the interlocutory orders can be challenged in higher courts causing further delay. As mentioned in *Crime in India*, 2007, only

13% of the cases pending trial under various section of IPC were disposed of during the year, and that most of these disposed of cases were old cases.

A survey of CBI cases in two States indicates that only 1% of the public servants booked by CBI were in jail. It must be understood that in the fight against corruption CERTAINTY is more important than the ENORMITY of Punishment.

13. India's performance on the 2007 Global Integrity Index indicates a huge gap between anti-corruption policies and practice. Although the legal and institutional frameworks against corruption are well developed, law enforcement, however, remains very weak, suffering a lack of political will to address the challenges of corruption. Shri Pratyush Sinha, the Central Vigilance Commissioner whom we had interviewed in the course of our project, felt that the weakest points in India's anti-corruption drive are:

1) It is perceived that fighting corruption is not the job of the concerned departments which completely abdicate their responsibility.

2) Although there are good institutions like CVC to fight corrupt practices of Ministers and Bureaucrats, there is no specific institution to tackle political corruption. The corrupt politicians in turn influence the corrupt civil servants.

3) Corruption has ceased to be an issue in the society. Earning more money means earning more respect. The young generation is likely to be unaware of the issue of the corruption.

14. The Central Vigilance Commission is the Nodal Agency in India to take action against corrupt public servants. However, from the following Charts (Figures 8.3–8.6), it may be seen that the number of cases received in the Commission has been decreasing since 2004 and the number of penalties imposed is also decreasing since 2004.

The number of penalty imposed to number of cases received (in %) was maximum in 2004 (73.4%) and thereafter remained close to 50–55%. The number of cases disposed of by the Commission also decreased since 2003 as may be seen in Figure 8.4. The senior officials in the Commission could not give any satisfactory reason for

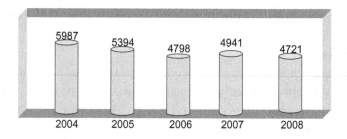

Figure 8.3 Number of cases received in the Commission

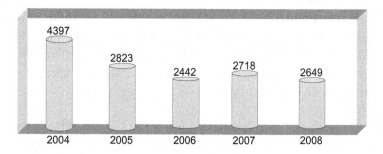

Figure 8.4 Number of penalties imposed

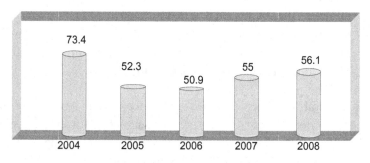

Figure 8.5 Number of penalties imposed to number of cases received (in %)

such drop in the number of cases registered, but it may be a reflection on the lack of confidence in the mind of general public.

15. Complaints are the starting point in the fight against corruption. General Public can complain only if there are enhanced awareness on

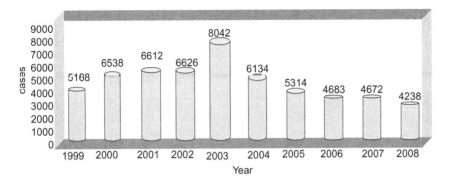

Figure 8.6 Number of cases disposed of by the Commission

the need to complain and also if they have faith in the Administration. The CVC receives complaints from various sources including individuals, Chief Technical Examiners' reports, employers, press, civil society etc. Large number of complaints are also received through the Complaints Lodging Facility in the Website of the Commission.

In the year 2008, the CVC received (and brought forward from the previous year) a total of 10,330 complaints out of which 10,188 were disposed of in the same year. Out of these disposed of complaints, 1,147 complaints was sent to the CBI/CVO for investigation and further penal action. The fate of the enquiry into these 1,147 complaints was not available.

Figures 8.7 and 8.8 indicate the nature of complaints (% share) and action taken on complaints (% share) received by the Commission. Although the percentage of the verifiable complaints was only 11.3%, confidence of general public can be restored if the investigating agencies could quickly complete these enquiries, and strong action is taken against those public servants found guilty.

16. It was mentioned by the senior officials of the CVC that PIDPI (Public Interest Disclosers & Protection of Informers) Resolution has been giving good results in the enquires undertaken by the CVC. PIDPI safeguards complainant's interest and also ensures that the investigation reports are submitted within 30 days. Confidentiality of the identity of the complainant and fixed time limit for completion of the enquiry are the two strong points of PIDPI resolution.

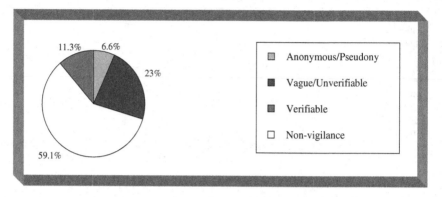

Figure 8.7   Nature of complaints (% Share)

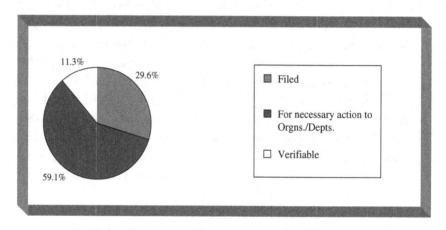

Figure 8.8   Action taken on complaints (% Share)

In 2008, the Central Vigilance Commission received 276 complaints under the PIDPI resolution. Table 8.7 indicates the nature of complaints (% share) and action taken of complaints (% share). It may be seen that 27.3% of these complaints were verifiable, as against only 11.3% of general complaints as seen in Figure 8.7.

The Central Vigilance Commission also maintains details of penalty imposed in cases for all category of officers handled by the CVO. Table 8.8 would show that as many as 12,539 officers were punished during this year, out of whom 819 corrupt public servants were

Table 8.7 Complaints received and disposed of during 2008 under the PIDPI resolution

Complaints received	Nos.	Action taken
No. of complaints received	276	
Anonymous/Pseudonymous	46	Filed
Vague/Vigilance	144	For necessary action to Orgns./Depts.
Verifiable	83	For investigation to CVO/CBI
Total disposed of	273	
Pendency	3	

Table 8.8 Details of penalties imposed in 2008 cases for all category of officers handled by the CVOs

Sl. No.	Nature of penalty	No. of officers
	Major Penalty	3,528
1.	Cut in Pension	67
2.	Dismissal/Removal/Compulsory retirement	819
3.	Reduction to lower scale/rank	1,664
4.	Other major penalty	978
	Minor Penalty	9,011
5.	Minor penalty other than censure	5,252
6.	Censure	3,759

dismissed or removed from service, which indicates that the CVC took strong action against the public servants found guilty.

19. The Government of India has recently taken various steps to increase transparency in public service. The Right to information (RTI) Act was enacted in 2005 and under this Act any citizen may request information from a "Public Authority" which is required to reply within 30 days. In the first year of its application, as many as 42,876 applications for information were filed to Central Public Authorities. The WHISTLEBLOWER resolution adopted recently has given the confidence in the mind of Government public servants to lodge complaint against higher officials, particularly his superiors without disclosing his identity. However a complete act with clauses of

safeguard and protection of the informant is yet to be enacted. E-governance has considerably increased the speed of Government services in many areas and reduced the opportunity for bribery. But lack of accountability in key areas and due to overlapping and conflicting mandates between institutions addressing corruption, the anti-corruption drive of the Government suffers badly. Influential politicians and senior officials are rarely convicted on charges of corruption, thereby eroding public confidence in the political will to tackle corruption.

20. During their first week in office, Columbian Judges and other officials involved in anti-drug efforts often receive a message asking "PLATA O PLOMO?". It reminds the public officials that there is an alternative to fighting drugs and receive PLOMO (Spanish for lead, as in bullets) which is not fighting drugs and receiving PLATA (Spanish for Silver or Money, as in a bribe). A country like India with high corruption and not-so-good officials can change for the better if it can reduce the risk of PLOMO and the allurement of PLATA for the public officials.

Conclusion

In this study, we have made an endeavor to find out whether there is a direct connection between crime and corruption, and economic growth in the Indian context. We have studied the pattern of crime and corruption in various states and attempted to find out a correlation between the two. We have also conducted a Sample Survey covering a large cross section of people including Students, Teachers, IT Professionals, Members of Chamber of Commerce and Industries, Office Bearers of Transport Organizations, NGOs etc. Interestingly, the public perception regarding the more corrupt states do not readily match with the number of corruption cases registered by the Anti-Corruption Bureaus in those states. Nor do we find out a direct connection between the Economic Growth in various states with the figures of Crime and Corruption and the ranking of the states from corruption point of view as drawn up by the Transparency International.

In India there exists a federal structure and each of the States has its own police Force and Anti-Corruption Bureau. It is often alleged that the Police and other Investigating Agencies do not record all cases of Cognizable Crime. As such, the data of Crime and Corruption do not always reflect the actual figure. This possibly gives an incorrect picture of correlation between Economic Growth vis-à-vis crime and corruption in various States. While it is difficult to get the actual crime figure (particularly those received but not recorded at PSs and Anti-Corruption Bureau), the public perception which came out during our survey more or less indicated that the most corrupt states as perceived had the least indicators of Economic Growth in the relevant years.

Recommendation

Paolo Mauro in his famous book (1997) concluded that corruption definitely affects economic growth in the long run. In our studies also we found out that the states which are perceived to be highly corrupt had poor economic growth during the period. However, in a large democracy like India with strong regional variations and different levels of anti-corruption drives, a deeper study has to be made to find out how crime and corruption actually affect economic growth. Nevertheless, in the national perspective it is highly important that we intensify the drive against corruption by taking timely action against corrupt public servants, both by way of Court Proceedings and/or Departmental Actions. Delay and lack of transparency in Government Departments need to be eliminated by taking necessary Administrative Reforms. As mentioned in our paper, the Criminal Justice System in India is overburdened with huge pendency of cases. Court trials need to be expedited so that important evidences are not lost due to long passage of time. We once again reiterate that **Certainty of punishment is more important than Severity of punishment**. Lastly, there should be proper enactment to tackle the corrupt politicians. Introduction of Lok Pal system to enquire into charges of corruption against Ministers and other senior politicians, both at the national and state levels would perhaps bring in the required changes. The civil society must also rise up and protest against corruption at all levels of public life. Social acceptance of corruption is also eating into the moral fabric of the society. The Civil Society Groups should spread awareness amongst the citizens regarding their rights and responsibilities and the need to report acts of corruption at respective institutions. We feel that the Anti-Corruption Laws in India are adequately strong but their implementation needs to be more effective so as to achieve the desired results.

References

1. *The Arthashastra* — Chanakya (C 350–283 BC).
2. *Crime in India*, 2007 — National Crime Records Bureau Ministry of Home Affairs Govt. of India.
3. Global Corruption Report, 2007 — Transparency International.
4. TII-CMS India Corruption Study, 2007 — Transparency International India.
5. Corruption and Growth — P. Mauro — *The Quarterly Journal of Economic*, 1995.
6. *Corruption and the Global Economy*, 1997 — P. Mauro — Adelinotorres.com
7. Global Integrity Report, 2007
8. The Prevention of Corruption Act, 1988 (India)
9. CVC Act, 2003 (India)
10. Vigilance Manual (India)
11. CVC Annual Report, 2007
12. Circulars and Guidelines of CVC — www.cvc.nic.in
13. The Right to Information Act, 2005 (India) (No. 22 of 2005)

Chapter 9

Comparative Crime and Corruption in Different Indian States in the Context of Economic Development

Surajit Kar Purkayastha, IPS

Commissioner of Police, Kolkata, India

Abstract

The relationship between crime and economic growth, and corruption and economic growth is complex in nature. It is also difficult to compare crime rates both internationally and nationally due to variation not only in legal definition of crime but also in its reporting systems, counting methods, and data quality. In India, average number of offences during the study period is ₹54.77 lakh of which ₹18.48 lakh under Indian Penal Code and ₹36.29 lakh under special and local laws. Crime against body, crime against properties and riots are falling but crime against women and economic offences are rising. This study covers 5 Indian States representing northern, southern, eastern and western part of India including West Bengal. Kerala, a southern state has the highest crime rate but remarkably better in overall functioning of the Criminal Justice System. On the other hand, West Bengal has lowest crime rate but requires improvement in Criminal Justice System. Unlike criminality rate and economic growth, the interrelationship between corruption and economic growth is perceived to be direct and strong. The rank correlation coefficient between 'corruption perception index' and 'per capita GDP rank' is 0.78 for selected 19 countries and 0.46 for selected Indian states. But there is an inverse relationship between crime and state domestic product. In addition, the data collected from wide range of people under this study reflects that rich persons are responsible for crime and corruption. Most of the respondents are not satisfied with anti-corruption measures. Lack of education, poor salary and poverty are considered to be the most important cause for corruption. People's active involvement in eradicating crime and corruption hold the key.

Keywords: Crime, corruption, economic development, rank correlation.

Introduction

India is a vast country having an area of 3.3 million sq. km and a population of more than one billion. It is divided into 28 States and 7 Union Territories, with a wide mix and variety of religion, ethnicity, cultural groups and languages etc.

Before going into the country specifics, we deem it necessary to sensitize our readers about the comparability of the crime data of India vis-à-vis other important countries in the world. We should mention that the crime data across countries are not strictly comparable for many reasons. The legal definition of crime itself may vary. While stating the difficulty in comparing crime rate between the United States and other countries, Reinhart[i] observes a number of contributing reasons 'including difference in criminal justice systems, rates at which crimes are reported by victims and recorded by police, crime reporting systems and counting methods, definitions, and data quality'. Note that we are confronted with most of these difficulties as we can only compare the inter-country crime data as registered with the government agencies and not the actual number of occurrences.

While scanning the world crime scenario, the readers may find the crime rate in India being strikingly less compared to many economically developed countries. Consider the criminality rates in few of them — the number of crimes per 100,000 population of Sweden (13,493), Denmark (6,813), Netherlands (7,439), Canada (8,317), Germany (7,628), USA (3,765), Italy (4,715), Japan (1,603) etc. vis-à-vis India with the rate hovering around a meagre 443.[ii]

It seems plausible that the lack of education, awareness and material resources discourage socially disadvantaged people from having recourse to the criminal justice system thus accounting for a noteworthy low criminality rate in India. As observed from state-wise data (furnished in later part of this report), it appears that the criminality rate is higher in a

Table 9.1 Aggregate crime incidents in India: 2003–2007

Year	Number of offences			Ratio	
	IPC	SLL	Total	(IPC:SLL)	Rate per million population
2003	17,16,120	37,78,694	54,94,814	1:2.20	51.44
2004	18,32,015	41,96,766	60,28,781	1:2.30	55.53
2005	18,22,602	32,03,735	50,26,337	1:1.76	45.58
2006	18,78,293	32,24,167	51,02,460	1:1.72	45.57
2007	19,89,673	37,43,734	57,33,407	1:1.88	50.45
Average	18,47,741	36,29,419	54,77,160		

Source: Crime In India 2007: *National Crime Records Bureau*, p. 23.

number of high-income states compared to the poorer ones. Do the richer states have relatively faster moving criminal justice system which encourage the people to use it in greater measure for redress of their grievances? Yes or no, this warrants more study.

With the benefit of this brief sensitization exercise let us look into the details of crime scenario of India as reflected in the available official data. Table 9.1 gives a summary view of aggregate crime incidences registered under both Indian Penal Code (IPC) and Special & Local Laws (SLL) over a period from 2003 to 2007.

As can be seen the IPC crimes and SLL crimes 2007 accounted for 34.7% and 65.3% of total cognizable crimes. Category wise examination follows.

Crime Data: Break-Up

The composition of IPC crimes shows that 22 specified heads accounted for nearly 58.3% of total IPC crimes with 'others' accounting for 41.7%. As individual groups, incidents of crime against body (CAB) constituted the highest percentage of the total (22.7%), followed by crime against property (CAP) (20.3%), economic crimes (4.2%) and crime against public safety (3.5%).

The nature of SLL crimes was more variegated. This can be appreciated from the fact that 21 individually specified heads constituted only

22.0% of the 'total', while the remaining 78% were clubbed under 'other SLL crimes'. As individual categories, crimes under the Prohibition Act and the Gambling Act were largest in terms of occurrence accounting for 14.1% of total SLL crimes. The next in order were crimes under Excise Act (3.8%) and Arms Act (2.0%).

Crime Rate: A Better Indicator

In the context of the rapidly rising population in India, the crime rates (number of incidence per one million people) seem to be more meaningful than the absolute number of occurrences. Accordingly we have constructed a small table that gives a reasonably good idea of the IPC related crime rates in the present decade. Some approximations are used as mentioned at the end of the Table 9.2 but that does not reduce the significance of the observations. Let us examine:

Table 9.2   Crime rates in India: 2001–2007

Year	CAB-rate	CAP-rate	CAW-rate	RIOT-rate	EC-rate	Others-rate	Total-rate
2001	4.11	3.81	1.13	0.74	0.59	6.81	17.20
2006	3.87	3.60	1.22	0.51	0.66	7.0	16.86
2007	3.99	3.64	1.37	0.53	0.73	7.33	17.59

[Crime against body (CAB) includes murder, attempt to murder, kidnapping & abductions, hurt, causing death by negligence, culpable homicide not amounting to murder; Crime against property (CAP) includes dacoity, robbery, preparation and assembly for dacoity, burglary and theft; Crime against women (CAW) includes dowry death, molestation, rape, sexual harassment, cruelty by husband & relatives, and importation of girls; Economic crime (EC) includes criminal breach of trust, cheating, and counterfeiting.]

Note: Normally the mid-year population is used to calculate crime rate. However, owing to their non-availability, we have used population figures as at 1st March of 2001, 2006 and 2007 from the Census of India website and then correlated these to crime figures available from the latest publications of NCB.

Crime Pattern — A Broad View

As the readers may notice, despite the rapidly rising population and many regressive forces in operation, the crime situation has remained within a reasonable limit.

The crime rate has been under appreciable control as regards 'crime against body', 'crime against property' and 'riots'. The rate however shows a clearly rising trend relating 'crime against women' and 'economic offences'. These increases can be understood in the context of rising awareness of women about their rights and the impact of fast economic growth with uneven opportunities to social cross sections.

Interestingly, somewhat similar contextual correlation can be found in higher share of the mega cities in the form of crimes like auto theft, other thefts, cheating, preparation and assembly for dacoity, counterfeiting, criminal breach of trust and burglary whereas their contribution to other crimes remain less pronounced.[iii]

Crime & its Impact On Economic Growth — Empirical Evidence

We have already seen that many economically developed countries have high criminality rates. In this context interested readers may glean through the 'criminality ranks' awarded to various countries in a survey conducted by the United Nation's Office on 'Drugs and Crimes'.[iv]

We observe a somewhat similar phenomenon while analyzing state-wise crime and economic data in India. We invite readers' attention to Table No. 5 that explores the interrelations of economic growth with each of crime and corruption across select Indian states. Interestingly, there appears to exist a moderately strong direct relationship between 'crime rates' and 'economic growth'. This obviously does not link economic progress to higher crime rates, but possibly indicate that the crime registration rate is higher in economically advanced states. To delve deeper into this paradox, we had also undertaken a more detailed review of functioning of the criminal justice system across five representative states viz., Bihar, Gujarat, Kerala, Punjab and West Bengal, based on ten (10) key parameters. The consideration for choosing the four states excluding the domain state of West Bengal are (a) geographic coverage — east, west, north & south; (b) income variation — high, medium and low. The relevant data are furnished in Table 9.3.

The Ten Parameters

At first, let us look at the criminality rank. The greater the rank, the lesser is the rate of crime. For example, West Bengal with a rank of 31 has the lowest crime rate amongst the select five states. The second parameter

Table 9.3 Functioning of the criminal justice system based on key parameters

	India	Bihar	Gujarat	Kerala	Punjab	W. Bengal
1. Criminality Rank: IPC		28	8	4	24	31
SLL		28	7	9	14	30
2. Recovery of property: Rate	**26.0**	16.2	23.8	8.6	54	16.4
3. Charge sheeting rate: IPC	**80.1**	73.5	81.5	90.6	75.5	75.4
SLL	**95.8**	87.3	99.8	92.7	96	92.4
4. Remand prisoners %-police: IPC	**19.2**	35.7	8	16.5	36.3	34.4
SLL	**5.6**	38.6	7.6	5.6	43.1	47.5
5. Remand prisoners %-court: IPC	**84.7**	89.5	92.9	76.3	80.5	91.9
SLL	**63.4**	86	87.8	68.2	78.6	90.1
6. Percentage of pending court cases: IPC	**84.2**	88.2	92.1	76.6	84.8	94.3
7. Percentage of conviction-court: IPC	**42.3**	16.7	42.3	44.5	37.6	13.2
8. Percentage of pending court cases: SLL	**60.4**	85.8	86.9	67.2	80.1	91.1
9. Percentage of conviction-court: SLL	**83.8**	28.6	63.8	78	77.5	36.3
10. Duratn.-court proceedings: <3 yrs	**63.9**	31.1	68.1	68	68.7	59.3
Between 3 and 10 years	**33.2**	63.3	30.4	31.6	30.8	35.8
More than 10 years	**2.9**	5.6	1.5	0.4	0.5	4.9

Data sources: Crime In India 2007, NCB: pp. 200, 202, 454, 346, 352, 541, 543, 545, 547, 358, 364, 374 and 381 for parameters 1–10 respectively.

Notes: (1) Except item no. 1, rest of the items show data in percentage terms.

(2) India figure or the national average includes all states and union territories.

considers the efficiency of the police in recovering properties lost due to theft, burglary, etc. The rest of the parameters are not crime-specific but reflect the general health of the criminal justice system that includes both police and judiciary. The third item reflects on the efficiency of the police in submitting charge sheets. The fourth and fifth parameters shed light on that segment of the 'prison population' against whom no charge sheet has been filed by the police and no conviction pronounced by any court of law. Items 6 to 9 reflect the speed of disposal of the court cases and the percentages of conviction. The last item i.e., 10 gives a rough but ready idea of time taken by various courts in disposing of cases.

Key Observation

Prima facie, there appears to exist an inverse relationship between 'crime rates' (reflected through 'criminality rank') and overall efficiency of the police and the judiciary. For example, Kerala has the highest crime rate but it has also remarkably better performance in the matter of filing charge sheets, disposal of court cases, conviction rate, etc. To a large extent the same thing applies to Gujarat. On the other hand, states such as West Bengal and Bihar have very low crime rates but the overall functioning of the criminal justice system requires to be improved. Does this phenomenon influence lodging of formal complaints or 'crime registration' as well? This paradox merits more attention.

Corruption
The multiplier effect

An internationally accepted definition of 'corruption' has been the use of 'public office' for 'private gains'. The beneficiaries are often powerful officials who misuse their power to favor certain persons, groups or organization to the detriment of the general interest of the society. Corruption at higher echelons, also known as kleptocracy, cripples a country through multiplier effect. As the eJournal USA observes:[v]

"Large-scale corruption by high-level public officials — kleptocracy — is a particular threat for democracy and rule of law in developing countries. Such corruption undermines financial accountability, discourages foreign investment, stifles economic performance, and diminishes trust in legal and judicial system".

In India, corruption has been a more difficult issue to tackle, being disguised but pervasive. Corruption often occurs clandestinely with both the 'giver' and the 'taker' taking pains to keep the transaction under wrap.

It may be considered to be one of the worst forms of crime as other crimes often involve two or a few persons whereas corruption breaks the backbone of the society through its multiplier effect.

Corruption in India-background

There are little official data available on corruption in India. To estimate its scale, we have to depend on surrogate sources including studies, surveys and possibly specific action programmes. We may consider a few of these:

The Transparency International provides a reliable assessment of the magnitude of corruption in the country through the corruption perception index. The latest global survey[vi] (2008) gives India a discomforting rank of 85 out of a total of 180 countries. And remember this rank is an improvement over the past after pursuing nearly two decades of de-regulation and liberalization.

The Indian Chapter of the Transparency International has been conducting periodical surveys to understand the nature and magnitude of corruption in public services and these made a number of startling observations. India corruption study 2005 conducted by the TII in alliance with Centre for Media Studies (CMS) delved into corruption faced by common man in availing 11 public services in 20 major states. While projecting an insight into the menace, the survey also awarded corruption ranking to individual states.

Unearthing black money

Another approach to measure the extent of corruption is to assess the quantum of black money. There have been occasional government actions in unearthing such money. Since independence the federal government declared five amnesty schemes allowing conversion of black money into 'white' subject to specified terms and conditions. The last one christened as VDIS or Voluntary Disclosure Scheme announced in the year 1997 was able to mobilize ₹30,000 crore of black money, which was either earned by or with the help of 'corrupt public officials'.

Corruption and Economic Growth

Unlike 'criminality rate' and 'economic growth', the interrelationship between 'corruption' and 'economic growth' is perceived to be direct and

Table 9.4   Rank correlation between corruption & per capita GDP

19 Countries including India

Country	GDP rank	CP rank
Singapore	1	2
USA	2	6
Australia	3	3
UK	4	5
Germany	5	4
France	6	7
Italy	7	10
Newzealand	8	1
South Korea	9	8
Russia	10	19
Malaysia	11	9
Iran	12	18
Thailand	13	12
China	14	11
Srilanka	15	14
Indonesia	16	16
India	17	13
Pakistan	18	17
Nepal	19	15
19 Countries		
Rank Correlation Coefficient	+ 0.785965	

Data sources:
1. http://www.transparencyindia.org/pdf/CPI_2008_table.pdf.
2. https://www.cia.gov/library/publications/the-world-factbook/rankorder/
2004rank.html.

close. We observe it working at the global level as well as in India through analyses of relevant data.

For global analysis, we used data (as available in year 2008) relating to 19 countries including India. These are furnished in the Table 9.4. We have used 'corruption perception index rank' and 'per capita GDP rank', the latter to represent the strength of economic growth of a country. The least corrupt country was given rank 1 and the country with the highest per capita GDP was also given rank 1. Finally we calculated the rank correlation coefficient (RCC) to understand their interrelations. The RCC worked out to 0.78 indicating a direct and strong relationship.

A similar but more encompassing analysis (relating economic growth to both corruption and crime) was carried out involving select 19 Indian states where we have used similar methodology with the per capita GDP replaced by per capita SDP or State Domestic Product.[vii] The corruption perception index rank was collected from a survey done by Transparency International India. The criminality rank was taken from the "Crime in India 2005' published by National Crime Records Bureau.[viii]

Whereas the methodology of this table has been mentioned in the list of references,[ix] few words about the tool of rank correlation coefficient may be in order here. The rank correlation can take any value between –1 to +1. When the value is +1 there is complete agreement in the order of the ranks and the ranks are in the same directions. When the value is –1, there is complete agreement in the order of the ranks but they are in opposite directions. The rank coefficient of correlation r has been calculated using the formula $r = 1 - 6 \Sigma D^2 / N(N^2 - 1)$, where D refers to the difference of ranks between paired items in two series and N refers to the number of ranks.[x]

In the present case, the rank correlation coefficient between per capita SDP and Corruption Perception worked out to (+)0.46, suggesting a positive but moderate degree of relationship. On the other hand the RCC w.r.t. crime worked out to (–)0.40 which shows a rather inverse relationship. Please refer to Table 9.5.

Crime and Corruption in India: Our Own Survey

The background

As said more than once already, in terms of 'criminality rate' India seems to be much better than many others including economically developed

Table 9.5 Rank correlation between per capita SDP, corruption & crime

States	Corruption perception	Per capita SDP	Crime rate
Kerala	1	7	18
HP	2	6	11
Gujrat	3	5	13
AP	4	11	12
Maharastra	5	3	8
Chattisgar	6	12	10
Punjab	7	4	3
West Bengal	8	10	2
Orissa	9	17	6
UP	10	18	1
Delhi	11	1	19
TN	12	8	16
Haryana	13	2	9
Jharkhand	14	16	5
Assam	15	15	7
Rajasthan	16	13	15
Karnataka	17	9	14
MP	18	14	17
Bihar	19	19	4
Rank correlation coefficient-SDP/CP	**0.45964**		
Rank correlation coefficient-SDP/Crime			**−0.403508772**

Data sources:
1. http://sampark.chd.nic.in/images/Statistics/SDP2005R5.pdf.
2. http://www.transparencyindia.org/Publication/India%20Corruption%20Study%202005%20in%PDF.pdf.
3. Crime in India 2005: National Crime Records Bureau, Ministry of Home Affairs, GOI.

countries. However, we cannot draw any comfort from this comparison unless we are sure that this apparent tranquillity does not conceal deeper problems of lack of public confidence in the system resulting in low-registration of crime. This doubt gets reinforcement after analyzing the correlation between economic growth and criminality rank across various states in the country. As regards corruption, the latest ranking of India by the Transparency International has been agonizingly high 85 out of a total of 180 countries. As mentioned earlier the TII or the Indian Chapter of the TII has also conducted surveys with regard to specific target group and or specific services. These too have portrayed grim pictures.

As a part of our study, we made an attempt to supplement these valuable work in a modest way by trying to get a first-hand account of the perceptions of a cross section of 'general' Indian citizens on the status of both 'crime' and 'corruption' in the country and their impact on the economic growth of the country. This 'on the field survey' is basically a perception study and should help us understand the phenomena of crime and corruption in the country as perceived by the citizens and their attitudinal orientation towards these evils and their eradication. A significant value addition is in its recentness — conducted over last few months preceding this report.

Sample design

For this purpose, we have chosen a moderate but highly representative sample of respondents. In terms of occupations the respondents represent categories like salaried, businessman, non-governmental organization, industrialist, trade body, and trade union. The educational qualifications of respondents range from higher secondary to PhD with most of them holding graduate degree or above. The respondents were selected with due care so that they understand this complex issue and provide meaningful feedback.

Questionnaire

The respondents were given an objective type questionnaire (A specimen of the questionnaire is enclosed as ready reference).

Study of the responses

Extent of concern

There was a broad consensus that India was a corrupt or highly corrupt country — nearly 90% respondents felt that way (Ref. Q.1). There was also a general consensus (82%) on identifying the reason for corruption — being 'politics and politicians' (Ref. Q.2). Between crime and corruption in the country, again 82% perceived an active interrelationship (Ref. Q.3).

Responsible for corruption and crime

Many respondents (73.6) felt that very rich and rich persons are responsible for propagation of corruption in India (Ref. Q.4). Most respondents (82.3%) opined that very rich and rich people were mostly responsible for crime including white collar crime and economic offences (Ref. Q.5).

Most corrupt

On the issue of ranking the five most corrupt segments in descending order, nearly every respondent perceived 'politicians' as most corrupt, followed by 'police'. The 'judiciary' was perceived to be least corrupt — at least 45% felt that way. 32.5% felt that the 'health services' were less corrupt than the other four. It appears plausible that the ranking was influenced by the direct experience of the respondent in dealing with the concerned government machineries to an extent. Thus, truck operator associations ranked 'police', some businessmen rated 'public works department' as the most corrupt, and so on (Ref. Q.7).

Impatience with anti-corruption measures

The frustrations with the working of the anti-corruption agencies in the country were evident. The sample nearly unanimously voiced their dissatisfaction, with 53% of them suggesting 'complete overhauling' of these entities (Ref. Q.9). As regards new enactments to curb corruption, majority (50%) did not deem this a necessity. On the contrary, they felt that the existing laws were sufficient but the implementation lacked and therefore merited attention. Another 30% held extremely pessimistic view and opined that laws to curb corruption would not at all work in the present system (Ref. Q.10).

Sunshine laws

The respondents were divided over the efficacy of Right to Information Act. About 49% of the respondents felt that the new Act has the potential to curb corruption. But 28% did not share such optimism based on the experience post-enactment — they felt the RTI Act was not able to deliver or achieve its purpose (Ref Q.11).

Impact of education and poverty on corruption and crime

The general view was that the 'lack of education' contributed to both 'corruption' and 'crime'. However the impact was deemed to be more decisive in relation to 'crime' — whereas 63% respondents felt lack of education as 'important' or 'very important' cause for corruption, the percentage was nearly 72% in relation to crime (Refs. Q.14 and Q.15). An even larger percentage of 84% felt poverty is responsible for crime and 58% felt poverty is responsible for corruption. The role of poverty as a trigger for corruption as perceived by respondents is however debatable — it is possible the respondents did not consider the technical definition of 'corruption' while responding but treated in a general way (Refs. Q.16 and Q.17).

Poor salary structure of government officials and corruption

Many respondents (74%) shared the perception that the poor salary of government officials could be a cause of corruption. Included in them were 24% who strongly believed this as a reason (Ref. Q.18).

Transparency and honesty in private sector

Most respondents (88%) believed that to achieve higher economic growth not only in government and public sector, transparency and honesty were as much required in the private/corporate sector (Ref. Q.20).

The preferred bureaucrat — efficiency and corruption dimension

The respondents were asked to choose from three types of bureaucrat — 'highly efficient but corrupt', 'partly efficient and partly corrupt', 'fully honest but not efficient'. Many (35%) declined to respond to this item as none constituted their choice. This suggests that quite some people still have not given up hope — they believe they would eventually get bureaucrats who are both 'honest and efficient'. Interestingly, 32.5% said they would prefer to deal with highly efficient bureaucrats even if corrupt. 22.5% opted for 'partly efficient and partly corrupt'. This perhaps explains both 'helplessness' and also 'impatience' of people with bureaucratic inefficiency in a fast changing world where time mattered (Ref. Q.23).

The ideal bureaucrat — reality or mirage?

To a question what percentage of bureaucrats are 'both honest and efficient', a number of respondents did not reply. Considering the feedback provided by the rest, the average of the percentages of such bureaucrats is estimated around 20%. The figure is significant and reinforces some faith in the much maligned 'bureaucracy' in the country (Ref. Q.24).

Taking the bull by horns

Half of the respondents felt that corruption could be 'reduced' in India essentially through institutional mechanism (Ref. Q.25). To a question on how to 'remove' corruption, an overwhelming percentage (95%) felt that the task demanded conscious and sustained efforts from all concerned. The majority of the respondents also felt the efforts in this direction should be supplemented by overriding technological growth (Ref. Q.26).

India's ranking in corruption index by Transparency International — a shock?

One-fifth of the respondents said they felt highly disturbed at the ranking. Hopefully, large majority (72.5%) overcame the 'stunned feeling' and wanted something concrete to be done immediately to improve the situation (Ref. Q.27).

Five most corrupt and least corrupt states

The respondents differed considerably on the 'ranking of States' in terms of corruption. It looked most did not have direct experience and relied on what they heard and read. Amongst most corrupt, the two common names were Bihar and Uttar Pradesh whereas Gujarat and Kerala received more votes than others as least corrupt States (Refs. Q.28 and Q.29).

Who can play the crusader?

In identifying key role player, respondents have given their preferences. In terms of a preference index that has been developed, respondents put maximum emphasis on the role of political leaders in curbing corruption, followed by judiciary.

Conclusions

Crime

A quiet crime data trend, especially in terms of criminality rank, is not comforting for reasons stated earlier. A hugely higher criminality rates in developed countries compared to India portends questions as to the degree of public confidence on the criminal justice system in the country. The inter-state data also indicate similar possibility. There is a real risk of 'transmission loss' i.e., difference between the actual crime incidents and criminal complaints lodged. The challenge before the policy planners and bureaucrats is to minimize this loss or to be able to capture maximum number of incidents by increasing the credibility of the entire criminal justice system. Whether or not the apprehension is true can be found out through the alternative method of 'sample survey' of the crime victims. The findings could indeed be valuable to the policy-making.

Corruption

As regards efforts on ground to tackle corruption through governmental actions, not enough seems to have been done. Comparing to the huge dimension, the number of cases filed, conviction etc. are clearly inadequate. The general public has grown so much accustomed to corruption that its eradication seems to be that much difficult. Worse, the society seems to be gradually losing its will power to fight corruption. The result obviously has been loss of efficiency and productivity, and throttling of well-distributed entrepreneurship across the country. Fortunately harsh periodical reminders from International bodies e.g., Transparency International in the form of alarm bells awakens us to the problem. Also the difficulties experienced by powerful business houses from abroad trying to set up establishments in India also reminds the government that some urgent steps are indeed called for.

Given the dynamics of the corruption situation, the first major assault has to be in the form of policy correctives. The Federal Government has been doing precisely that since 1991 through series of measures aiming at deregulation and economic liberalization which encompassed the areas of imports, foreign exchange, capital issues, industrial licensing, taxation etc. These measures are working to constrict the discretionary powers of bureaucrats. Secondly, the government has been attempting to facilitate public view of the inner working of various government departments through enactment of sunshine measures and legislations like Citizens' Charter, Social Audit, e-Governance, RTI Act, Consumer Protection Act, etc. These are yet in infancy but likely to play important role in curbing corruptions in course of time. Media — print and electronic — are also playing a role sometimes on their own and some other times due to competition for the eye-balls. Yet another governmental initiative has been to improve the pay and service conditions of government officials in recent years to ensure that they grow less vulnerable to the lures of easy immoral money.

At the end, it is important to appreciate the distinction between 'perception of corruption' and 'actual corruption'. It is true that the perception of corruption is often fed by actual corruption but it runs the risk of multiplication due to exaggeration and media hypes. The danger here lies in two forms (a) undermining of public morale — that, it is impossible to get a service without bribe or contact, (b) self-fulfilling prophecy playing out itself — the public expectation that the service providers would provide service against money. Tackling these dual menaces call for co-ordinated actions not only through policy initiatives and enforcements but also active, constructive participation by the media. Last but not the least, the people themselves have to come forward determined to eradicate this evil, as was echoed in the responses to our survey.

Endnotes

   i. *Crime Rate* by Christopher Reinhart, Senior Attorney in http://www.cga. at.gov/2008/rpt/2008-R-0347.htm <DOA 24 MAY 2009>.

  ii. http://www.unodc.org/documents/data-and-analysis/All_countries.pdf.

 iii. *Crime In India* 2007: National Crime Records Bureau p46.

 iv. *Crime In India* 2007: National Crime Records Bureau p63.

  v. Combating Kleptocracy: eJournal USA, American Information Resources Center: Issues of Democracy, December 2006, p9.

 vi. http://www.transparencyindia.org/pdf/CP1_2008_tabl.pdf <DOA 24 MAY 2009>.

 vii. http://sampark.chd.nic.in/images/Statistics/SDP2005R5.pdf: The ranking was done based on SDP data related to the year 2003-04.

viii. http://www.transparencyindia.org/Publication/India%20Corruption%20Study%202005%20in%20PDF.pdf

 ix. a. *This analysis examines the correlation between economic growth on one hand and crime and corruption on the other hand, in 19 important states in India including the five states constituting our sample;*

     b. *The economic growth has been measured through 'Per capita State Domestic Product', the crime through the 'criminality rank' obtained from the 'Crime in India' a NCB publication, and the corruption through 'Corruption Perception Index' available in the TII-CMS study.*

     c. *Since this is a 'rank correlation' study, we have considered only the ranks of these nineteen states under each of these three heads. As regards 'Per capita SDP', the state with the highest per capita SDP was given the rank no. 1. In case of 'criminality rank', the state with lowest rate of crime rate has been awarded rank no. 1. Similarly, the state perceived as the least corrupt was given rank no. 1. Our objective has been to find out the kind and nature of correlation, if any, between economic growth with the other two separately.*

d. *The homogeneity of the period for the three sets of data is desirable. The best available set as on date is that of year 2005 for both criminality rank and corruption perception and year 2003–2004 in respect of Per Capita SDP. This is because of non-availability of data for the latter two categories beyond the stated period. However, we consider that the available data are sufficient for our present purpose. Out of a total of 28 states, we chose a set of 19 important states in respect of which data were available for each of the three heads. The ranking interse these 19 states was recalculated and used.*

x.   Statistical Methods Dr. S. P. Gupta, Sultan Chand & Sons 1983, p E 10.33.

Annexure

Response Sheet on Crime, Corruption & Economic Growth

Name   :-

Address   :-

Phone   :-

E-mail ID   :-

Age   :-

Educational Qualification   :-

Occupation   :-

This Response Sheet is designed to receive feedback on the perception and opinion of the person concerned w.r.t. various facets and parameters of corruption with special reference to India.

The answers are objective type and based on the feedback from the respondents perceptions on the various issues are expected to be reflected.

1. How do you feel India rates as a country in terms of corruption:

   ☐ Highly Corrupt
   ☐ Corrupt
   ☐ Moderately Corrupt
   ☐ Not so Corrupt

2. How do you feel India's corruption perception is relevant w.r.t the following:

☐ Vast Size	[a]	[b]	[c]	[d]
☐ Linguistic Variations	[a]	[b]	[c]	[d]
☐ Cultural Diversity	[a]	[b]	[c]	[d]
☐ Political Reasons	[a]	[b]	[c]	[d]

Note: (a) Major Cause (b) Important Cause (c) Fairly Important (d) Not so Important

3. Do you feel corruption is a result of crime & vice versa:

   ☐ Fully related
   ☐ Partly related
   ☐ Not linked
   ☐ Two are completely different phenomenon

4. Which category of people do you feel are more responsible for propagation of corruption:

   ☐ Very Rich
   ☐ Rich
   ☐ Middle Class
   ☐ Low Income Group
   ☐ Do not know

5. Which category of people do you feel are mostly responsible for crime including White Collar Crime & Economic Offences:

   ☐ Very Rich
   ☐ Rich
   ☐ Middle Class
   ☐ Low Income Group
   ☐ Do not know

6. Economic Growth is impeded by:

   ☐ Corruption more than crime
   ☐ Crime more than Corruption
   ☐ Equally by Crime & Corruption
   ☐ Neither is very relevant

7. Please rate the following in terms of corruption starting from the most corrupt in descending order:

   Rank (1 – Most corrupt)

Health Services	☐
Judiciary	☐
Police	☐
Politicians	☐

PWD   ☐

Any other   ☐ Please specify:

8. Corruption is a result of

   ☐ People's own desire for small gains
   ☐ Greed of service provider
   ☐ Combination of both
   ☐ Lack of leadership

9. Anti-corruption agencies functioning in India are

   ☐ More than adequate
   ☐ Adequate
   ☐ Not up to the mark
   ☐ Needs complete overhaul
   Comments if any:

10. Do you think laws are to curb corruption in India:

    ☐ Stringent
    ☐ Need more Stringency
    ☐ Laws are enough but need better implementation
    ☐ Will not work in the present system/Ineffective

11. How effective an Instrument do you think RTI (Rights to Information) Act is in combating corruption:

    ☐ Effective
    ☐ Not so effective
    ☐ Has the potential to be effective
    ☐ Time will say as still not tested properly

12. Watch dogs and recently created Institutions like Human Rights Commission (National & State level) have been effective in curbing corruption

    ☐ Fully agree
    ☐ Partly agree
    ☐ Do not agree

13. An active Media and its penetration in various Govt. Sectors have contributed towards reduction in corruption

    ☐ Fully agree
    ☐ Partly agree
    ☐ Do not agree

14. How do you feel lack of Education as a cause of Corruption:

    ☐ Very Important Cause
    ☐ Important Cause
    ☐ Not so Important Cause
    ☐ Irrelevant

15. How do you feel lack of Education as a cause of Crime:

    ☐ Very Important Cause
    ☐ Important Cause
    ☐ Not so Important Cause
    ☐ Irrelevant

16. How do you link Economic Poverty to spread of Corruption:

    ☐ Highly Linked
    ☐ Linked
    ☐ Not so much Linked
    ☐ Not related

17. How do you link Economic Poverty to spread of Crime:

    ☐ Highly Linked
    ☐ Linked
    ☐ Not so much Linked
    ☐ Not related

18. Do you agree that poor Salary structure of Govt. servants should be a cause for Corruption:

    ☐ Could be a major cause
    ☐ May be a cause for some of the Govt. Servants
    ☐ Varies from State to State
    ☐ Not relevant

19. Do you think attempt to curb corruption in Govt. Sector should be the only focus area for attaining Economic Growth

☐ Agree completely
☐ Agree to a large extent
☐ Do not agree
☐ Govt. Sector reform can come only as part of overall social change

20. How important do you think are Transparency & Honesty in Corporate/ Pvt. Sector for economic growth.

☐ Extremely Important
☐ Very Important
☐ Not so Important
☐ Corporate Sector & Govt. Sector Integrity are Mutually Dependent

21. Corruption in a Country's environment.

☐ Mainly affects the Economic Development
☐ Causes more Social & Cultural anxiety than concern for Economic process of Development
☐ Affects the quality of Public life
☐ Has limited impact on Economic Development

22. For proper Economic growth which one should be given priority.

a) Reduce corruption as a pervasive phenomena across the society
b) Control selected but high level of corruption in Govt./Political/ Corporate World that does not permeate the common men
c) 'a' followed by 'b' or vice versa
d) Both at a time

23. In a limited situation which kind of a Bureaucrat/Political Leader would you prefer to have in a developing economy like India.

☐ Highly efficient who can deliver but corrupt
☐ Partly efficient & partly corrupt
☐ Fully honest but not efficient

24. What percentage of Bureaucrats/Political Leaders do you feel are highly efficient & at the same time highly honest.

%

%

25. In a country like ours do you think corruption will be reduced by:

☐ Individual Effort
☐ By Political Leadership
☐ Institutional Mechanism

26. Do you feel corruption in our country can be minimized:

☐ Through advent of technology like IT revolution etc.
☐ By conscious and sustained effort from all concerned irrespective of technological advent
☐ By conscious and sustained effort from all concerned along with overriding technological growth
☐ Through gradual but natural process of evolution with time

27. Looking at India as one of the countries on the darker sides in terms of corruption as per Transparency International how do you feel.

☐ Highly disturbed.
☐ Feel that something should be done urgently.
☐ Feel that it is normal for a country which is evolving
☐ No reaction.

28. Please name five states in India which according to you are most corrupt:

1.
2.
3.
4.
5.

29. Please name five states in India which you think are least corrupt:

    1.
    2.
    3.
    4.
    5.

30. In India who amongst the following do you think can play a key role in curbing corruption. Please rank in order of preference:

    ➢ Bureaucracy   ☐
    ➢ Judiciary   ☐
    ➢ People at large   ☐
    ➢ Political Leaders   ☐
    ➢ Vigilance Commissions   ☐
    ➢ Any other:

Chapter 10

A Certain Uncertainty; Assessment of Court Decisions in Tackling Corruption in Indonesia

Rimawan Pradiptyo[*,†]

Department of Economics, Faculty of Economics and Business Universitas Gadjah Mada, Indonesia

Abstract

This chapter aims to assess court decisions for eradicating corruption in Indonesia. The data were based on Indonesia Supreme Court decisions from 2001 to 2009. The dataset comprises of 549 cases involving 831 defendants. After the end of Suharto's regime, the Anti-Corruption Bill was ratified in 1999 and was refined in 2001. As Indonesia follows a civil law system, legal certainty has been manifested by stating the level of punishment clearly for each type of offences in the Bill. Despite a clear guidance on the intensity of punishments for each corruption type, judges' decisions on the intensity of punishments sentenced across defendants are far from consistent. Using logistic regressions, we found that the probability of judges in sentencing defendants with financial

*I would like to thank Paripurna P. Sugarda, Hifdzil Alim, Edy OS Hiarej and Arti Adji Kompas for thoughtful and constructive discussions. I am indebted to Harri Gemilang, SH Seri Damayanti, Surya Dharma Putra, Sony Saputra, and Abraham Wirotomo for their excellent assistance in collecting and inputing data. Constructive feedback from participants conferences in Perth, Australia, Toronto, Canada and Yogyakarta, Indonesia are gratefully acknowledged. All remaining errors are my responsibility.
†Corresponding contact details: E-mails: Rimawan@Gadjahmada.edu, Rimawan@feb.ugm.ac.id.

punishments (that is, fines, compensation and the seizure of evidence) does not depend on the level of economic losses inflicted by the defendants. On the contrary, the judges' decisions tend to be more lenient toward defendants with particular occupations but harsher toward others. The intensity of punishments has been sentenced idiosyncratically and has weakened the deterrence effect of the punishments. In estimating the social cost of corruption, prosecutors have estimated only the explicit cost of corruption, therefore the impact of corruption to Indonesia economy is underestimated. Brand and Price (2000) defined that the social costs of crime includes the costs in anticipation of crime, the costs as a result of crime and the costs in reaction of crime. The total explicit cost of corruption from 2001 to 2009 was Rp73.1 trillion (about US$8.49 billion), however the total financial punishment imposed by the Supreme Court was Rp5.33 trillion (about US$619.77 million). The data show that corruption is mostly committed by people with medium-high income and they usually have good careers.

Keywords: Corruption, legal certainty, financial punishment, Social Costs of Crime, explicit cost of corruption, Deterrence Effect.

Introduction

In the deterrence theory literature, the debate primarily focuses on whether increasing the severity of punishment is effective in deterring individuals in committing an offence. It is assumed that any potential offender is rational and committing an offence is a rational choice. Individuals are going to commit an offence if the expected benefits of the activity exceed the expected costs of offending. Consequently, in order to deter an individual from committing an offence, the authority may increase the expected costs of offending to be borne by potential offenders.

A group of economists tend to use decision theory in order to analyze why individuals commit an offence and how to deter individuals from committing such activity. It is argued that the severity of punishment does matter in deterring individuals from committing an offence. This approach is pioneered by Becker (1968), and excellent literature surveys in this area have been conducted by various authors including Garoupa (1997), Eide (2000; 2004), Bowles (2000) and Polinsky and Shavell (2000; 2007).

The other group of economists tend to use the game theory in analyzing phenomena in criminal justice. Tsebelis (1989; 1991; 1993) pionereed in using this approach and argued that any attempt to increase the severity of punishment reduced the probability of criminal justice authority in enforcing the law but it did not affect the probability of individuals from offending. This counter intuitive result triggered a long debate involving several authors including Bianco *et al.* (1990), Weissing and Ostrom (1991), Hirshleifer and Rasmusen (1992) and Andreozzi (2004). Pradiptyo (2007) refined the inspection game proposed by Tsebelis (1989) and showed that there is not so much discrepancy in the solution between decision theory and game theoretical approaches. Pradiptyo (2007) showed that any attempt to increase the severity of punishment is going to reduce the likelihood of offending if certain conditions hold. In addition, he proved that crime prevention initiatives are more effective in reducing the likelihood of offending in comparison to increasing the severity of punishment.

Attempts to increase the expected costs of offending can be conducted in several ways. The criminal justice authority may endeavor either to increase the probability of detection, or alternatively, they may increase the severity of punishment. Indeed both possible scenarios are costly. In order to achieve the optimum level of deterrence, however, the criminal justice authority has two possible scenarios either by setting low probability of detection combined with high intensity of punishment or by setting high probability of detection together with low intensity of punishment.

A similar approach as mentioned above can be used in eradicating corruption. Any potential corruptor is rational and accordingly would conduct costs-benefits analysis prior to committing corruption. As applicable to other type of offences, the intensity of corruption can be divided into several groups for instance small, medium and large scales of corruption. The classification of the groups depends on the intensity of misallocation of resources owing to corruption in Indonesia. There are various types of punishment for corruptors, ranging from imprisonment, fines, compensation order and the seizure of the illegitimate assets. In several countries, corruptors may receive capital punishment. In an ideal world, the higher the intensity of corruption, the higher the probability of corruptors to receive harsher punishments.

One aspect in the deterrence theory that has not received sufficient attention is the role of consistency of court decisions. The consistency of court decisions builds reputation of the criminal justice system and to some extent is going to affect the deterrence effect for any act imposed. The consistency of court decisions with the type and intensity of punishments may be sensitive to the penal system that has been embraced across countries.

This chapter aims to assess court decisions for the case of corruption in Indonesia. The study uses 549 cases, involving 831 defendants, which have been sentenced by the Supreme Court of the Republic of Indonesia in 2001–2009. All cases have been published in the official website of the Supreme Court in the following URL: http://putusan.mahkamahagung. go.id.

Corruption Erradication Programmes in Indonesia

Various attempts have been made by the Government of Indonesia (GoI) to tackle corruption. Back in the 1950s, during President Soekarno's era, the GoI had launched a programme to tackle corruption. Similarly, under President Suharto's era in the 1970s until the mid-1990s, the GoI also launched several programmes to eradicate corruption. Nevertheless the effectiveness of the programmes was questioned as both Presidents tend to embrace absolute power, which tend to be corrupt.

After President Suharto stepped down in 1998, Indonesia had been undergoing reformation in various aspects of the society. The main focus of the reformation was to abolish corruption, collusions and nepotism — the very problems which flourished under Suharto's regime.

Several measures have been taken in order to combat corruption. In 1999, the anti-corruption act was ratified and then refined in year 2001 (see the summary in Appendix A). In 2002 corruption eradication committee (KPK) was formed and the institution has been fully functional since 2004. In 2003, the money-laundering act was ratified and along with this act was the formation of Financial Transaction Report Analysis Centre (PPATK), which serves as a financial investigative unit in Indonesia. The PPATK has been fully functional since 2005. Recently, in October 2010 the amendments of the money laundering act were ratified which provide

Anti-Corruption Programmes in Indonesia

Figure 10.1   Various programmes in combating corruption in Indonesia

the basis of more active link between PPATK and other criminal justice agencies, including KPK, in attempts to combat corruption and money laundering (see Figure 10.1).

Anti-Corruption Programmes in Indonesia

A preventive measure to reduce corruption by civil servants is the initiation of bureaucratic reformation programmes since 2003. The programme has been initiated for the first time within the Ministry of Finance. The programme provides substantial improvement on civil servant salary but at the same time the transparency of civil servant performance has been promoted. Currently, most government departments have embraced bureaucratic reformation.

Indonesia follows civil law, which has been influenced by the Dutch since the colonial era. Criminal Code of Indonesia (KUHP) has been used in Indonesia. Although Indonesia achieved independence in 1945, its penal code is still based on the Dutch Criminal Code of 1811 (Wetboek van Strafrecht). Ironically, the Dutch themselves no longer implement the code as they embraced a new code in 1979.

Corruption is an extraordinary crime and there was a need to create a special measure to tackle corruption by creating anti-corruption act. The anti-corruption act was ratified in 1999, and again it was refined in 2001. In essence, both laws are similar and the only difference is that the intensity of punishment of the latter do not refer to Criminal Code of Indonesia (KUHP) which is based on the Dutch Criminal Code of 1811 (Wetboek van Strafrecht).[i]

The KPK is an independent body financed by the government and the main task of the KPK is to eradicate and to prevent corruption in Indonesia. It seems KPK tasks may overlap with police and prosecutors, however, KPK deals only with large scale corruption cases (i.e., the value of the corruption is at least Rp1 billion (US$116,279). Below the threshold, corruption cases are to be dealt by police and district prosecutors.

The Complexity of Corruption in Indonesia

A survey by Hong Kong-based Political & Economic Risk Consultancy Ltd. in 2010 placed Indonesia as the most corrupt country in Asia-Pacific region. It turns out that problems of corruption in Indonesia are more acute than in other countries in the region such as Cambodia, the Philippines, India, Thailand and Vietnam. Furthermore, the Corruption Perception Index in 2010 by the Transparency International placed Indonesia as the 110th country out of 178 countries in the world.

Figure 10.2 shows the model of complexity of corruption in Indonesia. The corruption may start from stage 1 whereby an individual committed an offence (either conventional offence or even some kind of corruption). At this stage, potential offenders interact with police by playing an inspection game. The potential offenders have two alternative strategies, offence and not offence, whereas the policemen have also two strategies, inspect and not inspect. It should be noted that in this model, it is assumed that the game is played by a representative agent.

Suppose in Stage 1 an individual commits a corruption while the police inspects, then the individual is caught. Given the individual is caught, the game moves to the Stage 2. In this stage, the police should process the case and then refer the case to district prosecutors. Prior to processing of the case, the offender may offer a bribe to the police or alternatively a corrupt policeman may extort money from the defendant. At this stage, both parties may involve in a bargaining process. Stage 2 modelled corruption by police officers. Bowles and Garoupa

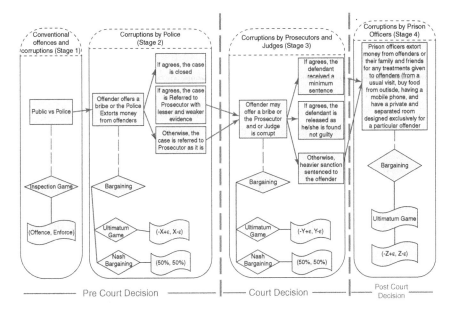

Figure 10.2   Modelling the complexity of corruption in Indonesia

(1997) provided extensive and excellent analysis of modelling police corruption.

There are various possible outcomes from the bargaining. If the bargaining is agreed, there is an opportunity that the policeman stops the process of investigation and decides not to record the case. Another alternative outcome if the bargaining is agreed is that the police may continue to process the case and refer the case to prosecutors but with lower gravity of offending and weaker evidence. This case may occur when the case is considered as high profile whereby the press has reported in the media. Nevertheless, if the policeman is a righteous person, any attempt to offer a bribe by the offenders may adversely affect them. In the referral to the prosecutors, the policeman may include information that the offenders attempted to offer a bribe to him/her. If this scenario occurs, the offenders will be prosecuted more severely.

Stage 3 provides a model of corruption involving prosecutors and judges. At this stage, the defendants may offer a bribe to prosecutors and/ or judges. Alternatively, the prosecutors or judges may extort money from defendants. The fact that Indonesia follows civil law provides plenty of room of manoeuvre for prosecutors and judges to extort money from defendants. There are various acts in Indonesia, and since Indonesia follow civil law, it is compulsory that each act states clearly the intensity of punishment to those who violate the law. In the banking act in 2004 for instance, the maximum fines for offenders can be Rp100 billion rupiah. On the other hand, the anti-corruption act stated that the maximum fines worth only Rp1 billion rupiah. Obviously the difference in the intensity of punishment between some acts creates opportunity to prosecutors and judges to extort money from defendants in exchange to reduce charges to less intensive punishments.

Similar to the process at stage 2, there is a bargaining process in stage 3 to determine the amount of money bribed or extorted and the possible outcomes in the court. If the bargaining is agreed, the defendant may be charged with not guilty or even if the defendant is found guilty he/she may receive much less intensive punishment. Nevertheless, bribing is uncertain business as the defendant may not know the types of prosecutors or judges. If the prosecutors and the judges are righteous individuals, then offering bribe to them may result in more severe punishment for the defendants.

It should be noted that corruption in courts in Indonesia is not limited only at district courts, but it may occur in high courts and even in the supreme courts. There are several cases of corruption involving judges in the supreme courts. It should be noted also that under Indonesia's penal law system, the decision whether defendants are guilty or not and also the intensity of punishment is determined by the judges. There is no jury system in Indonesia. Consequently, the desire to offer a bribe to judges is paramount as the judges have tremendous power to determine whether the defendants are guilty or not and they also hold the right to determine the type and the intensity of punishment.

In the final stage, corruption may be committed by officers in prisons. The type of corruption committed in prison may range from asking money to the family of offenders during the scheduled visits allowing offenders to spend several nights to stay at home with their family. There are two famous cases of corruption in prison in Indonesia. The first is the case of Artalita who managed to bribe prison officers to allow her to have her own five star very spacious private room within the prison area. Furthermore, she has another spacious room for organizing monthly meeting with her staff to run her multi-billion businesses. Secondly there is the case of

Gayus Tambunan, who managed to bribe prison officers to allow him to go on holiday in Hong kong with his wife and to watch international tennis match in Bali.

The complexity of corruption in Indonesia is paramount if consideration is taken for the existence of *markus* or case broker in every single level of criminal justice authority in Indonesia. *Markus* stands for *makelar kasus* (*makelar* is from the Dutch word *makelaar* which means broker, and *kasus* means case, thus *markus* is a case broker). The *markuses* exist in every single part of criminal justice system in Indonesia. The *markus* may not necessarily be a criminal justice officer, but it can be anybody as long as the person has a good connection with officers in the criminal justice system. As a broker, the *markus* works by intermediating between defendants and officers in criminal justice system. Indeed, the existence of the *markus* occurs due to the uncertainty in bribery and extortion whether the offer would be accepted by the other party. The *markus* serves as the intermediary between both parties to smooth the process and to reduce error types I and II in offering bribery or asking for extortion. The problem of the *markus* is paramount such that the GoI has formed a special task force for cracking the Markus within the criminal justice authority.

Judicial System in Indonesia

Under Indonesia's criminal justice system, all criminal cases should be trialed before District courts. Each District court is situated in a Kabupaten (district) and there are 502 districts in Indonesia. Judges' decisions in a district court may be appealed either by defendants or prosecutors if they are dissatisfied with the decisions. In the event that the defendant does the appeal, which occurs in most corruption cases, then the case is referred to a high court, which is situated in the capital of each province. If the defendant is not satisfied with judges' decisions in the High court, a further appeal can be made to the supreme court. On the contrary, if the prosecutor is not satisfied with judges' decisions in the District court, the case may be appealed directly to the supreme court (see Figure 10.3).

Figure 10.3 shows that after a case is sentenced by the supreme court, there is still an opportunity for conducting further appeal called a judicial re-examination by the supreme court. The judicial re-examination can

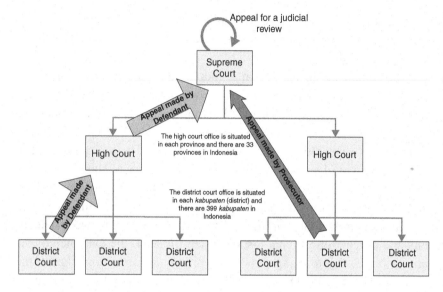

Figure 10.3   Appeal process in Indonesia's criminal justice system

only be pursued if there is new evidence, which has not been put before trial previously. It should be noted that the cost of court in Indonesia is economical. The judicial system in Indonesia rules that the there are three possible values of the court costs, namely Rp2,500 to Rp10,000 (US$0.29– US$1.16), irrespective of how long the trials have been conducted.

Owing to the structure above, it is highly likely that a defendant will make an appeal until reaching the supreme court. Almost all corruption cases that have been dealt by district courts were appealed up to the Supreme court. This occurs partly due to the fact that most defendants who were prosecuted for corruption cases tend to be more educated in comparison to defendants for other conventional offences (e.g., theft, robbery, criminal damage, etc.).[ii] From game theoretical analysis, it is rational for defendants to appeal their case until the supreme court as the system allows it of doing so and the court cost, apart from hiring a lawyer, is economical.

The cases appealed in Indonesian judicial system looks like a tube or a pipe, whereby there is no difference between the number of cases dealt by the district courts and the number of cases dealt by the supreme court

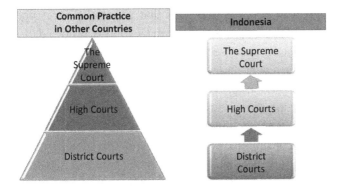

Figure 10.4   Comparison of the distribution of cases across level of courts

(see Figure 10.4). This occurs since almost all corruption cases which were trialed in the district court have been appealed. Once an appeal has been made by either a defendant or a prosecutor, then the case would certainly end up in the supreme court. Obviously this structure is different from the distribution of cases dealt by different level of courts in countries which follow common law. In those countries, some cases in either the magistrate's court or crown court may not be able to appeal in high courts. Similarly, some cases in high courts may not necessarily be able to be appealed in the supreme courts. Consequently, the structure of the distribution of cases in each level of court in those countries looks like a triangle.

The data used in this study were based on the Supreme court's decisions in the period 2001–2009. Indeed the use of decisions by the supreme courts create unobserved heterogeneity and the source of the unobserved heterogeneity are as follows:

1. Some appeals went through high courts, but some went directly to the supreme court (being accommodated in the model);
2. The number of cases terminated in high courts is unknown (unsolved);
3. The number of cases terminated in district courts is unknown (unsolved);
4. The number of cases reported to Police is unknown (unsolved).

The last source of unobserved heterogeneity may be unsolvable and this occurs in various empirical studies in the economic analysis of a crime. Nevertheless, information and judgment from practitioners and experts in the area of corruption show that, especially in corruption cases, almost certainly the decision in the district court is followed by an appeal either by defendants or prosecutors.[iii]

Another consequence to the structure of case distribution across courts is the tremendous pressure on the task of the supreme court judges. Currently, there are 46 supreme court judges in Indonesia. This number is much higher above the number of the supreme court judges in the USA, which only have 9 supreme court judges. In terms of population, the USA has the third largest population in the world, whereas Indonesia is in the fourth place. Nevertheless, due to different law systems that have been embraced by both countries, the number of the supreme court judges is totally different.

Table 10.1 shows the extent of the burden faced by judges across various level of courts in Indonesia. The number of cases appealed to the supreme court is higher than those of the high courts. The ratio of the cases appealed to the supreme court as opposed to the high courts is about 3 to 1. Unfortunately there are only 46 judges in the supreme court in Indonesia, as opposed to 334 judges in the high courts, therefore it is not surprising that the average case per judge is much higher in the supreme court (540 cases) relative to that of the high court (25 cases). The judges in the high court managed to complete 77.44% of cases appealed, whereas the supreme court judges only managed to complete 43.16% of cases appealed to the supreme court.

The Cost of Corruption

Each criminal offence creates burdens or social costs to the society. There are various ways to estimate the social costs of crime (see Brand and Price, 2000, Dubourg *et al.*, 2005, among others). Brand and Price (2000) proposed the social costs of crime consist of three main elements, which are the costs in anticipation of crime, the costs inflicted to victims and the costs in reaction of crime. Corruption is an extraordinary crime, however, corruption may not necessarily affect victims. To some extent, corruption may be considered as a victimless crime if we compare it with other types of offences, which involve some physical impacts to victims such as robbery, the violence against the person, sexual offences, etc.

Table 10.1 Number of cases and sentences made by judges in Indonesian judicial
system 2006

Courts	Number of cases	Number of cases sentenced	(%)	Number of judges	Average cases per judge	Average sentenced cases per judge
Supreme court	24,826	10,714	43.16	46	540	233
High court						
a. Common court	8,202	6,352	77.44	334	25	19
b. Religious court	1,952	1,592	81.56	239	8	7
c. State Administration court	621	523	84.22	30	21	17
d. Military court	425	303	71.29	9	47	34
District court						
a. Common court	2,636,689	2,601,551	98.67	2,787	946	933
b. Religious court	206,780	171,573	82.97	2,203	94	78
c. State Administration court	1,203	840	69.83	180	7	5
d. Military court	4,628	3,838	82.93	73	63	53

Source: The Supreme Court Annual Report 2006.

Corruption creates misallocation of resources and to some extent it
may reduce the welfare of many individuals in the society. Using a similar
framework as proposed by Brand and Price's (2000), the social cost of
corruption may be estimated using four elements as follows:

1. The costs in anticipation of corruption,
2. The explicit cost of corruption,
3. The implicit costs of corruption,
4. The costs in reaction to corruption.

In measuring the misallocation of resources owing to corruption, the
explicit and the implicit costs of corruption may not be separated. The
explicit cost of corruption measures the amount of public money that was

misallocated to personal purpose. The implicit costs of corruption measure the opportunity costs of misallocating the resources, namely the loss in economic multiplier due to the misallocation of public money to personal purpose.

According to the anti-corruption act, any conduct by an individual or corporation which is either against the law and or abuse the power which may inflict losses to economy or national budget is considered as a corruption. The definition of corruption in the anti-corruption act is limited to misallocation of public money. Indeed, the coverage of offences in Indonesia anti-corruption act is narrower in comparison to that of the UN convention against corruption in 2003, though Indonesia is one of countries, which ratified it. The anti-corruption act does not cover corruption by private sector, moreover it does not taken into consideration that money politic is part of corruption. The latter is quite ironic since in Indonesian Criminal Code (KUHP) it is stated clearly that money politic is a criminal offence, unfortunately this type of offence has not been acknowledged as part of corruption in the anti-corruption act.

The main indicator of corruption in Indonesia is that whether or not such activity may inflict losses to the economy or the national budget. Ideally the estimation of losses in economy and national budget uses the economic approach by estimating both the explicit and the implicit costs of corruption. The common practice in Indonesia's judicial system is that the estimation of losses in economy or national budget due to corruption is limited to the explicit cost of corruption. The estimation of the losses has been conducted by prosecutors, who are obviously well versed in the area of law but they have limited knowledge in Economics. From the perspective of Economics, the use of explicit costs as a measure to prosecute an individual for committing a corruption contains high probability of making error types I and II in court sentences.

The estimation of explicit and implicit costs cannot be separated in every economic activity. In many cases, the explicit costs of a decision are overwhelmed by its implicit costs or implicit benefits. For instance, in order to compensate an increase in fuel prices, the Indonesian government provides transfer payment to households with low income for the first six months. If the explicit costs are the only measure used to analyze the initiative, than there is no merit of this initiative as it costs dearly to the taxpayers. Nevertheless, if the opportunity costs have been taken into consideration, then the benefits of the initiative may outweigh the cost.

Brand and Price (2000) estimated the social cost of crime by taking into consideration the offence multiplier for each offence. It is true that for almost all offences, the underlying number of offences is unknown. As a result, the recorded offences reported by Police may be seen as a tip of an iceberg, as the number of unrecorded offences is unknown. The number of unrecorded offences can be estimated by estimating the value of the offence multiplier. The offence multiplier is estimated by comparing the number of subjects in a particular survey who were victimized and they report to the police and those who did not report. This multiplier can be used to estimate the number of unrecorded offences. The underlying number of offences, then, is the summation of the number of recorded offences and the estimated number of unrecorded offences.

Thus far there is no comprehensive survey on crime and victimization in Indonesia, consequently the offence multiplier on corruption cannot be estimated. Owing to the lack of the information, the estimation of the cost of corruption does not take into consideration the number of unrecorded offences as used in Brand and Price (2000). It can be argued that the social cost of corruption in this paper is underestimated, as it does not taken into consideration the offence multiplier and also the opportunity costs of misallocation of resources due to corruption.

The estimation of the cost of corruption in this paper refers to the explicit cost of corruption as estimated by prosecutors and stated explicitly in the documents of Indonesia's Supreme court decisions. Based on constant price 2008, the explicit cost of corruption in Indonesia from 2001 to 2009 was Rp73.10 trillion (US$8.49 billion based on average exchange rate in August 2011 which is Rp8600: US$1). This is slightly higher than the value of fiscal expansion (Rp72 trillion or US$8.37 billion) allocated by the Indonesian government in order to reduce the impact of global crisis in 2009. The cost of corruption in the period of 2001–2009 was about 7.3% of Indonesian annual budget in 2009 or about 6.08% of the annual budget in 2011.

Table 10.2 shows that most corruptions in Indonesia were committed by males (93%). This occurs due to the fact that most important positions in public sector are still dominated by males. Of 544 offenders who were

Table 10.2 The explicit social costs of corruption in Indonesia 2001–2008 based on gender, location and occupation

		Number of offenders	(%)	Explicit costs of corruption (2008 Price)		
				Total	(%)	Average
Gender	Male	504	93.33	Rp73.05 trillion (US$8.49 billion)	99.92	Rp144.93 billion (US$16.85 million)
	Female	36	6.67	Rp19.98 billion (US$2.32 million)	0.03	Rp555.22 million (US$64,560)
	NA	4		Rp35.00 billion (US$4.07 million)	0.05	Rp8.75 billion (US$1.02 million)
Age	Below 60	479	88.70	Rp38.72 trillion (US$4.50 billion)	52.97	Rp80.84 billion (US$9.40 million)
	60+	60	11.11	Rp34.34 trillion (US$3.99 billion)	46.98	Rp572.37 billion (US$66.55 million)
	NA	5	0.93	Rp35.00 billion (US$4.07 million)	0.05	Rp8.75 billion (US$1.02 million)
Location	Jawa	241	44.63	Rp37.36 trillion (US$4.34 billion)	51.11	Rp155.03 billion (US$18.03 million)
	Greater Jakarta (Jabodetabek)*	78	32.37	Rp36.86 trillion (US$4.15 billion)	98.67	Rp472.64 billion (US$54.96 million)

(Continued)

Table 10.2 *(Continued)*

| | Number of offenders | (%) | Explicit costs of corruption (2008 price) | | |
			Total	(%)	Average
Outside Jawa	299	55.37	Rp35.70 trillion (US$4.15 billion)	48.89	Rp119.41 billion (US$13.89 million)
NA	4		Rp35.00 billion (US$4.07 million)	0.05	Rp8.75 billion (US$1.02 million)
Occupation Civil Servant	223	41.30	Rp470.15 billion (US$54.67 million)	0.64	Rp2.11 billion (US$245,226)
State-owned Enterprise Employee	68	12.59	Rp29.33 trillion (US$3.41 billion)	40.12	Rp431.31 billion (US$50,152)
Legislative	130	24.07	Rp216.65 billion (US$25.19 million)	0.30	Rp1.66 billion (US$193,837)
Private Sector	117	21.67	Rp37.75 trillion (US$4.39 billion)	51.64	Rp322.63 billion (US$37.51 million)
NA	6	1.11	Rp5.34 trillion (US$620.47 billion)	7.30	Rp889.33 billion (US$103.41 million)
Total	544		Rp73.10 trillion (US$8.50 billion)	100.00	Rp135.370 billion (US$15.741 million)

Source: Indonesia Supreme Court Decisions, 2001–2009.

found guilty by the supreme court, only 36 individuals are females (6.67%). The proportion of money that female corruptors took was only 0.03% as opposed to 99.92% by their male counterparts.

In terms of age, the majority of corruption cases were committed by individuals in their productive age (below 60 year old). Of 544 corruptors, 479 individuals (88.70%) were below 60 year old, while only 60 corruptors (11.11%) were 60 year old or older. This feature is different from the characteristics of offenders for conventional crimes, such as burglary, theft, robbery, etc. Bowles and Pradiptyo (2005) used British Offender Index data and found that offenders for conventional crime are age sensitive. They may start to have a criminal career as early as 8 or 9 years old, however they tend to stop offending when they reach the age of 40.

The proportion of senior corruptors was just 11.11%, however the total explicit cost they inflicted to Indonesian economy was Rp34.34 trillion (US$3.99 billion) or about 46.98% of the total explicit cost of corruption. Since the senior corruptors were only 60 individuals, the average explicit cost of corruption inflicted by senior offenders (aged 60 year old or above) is more than seven-folds to that committed by offenders at the productive age.

In terms of geographical distribution, of 544 offenders, 241 offenders (44.63%) committed corruption in the island of Jawa. The explicit cost of corruption in Jawa was accounted for Rp37.36 trillion (US$4.34 billion), of which Rp36.86 trillion (US$4.15 billion) or 98.67% occurred in Greater Jakarta (Jabodetabek, stand for Jakarta–Bogor–Depok–Tangerang and Bekasi). The average explicit cost of corruption in Jakarta was Rp472.64 billion (US$54.96 million) or more than three folds to that of corruption in Jawa or about four folds to that of corruption in outside Jawa.

The highest proportion of explicit cost of corruption was attributable by offenders from private sectors 51.64% or about Rp37.75 trillion (US$4.39 billion). Indeed the definition of corruption in Indonesia is limited to the misallocation of public money. The involvement of the private sector in corruption in Indonesia is primarily related to provision of goods and services in public sector. The highest average explicit cost of corruption, however, was attributable by state-owned enterprise employees. It is recoded that only 68 state-owned enterprise employees who were found guilty of committing corruption, however the average explicit cost of corruption they inflicted to economy was Rp431.31 billion (US$50.15 million). Most cases of corruption involving state-owned (and also local-government owned) enterprises' employees are related to procurement, embezzlement and their conducts during and post economic crisis in 1998, which were considered against the national interests.

Civil servants were involved in more than half of corruption cases in Indonesia, whereas members of the parliament (both in local and national levels) were involved in almost a quarter of corruption cases in Indonesia. In contrast to State-owned companies' employees, the average value of corruption of civil servants and senators were only Rp2.11 billion (US$245,226) and Rp1.66 billion ($193,837), respectively.

As mentioned earlier, the estimation of social costs using explicit costs implies that the value of the social costs of corruption has been underestimated. Given that the explicit cost of corruption in Indonesia is relatively high, in the absence of any attempt to recover the misallocation of resources, obviously the cost of corruption would be borne by the taxpayers. Unfortunately little attempt has been made by Indonesia's criminal justice system to recover the misallocation of resources created by corruptors.

It should be noted that there are various types of financial punishments in Indonesia's justice system, namely: fines, compensation, and seizure of evidence (monetary and non-monetary), court costs and other sentence. We defined total financial punishment which comprises fines, compensation order and the monetary seizure of asset or evidence. Non-monetary seizure of asset or evidence is not included in the variable as we are faced with the complexity of converting it to monetary value. The court cost is negligible as its values range between Rp2500 and Rp10,000 (US$0.29 to US$1.16), and other sentence is also negligible.

Table 10.3 shows the discrepancy between the explicit cost of corruption and the total financial punishment sentenced by judges in Indonesia's judicial system. Prior to the trial in a district court, prosecutors estimated the value of the explicit cost of corruption. In the trial, then, the prosecutions to offenders were made by the prosecutors. The value of explicit cost of corruption during 2001–2009 was Rp73.10 trillion (US$8.49 billion), however, surprisingly the defendants were prosecuted only Rp32.40 trillion (US$3.77 billion) or 59.37% of the total explicit cost of corruption.

In essence, this phenomenon can be analyzed as a bargaining problem. If the bargaining can be described as a modelling of splitting a pie, then the underlying size of the pie is the total explicit cost of corruption. Nevertheless,

Table 10.3 Comparison between explicit cost of corruption, and financial punishments across courts

	Number of offenders	Total (2008 Price)	Proportion to the explicit social costs (%)	Average (2008 Price)
Explicit Cost of Corruption*	544	Rp73.10 trillion (US$8.50 billion)	100	Rp135.37 billion (US$15.74 million)
Financial Punishment Prosecuted**	543	Rp32.40 trillion (US$3.77 billion)	59.37	Rp59.67 billion ($6.94 million)
Financial Punishment Sentenced by Judges in District courts**	468	Rp2.39 trillion (US$277.79 million)	3.27	Rp5.11 billion (US$594,186)
Financial Punishment Sentenced by Judges in the Supreme court**	544	Rp5.33 trillion ($619.77 million)	7.29	Rp9.80 billion ($1.14 million)

Notes: *The figure only estimated the amount of public money that was taken by offender(s). The figure only represents some parts of the social costs of crime (i.e., corruption) as suggested by Brand and Price (2000). **The figure was the summation of fines, compensation order, and seizure of financial evidence.

Source: Supreme court Decisions 2001–2009, estimated.

the data show that most district prosecutors did not realize that the underlying value of the pie was the explicit social costs of crime, which was Rp73.10 trillion ($8.50 billion) in total or Rp135.37 billion ($15.74 million) in average value. Instead of prosecuting defendants according to the explicit costs of corruption, they tend to prosecute only about 60% of the total explicit cost of corruption. Unfortunately, there is no further information on how this mechanism had been organized by the prosecutors.

From the perspective of economists, this phenomenon is puzzling, if it cannot be said as irrational. As the bargaining problem is a problem of 'splitting a pie', then it would be rational to prosecute a defendant with at least equal to the values of the explicit costs of corruption in order to incorporate the opportunity costs of the misallocation of resources. This notion is based on assumption that there would be some kind of 'negotiation' processes during the trials. This process can be analyzed by comparing the value of total financial punishment prosecuted and total financial punishment sentenced by judges in the District courts.

In the high courts, of 544 defendants who were found guilty by the district courts, only 468 defendants (86.03%) were also found guilty by the high courts. The total financial punishment sentenced by the high court has shrunk to Rp2.39 trillion ($277.79 million) or only 3.27% of the total explicit cost of corruption. In the final stage, when the cases were appealed to the supreme court, the total number of defendants who were found guilty by the supreme court was 544 individuals. The total financial punishment sentenced by the supreme court increased to Rp5.33 trillion ($619.77 million) or about 7.29% of the total explicit cost of corruption.

Table 10.4 shows the discrepancies between the explicit cost of corruption, the total financial punishment prosecuted, the total financial punishment sentenced by district courts and the total financial punishment sentenced by the supreme court. The overall ratio between the explicit costs of corruption with the total financial punishment prosecuted is 5 to 3. It is surprising that the defendants are only prosecuted 60% of the total explicit cost that the defendants inflicted to the society. As the trials can be seen as a bargaining problem, meaning that most likely judges sentenced the defendant much lesser than the prosecution asked for, it would be rational for the prosecutors to prosecute defendants with financial punishment much higher than the explicit costs that they had inflicted.

Table 10.4 Ratios between explicit cost of corruption and the financial punishment sentenced in district courts and the supreme court

		Total explicit costs (2008 prices)	Financial punishment prosecuted (B)	Financial punishment sentenced by judges in district courts (C)	Financial punishment sentenced by judges in the supreme court (D)	(B/A) (%)	(C/A) (%)	(D/A) (%)
Gender	Male	Rp73.05 trillion ($8.494 billion)	32.40 trillion ($3.77 billion)	Rp2.38 trillion ($276.74 million)	Rp5.31 trillion ($617.44 million)	44.35	3.26	7.27
	Female	Rp19.99 billion ($2.32 million)	12.33 billion ($1.43 million)	3.22 billion ($374,419)	Rp10.63 billion ($1.24 million)	61.68	16.11	53.18
Age	Below 60	Rp38.72 trillion ($4.50 billion)	3.84 trillion ($447 million)	Rp2.13 trillion ($247.67 million)	Rp2.73 trillion ($301.42 million)	9.92	5.50	7.05
	60 or Above	Rp34.34 trillion ($3.99 billion)	Rp28.56 trillion ($3.32 billion)	Rp259.22 billion ($30.14 million)	Rp2.59 trillion ($301.16 million)	83.17	0.75	7.54
Location	Jawa	Rp37.36 trillion ($4.34 billion)	Rp32.01 trillion ($3.72 billion)	Rp2.39 trillion ($277.91 Million)	Rp4.99 trillion ($580.23 million)	85.68	6.40	13.36
	Greater Jakarta	Rp36.87 trillion ($4.29 billion)	Rp31.56 trillion ($3.67 billion)	Rp1.95 trillion ($226.74 million)	Rp4.81 trillion ($559.30 million)	85.60	5.29	13.05
	Outside Jawa	Rp35.70 trillion ($4.15 billion)	Rp401.70 billion ($46.71 million)	Rp85.34 billion ($9.92 million)	Rp328.63 billion ($38.21 million)	1.13	0.24	0.92

(*Continued*)

Table 10.4 (*Continued*)

		Total explicit costs (2008 prices)	Financial punishment prosecuted (B)	Financial punishment sentenced by judges in district courts (C)	Financial punishment sentenced by judges in the supreme court (D)	(B/A) (%)	(C/A) (%)	(D/A) (%)
Occupation	Civil Servant	Rp470.15 billion ($54.67 million)	Rp219.38 billion ($25.51 million)	Rp120.94 billion ($14.06 million)	Rp135.76 billion ($15.79 million)	46.66	25.72	28.88
	State-owned Enterprise Employee	Rp29.33 trillion ($3.41 billion)	Rp29.16 trillion ($3.39 billion)	Rp150.08 billion ($17.45 million)	Rp2.48 trillion ($288.37 million)	99.42	5.12	8.46
	Legislative	Rp216.65 billion ($25.19 million)	Rp102.10 billion ($11.87 million)	Rp58.67 billion ($6.82 million)	Rp55.12 billion ($6.41 million)	47.13	27.08	25.44
	Private Sector	Rp37.75 trillion ($4.39 billion)	Rp2.92 trillion ($340 billion)	Rp2.06 trillion ($239.53 million)	Rp2.65 trillion ($308.14 million)	7.74	5.46	7.02

Source: The Supreme Court Decisions 2001–2009, estimated.

The reason to support this argument is the fact that the cost of corruption covers only the explicit cost and does not take into account the opportunity costs incurred due to the misallocation of resources owing to the corruption. Contrary to the prescription given by bargaining theory (Nash, 1951; Rubinstein, 1982, among others), in Indonesia there has been a strong tendency to prosecute defendants with financial punishment that is much lower than the explicit cost of corruption.

Information in the column ratio B/A represent the proportion of the total financial punishment prosecuted and the total explicit cost of corruption across gender, age, geographical distributions and occupations. Both values were estimated by the same individuals, namely the prosecutors, however, surprisingly both values are significantly different. The majority of corruption in Indonesia are committed by males, however there is a tendency that female corruptors (61.68%) were prosecuted with higher financial punishment as opposed to their male counterparts (44.35%). Corruptors in their productive age tend to be prosecuted with lesser financial punishment (only 9.92%) than offenders aged 60 year old or above (83.17%). Offenders who committed corruption in Jawa (86.68%), tend to be prosecuted much more heavily in comparison to those who conducted corruption outside Jawa (1.13%). In terms of occupation, offenders who previously worked as state-owned enterprise employees were prosecuted much heavier (99.42%) in comparison to corruptors who previously worked in other occupations. On the contrary, corruptors who previously worked in private sector were prosecuted most leniently in comparison to those from other occupations.

The column ratio C/A measures the proportion of financial punishment sentenced by the district courts and the total explicit cost of corruption. The column ratio D/A, furthermore, measures the proportion of financial punishment sentenced by the supreme court and the total explicit cost of corruption.

The estimations in the column ratio C/A are much lesser than those in column ratio B/A. This implies that the financial punishment sentenced by judges in the district courts is lesser than both the explicit cost of corruption and the financial punishment prosecuted by the prosecutors. In most cases, the ratios of C/A across gender, age, geographical distributions and occupations were less than 10%, unless for female corruptors (16.11%), and offenders who previously worked as civil servants (25.72%) and members of the parliament (27.08%).

Table 10.5 The average explicit cost and the average financial punishment across gender, age, geographical distribution and occupations

		Number of offenders	Average explicit costs (2008 prices)	Average financial punishment prosecuted	Average financial punishment sentenced by judges in district courts	Average financial punishment sentenced by judges in the supreme court
Gender	Male	504	Rp145.63 billion ($16.93 million)	Rp64.29 billion ($7.48 million)	Rp4.72 billion ($549,091)	Rp10.54 billion ($1.23 million)
	Female	36	Rp555.28 million ($64,567)	Rp342.5 million ($39,826)	Rp89.44 million ($10,401)	Rp295.28 million ($34,335)
Age	Below 60	479	Rp80.84 billion ($9.40 million)	Rp8.02 billion ($932.17 million)	Rp4.45 billion ($517,066)	Rp5.70 billion ($662,718)
	60 or Above	60	Rp572.33 billion ($66.55 million)	Rp476.00 billion ($55.35 million)	Rp4.32 billion ($502.36 million)	Rp43.17 billion ($5.02 million)
Location	Jawa	241	Rp155.02 billion ($18.03 million)	Rp132.82 billion ($15.44 million)	Rp9.92 billion ($1.15 million)	Rp20.71 billion ($2.41 million)
	Greater Jakarta	78	Rp472.69 billion ($54.96 million)	Rp404.62 billion ($47.05 million)	Rp25.00 billion ($2.91 million)	Rp61.67 billion ($7.17 million)
	Outside Jawa	299	Rp119.40 billion ($13.88 million)	Rp1.34 billion ($156,218)	Rp285.42 million ($33,188)	Rp1.10 billion ($127,802)

(*Continued*)

Table 10.5   (*Continued*)

	Number of offenders	Average explicit costs (2008 prices)	Average financial punishment prosecuted	Average financial punishment sentenced by judges in district courts	Average financial punishment sentenced by judges in the supreme court
Occupation Civil Servant	223	Rp2.101 billion ($245,151)	Rp983.77 million ($114,391)	Rp542.33 million ($63,062)	Rp608.79 million ($70,789)
State-owned Enterprise Employee	68	Rp431.32 billion ($50.15 million)	Rp428.82 billion ($49.86 million)	Rp2.21 billion ($256,635)	Rp36.47 billion ($4.24 million)
Legislative	130	Rp1.67 billion ($193,784)	Rp785.38 million ($91,324)	Rp451.31 million ($52,478)	Rp424 million ($49,302)
Private Sector	117	Rp322.65 billion ($37.52 million)	Rp24.96 billion ($2.90 million)	Rp17.61 billion ($2.05 million)	Rp22.65 billion ($2.63 million)

Source: The Supreme court Decisions 2001–2009, estimated.

The ratios of D/A across gender, age, geographical distribution and occupations tend to be higher rather than those in the column ratio C/A. This implies that the decisions by the supreme court provides positive corrections toward the sentences made by the district courts. The male offenders tend to receive lesser financial punishment (7.27%) by the supreme court as opposed to their female counterparts (53.18%). Both offenders who were in their productive age and more senior offenders received almost similar financial punishment by the supreme court, namely about 7% of the total explicit cost of corruption. A substantial gap in the ratios of D/A was found for offenders who committed corruption in Jawa and outside Jawa. Those who committed corruption in Jawa have the ratio of D/A 13.36%, whereas their counterparts in outside Jawa only received financial punishment by the supreme court 0.92% of the explicit cost of corruption.

The Supreme Court Decisions

There are various ways to assess court decisions. In this study, a logistic regression is used to various criminogenic factors which may influence decisions made by judges. A logistic regression uses a dependent variable in the form of binary alternatives (e.g., to be fined or not, to be imprisoned or not etc.) which will be on the left hand side of the equation, and various independent variables or explanatory variables on the right hand side of the equation. The criterion used to judge whether the covariates that are included are a significant part of the explanation is whether the value in the Sig column is less than 0.05 (for 5% significance level) and less than 0.01 (for 1% significance level).

The likelihood of conviction

The following econometric model is used to assess the decisions made by the Supreme courts to determine whether a defendant was found guilty as charged by the supreme court judges as follows:

$$
\begin{aligned}
SC\_guilty_i = {} & a + b_1 log\_Age_1 - b_2 Gender_i - b_3 D\_Jawa_i + b_4 D\_SOE_i \\
& + b_5 D\_MP_i - b_6 D\_Private_i - b_7 log\_ExplicitCost_i \\
& + b_8 DC\_guilty_i + b_9 SOE_i * log\_ExpCost_i + b_{10} D\_MP_i \\
& * log\_ExpCost_i + b_{11} D\_MP_i \times log\_ExpCost_i
\end{aligned}
$$

Whereby:

SC_*guilty*:	The Supreme court decisions, 1 = guilty, 0 = otherwise
Age:	Age of offenders when they were sentenced by District courts.
Gender:	1 for male and 0 for female
D_Jawa:	Dummy variable for location, 1 = the island of Jawa, 0 = outside Jawa
D_SOE:	Dummy variable for occupation, 1 = State-owned Enterprises Employees, 0 = otherwise
D_MP:	Dummy variable for occupation, 1 = members of the parliaments both in local and national levels, 0 = otherwise
D_Private:	Dummy variable for occupation, 1 = private sector, 0 = otherwise
Log_ExplicitCost:	log(explicit costs of corruption at nominal price)
DC_guilty:	Dummy variable whether district courts found the defendants guilty as charged; 1 = guilty, 0: otherwise
$D_{SOE} * \log\_ExpCost$:	Interaction between dummy variable whether defendant was a State-own Enterprise Employee and log(explicit cost of corruption inflicted by the defendant)
$D_{MP} * \log\_ExpCost$:	Interaction between dummy variable whether defendant was a senator and log(explicit cost of corruption inflicted by the defendant)
$D_{Private} * \log\_ExpCost$:	Interaction between dummy variable whether defendant was a civil servant and log(explicit costs of corruption inflicted by the defendant)

The equations above are based on assumption that the likelihood of conviction may be associated with various static and dynamic criminogenic factors. Gender and the district courts decisions are considered as static criminogenic factors, whereas age and occupations are classified as dynamic criminogenic factors. Under the Indonesian criminal penal system, the trials are conducted in the area where the offence has been committed. Although Jawa is one of 17,508 islands in Indonesia, however the island of Jawa is the centre of economic and political activities in Indonesia. The area of the island of Jawa is about 7% of the total area in Indonesia, however of the 240 million population in Indonesia, about 60% of them (about 114 million people) live in Jawa. It may not be surprising if the development in Jawa is more advanced than in the other islands in Indonesia. Based on this reason, a dummy variable has been generated in order to investigate whether there are differences in decisions between courts in Jawa and outside Jawa.

Results from descriptive statistic showed that the level of corruption varies across occupations (see Tables 10.1–10.5). This notion is accommodated in the model by generating three dummy variables to capture the role of occupation in relation to the supreme court decisions. In the model, the civil servant has been used as the reference group for a set of dummy variables which represent occupation.

The logistic regression models have been developed based on the assumption that the likelihood of receiving types of punishment may be associated with dynamic and criminogenic factors. Furthermore, it is expected that the types of punishment may correspond with the nominal value of the explicit cost of corruption. The use of nominal values for the explicit cost of corruption is based on assumption that both prosecutors and judges do not consider the real value of the explicit cost of corruption. Instead, they consider the explicit cost of corruption according to the current price as opposed to the constant price. The last three independent variables in the model are the interaction variables between dummy variables for occupations and the explicit cost of corruption.

Table 10.6 shows that there is a tendency that judges in the supreme court support the decisions made by judges in the district courts. This finding may be contradicted with the tendency that both defendants and prosecutors tend to appeal to any decisions made by judges in district courts if the decisions are not in their favor. In addition, defendants who committed corruption and were trialed in Jawa, tend to have a lower probability to be found guilty by the supreme court judges, even though

Table 10.6   Logistic regression analyses of the supreme court's sentences

Dependent variable: SC_Guilty_YN

Sample: 1,831; Included observations: 811; Excluded observations: 20

	Coeff.	S.E.	Prob.
C	1.445	2.15	0.501
DC_Guilty_YN	3.282	1.124	0.004***
Gender	0.118	0.368	0.748
Log(Age)	−0.922	0.511	0.071*
D_Jawa	0.44	0.219	0.045**
D_Greater Jakarta	−0.316	0.39	0.418
D_SOE_empl.	−5.016	3.883	0.196
D_MP	4.29	2.486	0.084*
D_Private	2.639	1.703	0.121
D_Appeal_HC	−0.62	1.125	0.582
D_JudRev	1.663	0.404	0.000***
Log_ExplicitCost	0.047	0.059	0.425
Log_ExpCost * D_BUMN	0.314	0.192	0.102
Log_ExpCost * D_MP	−0.24	0.126	0.057*
Log_ExpCost * D_Private	−0.116	0.086	0.175
Mean dependent var	—	—	0.663
S.E. of regression	—	—	0.377
Sum squared resid	—	—	113.3
Log likelihood	—	—	−359.9
Restr. log likelihood	—	—	−518
LR statistic (11 df)	—	—	316.2
Probability (LR stat)	—	—	0
McFadden R-squared	—	—	0.305

Notes: * Significant at 10%, ** Significant at 5%, *** Significant at 1%.
Source: The Supreme Court Decisions 2001–2009, estimated.

statistically the result is weakly significant. This finding is interesting since the average explicit cost of corruption inflicted by offenders in Jawa (Rp155.03 billion or US$18.03 million) was higher than that of offenders outside Jawa (Rp119.41 billion or US$13.89 million). Nevertheless, if defendants in Jawa are found guilty, then the average financial punishment sentenced by the supreme court was $2.41 million or about 18.86 time folds higher than their counterparts outside Jawa. The result also suggests that the detection rate of corruption outside Jawa tends to be higher than in Jawa, however prosecutors outside Jawa tend to be more lenient toward the defendants.

Imprisonment and probation

The logistic regression models for judges in the Supreme court to sentence defendants with imprisonment and probation are as follows:

$$
\begin{aligned}
SC\_Imprisonment_i = {} & a - b_1 log\_Age_i + b_2 Gender_i - b_3 D\_Jawa_i - b_4 D\_SOE_i \\
& + b_5 D\_MP_i + b_6 D\_Private_i - b_7 log\_ExplicitCost_i \\
& + b_8 DC\_Imprisonment_i + b_9 D_{Private} * log\_ExplicitCost_i \\
& - b_{10} D_{SOE_i} * log\_ExplicitCost_i - b_{11} D\_MP_i * log\_ExplicitCost_i
\end{aligned}
$$

$$
\begin{aligned}
SC\_Probation_i = {} & a - b_1 log\_Age_i + b_2 Gender_i - b_3 D\_Jawa_i + b_4 D\_SOE_i \\
& + b_5 D\_MP_i + b_6 D\_Private_i - b_7 log\_ExplicitCost_i \\
& + b_8 DC\_Probation_i + b_9 D_{Private} * log\_ExplicitCost_i \\
& + b_{10} D_{SOE_i} * log\_ExplicitCost_i + b_{11} D\_MP_i * log\_ExplicitCost_i
\end{aligned}
$$

Whereby:

SC_Imprisonment = the Supreme court sentenced offenders with imprison- ment, 1 = Yes, 0 = No

SC_Probation = the Supreme court sentenced offenders with probation, 1 = Yes, 0 = No.

The result in Table 10.7 suggests that the likelihood of sentencing defendants with imprisonment does not correspond with the explicit cost of corruption. There is no proof, whether the higher the explicit cost of corruption inflicted to the economy increases the likelihood of offenders to receive imprisonment. In addition, the higher the explicit costs

Table 10.7   Logistic regressions of the likelihood of imprisonment

	Dependent variable: SC_Imprisonment_YN Sample(adjusted): 4,831; Included observations: 472; Excluded observations: 356				Dependent variable: SC_Probation_YN Sample(adjusted): 2,830; Included observations: 463; Excluded observations: 366		
	Coeff.	S.E.	Prob.		Coeff.	S.E.	Prob.
C	−2.975	4.166	0.475	C	0.215	5.022	0.966
DC_Imprisonment_YN	1.661	1.643	0.312	DC_Probation_YN	−0.033	0.812	0.967
Gender	−0.198	0.846	0.816	Gender	0.577	1.067	0.589
Log(Age)	0.887	0.97	0.36	Log(Age)	0.148	1.134	0.896
D_Jawa	−0.385	0.428	0.368	D_Jawa	0.181	0.464	0.697
D_Greater Jakarta	1.177	1.179	0.318	D_Greater Jakarta	−0.521	0.869	0.549
D_SOE_empl.	3.959	8.93	0.658	D_SOE_empl.	2.612	8.445	0.757
D_MP	−10.829	6.311	0.086*	D_MP	−22.12	8.097	0.006***
D_Private	−2.34	4.263	0.583	D_Private	−10.238	4.467	0.022**
D_Appeal_HC	1.804	1.64	0.271	D_Appeal_HC	1.349	1.047	0.198
D_JudRev	1.668	0.845	0.049**	D_JudRev	−0.839	0.806	0.298
Log_ExplicitCost	−0.045	0.133	0.734	Log_ExplicitCost	−0.271	0.125	0.030**
Log_ExpCost*D_BUMN	−0.121	0.422	0.775	Log_ExpCost*D_BUMN	−0.132	0.442	0.765

(*Continued*)

Table 10.7 (*Continued*)

Dependent variable: SC_Imprisonment_YN
Sample(adjusted): 4,831; Included observations: 472;
Excluded observations: 356

	Coeff.	S.E.	Prob.
Log_ExpCost*D_MP	0.56	0.333	0.093*
Log_ExpCost*D_Private	0.135	0.224	0.547
Mean dependent var			0.888
S.E. of regression			0.248
Sum squared resid			28.087
Log likelihood			–107.3
Restr. log likelihood			–165.8
LR statistic (11 df)			117
Probability(LR stat)			0
McFadden R-squared			0.353

Dependent variable: SC_Probation_YN
Sample(adjusted): 2,830; Included observations: 463;
Excluded observations: 366

	Coeff.	S.E.	Prob.
Log_ExpCost*D_MP	1.036	0.379	0.006***
Log_ExpCost*D_Private	0.518	0.223	0.020***
Mean dependent var			0.06
S.E. of regression			0.233
Sum squared resid			24.4
Log likelihood			–93.9
Restr. log likelihood			–105.7
LR statistic (11 df)			23.5
Probability(LR stat)			0.052
McFadden R-squared			0.111

Source: The Supreme Court Decisions 2001–2009, estimated.

of corruption inflicted by MPs, are more likely to be sentenced with imprisonment in comparison with their civil servant counterparts, even though the impact is relatively weak.

The anti-corruption act 2000/2001 stated clearly that in some offences imprisonment and fines should be imposed together. The more serious an offence is considered, more severe the types and intensity of punishment [see Appendix A]. Imprisonment is an indicator that the type of offences committed by offenders may be quite serious. Similarly, the value of financial punishment prosecuted can be used as an indicator how serious the offence is, however, the results show that the decisions to sentence defendants with imprisonment do not take into consideration the scale of damage due to corruption.

The result in Table 10.7 shows that the higher the explicit cost of corruption the lesser the likelihood of the defendants to be sentenced with probation. The result does not support the hypothesis that the more serious corruptors tend to be sentenced with imprisonment as opposed to probation. There is a strong tendency that offenders with occupations as members of the parliament and in private sectors received lower sentences in comparison to their civil servant counterparts. Nevertheless, both members of the parliament and private sector who commit more serious type of corruption are less likely to be sentenced with probation as opposed to their civil servant counterparts.

In many countries in Europe, imprisonment is given to defendants only if the types of offences are considered quite serious, namely the offence gravity[iv] committed by the offenders is relatively high. The intensity of offences is estimated by how serious the impact of the offence to victims and even to the society. In the UK for instance, corruption is classified as one of the serious offences, therefore most likely individuals who were proven guilty of conducting corruption will be sentenced by imprisonment.

In Indonesia, corruption is considered also as extraordinary crime. As the social costs of corruption are high, then ideally judges can use the value of financial punishment prosecuted as a proxy to estimate how serious the case is. It is surprising, however, that judges in the supreme court do not take into consideration the value of financial punishment prosecuted as a means to determine whether or not the offenders should be sentenced with imprisonment or probation.

In the case for which the likelihood of receiving imprisonment does not correspond to the economic burden inflicted by offenders to the society, then judges' decisions, at least, do not take into consideration the concept of fairness proposed by Rabin (1993). Rabin (1993) argued that fairness should be seen as a reciprocal relationship rather than an altruistic behavior. Implementing Rabin's (1993) concept of fairness to sentencing, ideally, offenders who inflicted high social costs to society should be punished heavier, and imprisonment is a type of punishment which is considered tough.

The result shows that the defendants who worked as a member of the parliament were more likely to be sentenced with probation in comparison with other defendants with different occupations. Similarly, the social cost of corruption inflicted by a senator (the interaction variable between senator and the social cost) was more likely to be used as an indicator to determine probation order. It should be noted that these findings are valid only at a significant level 10%.

Fines and the subsidiary of fines

As Indonesia follows civil law, not only does the anticorruption act regulate any conduct that can be considered as corruption but also it states clearly the types and the intensity of punishment for each offence. The reason behind this is the aim to maintain the legal certainty, which is mainly interpreted by stating clearly the type of offences, the type of punishments and their intensity in an act. The question is whether or not judges follow the rules that were stated in the act.

A further exercise has been conducted to estimate factors which affect the likelihood of a defendant to be sentenced with fines and the subsidiary of fines by the Supreme Court, and the logistic regressions are as follows:

$$
\begin{aligned}
SC\_Fines_i = {} & a + b_1\ log\_Age_i + b_2 Gender_i + b_3 D\_Jawa_i + b_4 D\_SOE_i \\
& + b_5 D\_MP_i + b_6 DPrivate_i - b_7 log\_ExplicitCost_i + b_8 DC\_Fines_i \\
& + b_9 D_{Private} * log\_ExplicitCost_i - b_{10} D_{SOE_i} * log\_ExplicitCost_i \\
& + b_{11} D\_MP_i * log\_ExplicitCost_i
\end{aligned}
$$

$$SC\_Subs\_Fines_i = a - b_1 \log\_Age_i + b_2 Gender_i - b_3 D\_Jawa_i - b_4 D\_SOE_i$$
$$+ b_5 D\_MP_i + b_6 D\_Private - b_7 \log\_ExplicitCost_i$$
$$+ b_8 DC\_Subs\_Fines_i + b_9 \log\_Fines_i + b_{10} D_{Private_i}$$
$$* \log\_ExplicitCost_i + b_{11} D_{SOE_i} * \log\_ExplicitCost_i$$
$$- b_{12} D\_MP_i * \log\_ExplicitCost_i$$

Whereby:

SC_Fines = the Supreme court sentenced offenders with fines, 1 = Yes, 0 = Otherwise.

SC_Subs_fines = the Supreme court sentenced offenders with subsidiary of the fines, 1 = Yes, 0 = Otherwise.

The modelling of fines is similar to models in the previous sections. In the modelling of logistic regression for subsidiary of fines, the value of the fines has been included in explanatory variables. The notion of subsidiary punishment is based on assumption that the main punishment has little deterrence effect. It is expected that the higher the value of fines, the more likely the subsidiary of fines will be sentenced to offenders.

Table 10.8 shows that defendants were more likely to be sentenced by the supreme court judges with fines and or the subsidiary of fines if previously they were imposed fines and or subsidiary of fines in district courts. The value of explicit cost of corruption committed does affect the supreme court judges to sentence offenders with fines, even though the impact is weak. In contrast, the value of explicit cost of corruption affects significantly the likelihood of offenders to be sentenced with subsidiary of fines.

In contrast to Becker (1968), Pradiptyo (2007) argued that as opposed to other disposals, fines were not the best punishment. This is related to the low rate of payment, and fines have a deterrence effect only when they are paid by offenders. In the UK, the rate of fine payment is about 55% in England and Wales (DCA, 2004). If this disposition rate were translated into imprisonment, the result would be as if 45% of prisoners escaped (Bowles and Pradiptyo, 2004).

Empirical studies show that the costs to collect fines are substantial and may increase as the value of fines increases. According to Chapman *et al.* (2002), the costs of collecting fines in the UK is almost one-third of the value of the fines. This applies when the average value of the fine is £200, which is much lower than the average social costs of crime.

In addition, variations in the costs to collect fines in the UK are high, ranging from 11 pence to 44 pence per pound collected (DCA, 2004).

In order to make fines more credible, many authorities have to adopt a strategy of transforming the values of fines in relation to a term of imprisonment period — as a result, a failure to pay the fines will be compensated by serving time in prison. In the US, for instance, 25% of convicts sentenced by state courts in the year 2000 received fines as additional penalties (US DOJ, 2003). In Israel during 1997–2000, fines were used in combination with other penalties in 34.7% of the cases (Einat, 2004). The use of complementary sanctions shows that fines in themselves are not sufficient as a credible sentence. Furthermore, the costs of policing and enforcing fines may not necessarily be lower than other types of sentences, and the higher the fine, the higher the costs of enforcing and policing it. Any attempt to increase the value of fines may increase the number of defaults. In turn, this gives rise to an increase in the number of inmates in prison. As a result, fines may not be a good solution when tackling overcrowded prisons.

Table 10.8 shows that none of independent variables was significant in affecting the likelihood of judges to sentence offenders with subsidiary of fines. In order to make fines credible, imprisonment should be a complementary punishment with fines. Nevertheless, the finding shows that the decision to sentence with subsidiary of fines does not take into consideration the value of the fines itself. This result shows that the credibility of fines as a deterrence to prevent potential offenders to involve in corruption in Indonesia is questionable.

It should be noted that the subsidiary punishment for fines is asset recovery or imprisonment. Based on the anti-corruption act 2001, for every fine worth Rp50 million ($5,000) is equivalent to 12 months imprisonment or approximately Rp4.2 million ($420) per month. Nevertheless this formula has never been followed by judges in all courts when they decided the subsidiary sentence for fines. In one case, an offender was sentenced to pay fines Rp100 million and the subsidiary sentences are asset recovery or imprisonment for 2 months. In another case, an offender was fined with an identical amount, however, he/she received subsidiary sentences asset recovery or imprisonment for 6 months. Ideally the offenders should be sentenced with subsidiary punishment of two years imprisonment, however there is no evidence to support that judges follow this rule closely.

Table 10.8 Logistic regression of the likelihood of fines and subsidiary of fines

Dependent variable: SC_Fines_YN

Sample(adjusted): 4,831; Included observations: 516; Excluded observations: 312

	Coeff.	S.E.	Prob.
C	-8.103	3.564	0.023
DC_Fines_YN	4.195	0.511	0.00***
Gender	0.347	0.626	0.58
Log(Age)	0.786	0.777	0.312
D_Jawa	0.672	0.348	0.054*
D_Greater Jakarta	-0.479	0.706	0.497
D_SOE_empl.	4.297	5.801	0.459
D_MP	1.738	4.203	0.679
D_Private	2.41	3.272	0.462
D_Appeal_HC	-1.12	0.58	0.054*
D_JudRev	0.225	0.461	0.626
Log_ExplicitCost	0.198	0.103	0.055*
Log_ExpCost*D_BUMN	-0.158	0.285	0.579

Dependent variable: SC_Fines_Subs_YN

Sample(adjusted): 4,831; Included observations: 515; Excluded observations: 313

	Coeff.	S.E.	Prob.
C	-8.597	3.618	0.018
DC_Fines_Subs_YN	4.106	0.483	0.00***
Gender	0.108	0.647	0.867
Log(Age)	0.82	0.785	0.296
D_Jawa	0.671	0.351	0.056*
D_Greater Jakarta	-0.588	0.71	0.407
D_SOE_empl.	4.238	5.838	0.468
D_MP	2.356	4.245	0.579
D_Private	3.186	3.334	0.339
D_Appeal_HC	-0.962	0.553	0.082*
D_JudRev	0.376	0.471	0.425
Log_ExplicitCost	0.229	0.105	0.030**
Log_ExplicitCost*D_BUMN	-0.162	0.287	0.572

(Continued)

Table 10.8 *(Continued)*

	Dependent variable: SC_Fines_YN **Sample(adjusted): 4,831; Included observations: 516;** **Excluded observations: 312**			**Dependent variable: SC_Fines_Subs_YN** **Sample(adjusted): 4,831; Included observations: 515;** **Excluded observations: 313**		
	Coeff.	**S.E.**	**Prob.**	**Coeff.**	**S.E.**	**Prob.**
Log_ExpCost∗D_MP	−0.117	0.218	0.589	Log_ExplicitCost∗D_MP	−0.154	0.22	0.483
Log_ExpCost∗D_Private	−0.114	0.17	0.503	Log_ExplicitCost∗D_Private	−0.152	0.173	0.379
Mean dependent var			0.771	Mean dependent var			0.771
S.E. of regression			0.31	S.E. of regression			0.306
Sum squared resid			48.032	Sum squared resid			46.884
Log likelihood			−165.5	Log likelihood			−162.4
Restr. log likelihood			−277.4	Restr. log likelihood			−277.2
LR statistic (11 df)			223.8	LR statistic (11 df)			229.5
Probability (LR stat)			0	Probability (LR stat)			0
McFadden *R*-squared			0.403	McFadden *R*-squared			0.414

Source: The Supreme Court Decisions 2001–2009, estimated.

European countries tend to use fines more intensively than other developed countries such as the US and Israel. In 1986, for instance, 81% of adult offenders in Germany were ordered to pay fines (Tonry, 1997). In addition, fine payment covers 91% of court dispositions in Finland in 1979. In the US, however, fines have been used more often as an additional penalty, combined with a primary penalty of either imprisonment or community service, rather than as a sole sanction. In year 2000, of 28,810 convicts in the 75 largest counties, only 1% received a fine as a sole sanction (US DOJ, 2003). Similarly, Einat (2004) reported that in Israel during 1997–2000 fines were used as a sole sanction for only 11% of cases on average.

The ineffectiveness of a small fine was reported by Gneezy and Rustichini (2004), based on findings from their experiment. The results show that imposing a small fine fails to reduce the unwanted behavior. On the contrary, it increases the tendency to repeat the behavior for which fines were imposed. They argue that a fine will reduce the unwanted behavior only if it is imposed on a large scale. While this argument seems appealing, in the area of criminal justice there is an upper limit on the fines imposed, which is the wealth of offenders.

Compensation order and the subsidiary of compensation order

Further assessment has been conducted for the supreme court judges to sentence defendants to pay compensation for offences they committed and the subsidiary punishments of compensation. The logistic regressions to assess both notions are as follows:

$$
\begin{aligned}
SC\_Compensation_i ={}& a - b_1 log\_Age_i + b_2 Gender_i - b_3 D\_Jawa_i - b_4 D\_SOE_i \\
&+ b_5 D\_MP_i + b_6 D\_Private_i - b_7 log\_ExplicitCost_i \\
&+ b_8 DC\_Compensation_i + b_9 D_{Private} * log\_ExplicitCost_i \\
&- b_{10} D_{SOE_i} * log\_ExplicitCost_i - b_{11} D\_MP_i * log\_ExplicitCost_i
\end{aligned}
$$

$$
\begin{aligned}
SC\_Subs\_Compensation_i ={}& a + b_1 log\_Age_i + b_2 Gender_i + b_3 D\_Jawa_i + b_4 D\_SOE_i \\
&- b_5 D\_MP_i + b_6 D\_Private_i + b_7 log\_ExplicitCost_i \\
&- b_8 DC\_Compensation_i + b_9 log\_Compensation_i \\
&\pm b_{10} D_{Private_i} * log\_ExplicitCost_i + b_{11} D_{SOE_i} \\
&* log\_ExplicitCost_i + b_{12} D\_MP_i * log\_ExplicitCost_i
\end{aligned}
$$

Whereby:

SC_Compensation = the Supreme court sentenced offenders to pay compensation, 1 = Yes, 0 = Otherwise.

SC_Subs_compensation = the Supreme court sentenced offenders with subsidiary toward compensation, 1 = Yes, 0 = Otherwise.

Table 10.9 shows the likelihood of defendants to be sentenced with compensation order by the supreme court tends to decrease relative to the other type of occupations if the defendants are members of the parliament. Similarly, the higher the explicit cost inflicted by members of the parliament, the lesser the likelihood to receive compensation order. With respect to the compensation order, the supreme court judges tend to have opposite views with their counterparts in district courts. The other explanatory variables are not statistically significant. This means that when the supreme court judges made their decisions whether or not to sentence compensation order, they did not take into consideration the defendants' age, gender, occupation and also the value of financial punishment prosecuted.

According to Anti-Corruption Act 2000/2001, there is no particular term which regulates the level of compensation. Nevertheless, according to Indonesian Criminal Code (KUHP) apart from fines, judges have been permitted to sentence offenders with other types of financial punishments including: compensation, seizure of evidence (asset), court costs and other offence. Some prosecutors tend to prosecute a defendant to pay the compensation as much as the explicit costs that they inflicted on the society. Nevertheless, none of the judges in either district or supreme courts sentenced defendants to pay compensation as much as the explicit costs that they inflicted.

Similar to the fines, the compensation order has a deterrence effect if it is paid. The credibility of compensation order may be achieved if imprisonment was used as a complementary punishment for offenders who cannot afford to pay the compensation.

The result shows that judges' decisions to sentence offenders with subsidiary of compensation order was nothing to do with the value of the social cost and also the value of compensation order imposed to offenders. Instead, several factors which significantly affect the likelihood of

Table 10.9 Logistic regression of the likelihood of compensation

Dependent variable: SC_Compensation_YN Sample(adjusted): 4,831; Included observations: 517; Excluded observations: 311 + A99				Dependent Variable: SC_Subs_Compensation Sample(adjusted): 4,831; Included observations: 517; Excluded observations: 311			
	Coeff.	S.E.	Prob.		Coeff.	S.E.	Prob.
C	−2.934	3.225	0.363	C	−2.88	2.276	0.206
DC_Compensation_YN	4.101	0.362	0.000***	SC_Subs_Compensation_YN	0.004	0.009	0.662
Gender	0.525	0.572	0.359	Gender	0.586	0.431	0.175
Log(Age)	0.318	0.734	0.665	Log(Age)	−0.076	0.504	0.88
D_Jawa	0.756	0.32	0.018**	D_Jawa	0.244	0.22	0.267
D_Greater Jakarta	−1.272	0.509	0.012**	D_Greater Jakarta	−0.523	0.367	0.155
D_SOE_empl.	6.184	4.574	0.176	D_SOE_empl.	2.505	2.529	0.322
D_MP	7.834	3.642	0.032**	D_MP	4.333	2.937	0.14
D_Private	0.311	2.789	0.911	D_Private	1.053	1.961	0.591
D_Appeal_HC	−0.922	0.452	0.042**	D_Appeal_HC	1.589	0.367	0.00***
D_JudRev	0.291	0.421	0.49	D_JudRev	0.359	0.299	0.229
Log_ExplicitCost	−0.023	0.091	0.8	Log_ExplicitCost	0.029	0.067	0.665

(Continued)

Table 10.9 (*Continued*)

Dependent variable: SC_Compensation_YN

Sample(adjusted): 4,831; Included observations: 517; Excluded observations: 311 + A99

	Coeff.	S.E.	Prob.
Log_ExpCost*D_BUMN	−0.273	0.219	0.211
Log_ExpCost*D_MP	−0.393	0.185	0.034**
Log_ExpCost*D_Private	0.011	0.142	0.937
Mean dependent var			0.609
S.E. of regression			0.339
Sum squared resid			57.571
Log likelihood			−193.4
Restr. log likelihood			−345.9
LR statistic (11 df)			305
Probability (LR stat)			0
McFadden R-squared			0.441

Dependent Variable: SC_Subs_Compensation

Sample(adjusted): 4,831; Included observations: 517; Excluded observations: 311

	Coeff.	S.E.	Prob.
Log_ExpCost*D_BUMN	−0.106	0.123	0.39
Log_ExpCost*D_MP	−0.152	0.15	0.311
Log_ExpCost*D_Private	−0.038	0.1	0.702
Mean dependent var			0.472
S.E. of regression			0.473
Sum squared resid			112.4
Log likelihood			−322.9
Restr. log likelihood			−357.5
LR statistic (11 df)			69.3
Probability (LR stat)			0
McFadden R-squared			0.097

Source: The Supreme Court Decisions 2001–2009, estimated.

sentencing offenders with subsidiary of compensation order were: (a) age; (b) Jawa; (c) State-owned enterprise employee; and (d) the interaction between State-owned enterprise and the social cost of corruption.

It should be noted that not all compensation orders were accompanied by subsidiary compensation in the form of either asset recovery or imprisonment. Even if a compensation order were accompanied with asset recovery or imprisonment to improve the deterrence effect of the compensation, it turns out that the actual subsidiary orders tend to be more lenient relative to the idealized subsidiary orders.

Conclusion

The findings of this study show that most judges in all levels of courts do not follow the guidance on the intensity of punishment closely, as stated in the anti-corruption act 2000/2001. The lack of consistency in determining the intensity of punishments in sentencing has weakend the deterrence effect of the punishments.

The prosecution can be analyzed as a bargaining problem. Contrary to the theory, the size of pie shrinking rapidly by the time the cases have been prosecuted. On the average, the value of financial punishment only covers 60% of the total explicit social cost of corruption. The explicit cost of corruption were Rp73.1 trillion (about US$8.49 billion), however the total financial punishment imposed by the supreme court were Rp5.31 trillion (about US$617.44 million). Obviously, this discrepancy cannot be redeemed by the criminal justice system and in the end the taxpayers have to pay the burden inflicted by the corruptors.

The logistic regression analyses show that for all types of punishment, the likelihood of sentences do not correspond with the social cost of corruption inflicted by the offenders. Instead, there are strong tendencies that judges tend to be more lenient toward offenders with certain occupations. The sentences have been conducted idiosyncratically and they are far from being consistent with the guidance of sentences as stated in the Anti-Corruption Act 2000/2001. The implication of this finding is that the deterrence effect of the Anti-Corruption Act 2000/2001 and the role of KPK in eradicating corruption may be jeopardized. Even if the existence of KPK may improve the detection rate of corruption cases, however as judges tend to sentence offenders idiosyncratically, offenders who inflict high cost of corruption may receive light sentences. Obviously this weakend the deterrence effect of punishment, and potentially jeopardize corruption eradication movements.

The explicit cost of corruption is only a small fraction from the social cost of corruption, as Brand and Price (2000) defined that the social cost of crime includes the costs in anticipation of crime, the costs as a result of crime and the costs in reaction of crime. The data show that corruption are mostly committed by people with medium-high income and they usually have good careers, we suggest that a private solution could be implemented in punishing the offenders. This implies that the total financial punishment should be sufficient to compensate the social cost of corruption.

References

Andreozzi, L. (2004). Rewarding policemen increases crime. Another surprising result from the inspection game, *Public Choice*, 121, pp. 69–82.

Becker, G.S. (1968). Crime and punishment: An economic approach, *Journal of Political Economy*, 70, pp. 1–13.

Bianco, W.T., Ordeshook, P.C., Tsebelis, G. (1990). Crime and punishment: Are one-shot, two-person games enough? *American Political Science Review*, 84, pp. 569–586.

Bowles, R. (2000). "Corruption", in Boudewijn, B., De Greest, G. (eds.), *Encyclopedia of Law and Economics*, Vol. 5, The Economics of Crime and Litigation, pp. 460–491, Edward Elgar.

Bowles, R., Garoupa, N. (1997). Casual police corruption and the economics of crime, *International Review of Law and Economics*, 17, pp. 75–87.

Bowles, R., Pradiptyo, R. (2004). "An Economic Approach to Offending, Sentencing and Criminal Justice Interventions — Report to Esmee Fairbairn Foundation", presented to Esmee Fairbairn Foundation, London.

Bowles, R., Pradiptyo, R. (2005), A Study on Young Adults and the Criminal Justice System, *Barrow Cadbury Trust.*, London, UK. URL: http://www.bctrust.org.uk/snapshots/economics-young-adult-crime/economics-young-adult-crime.pdf.

Brand, S., Price, R. (2000). "The Economic and Social Costs of Crime", Home Office Research Series Paper 217. London: Home Office.

Chapman, B., Mackie, A., Raine, J. (2002). "Fine Enforcement in Magistrates' Courts", Home Office Development and Practice Report 1, London, Home Office.

Department for Constitutional Affairs (DCA) (2004). Magistrates' Courts Business Returns — Annual Report 2002–2003. London: Department for Constitutional Affairs.

Dubourg, R., Hamed, J., Thorns, J. (2005). "The Economic and Social Costs of Crime Against Individuals and Households 2003/04", Home Office Online Report 30/05. London: Home Office.

Ehrlich, I. (2004). "Recent Development in Economics of Crime", *German Working Papers in Law and Economics*, Paper 8.

Eide, E. (2000). "Economics of Criminal Behaviour", in Boudewijn, B., De Greest, G. (eds.), *Encyclopedia of Law and Economics*, Vol. 5, The Economics of Crime and Litigation, pp. 345–389, Edward Elgar.

Eide, E. (2004). Recent Development in Economics of Crime. German Working Papers in Law and Economics, Paper 8.

Einat, T. (2004). Criminal fine enforcement in Israel; administration, policy, evaluation and recommendations, *Punishment & Society*, 6, pp. 175–194.

Garoupa, N. (1997). The theory of optimal law enforcement, *Journal of Economic Surveys*, 11, pp. 267–295.

Gneezy, U., Rustichini, A. (2004). "Incentives, Punishment and Behavior", in Camerer, Loewenstein, Rabin (eds.), *Advances in Behavioral Economics*, Princeton University Press.

Hirshleifer, J., Rasmusen, E. (1992). Are equilibrium strategies unaffected by incentives? *Journal of Theoretical Politics*, 4, pp. 353–367.

Nash, J. (1951). Non-Cooperative games, *Annals of Mathematics*, 54, pp. 286–295.

Polinsky, A.M., Shavell, S. (2000). The economic theory of public enforcement of law, *Journal of Economic Literature*, 38, pp. 45–76.

Polinsky, A.M., Shavell, S. (2007) "The Theory of Public Enforcement of Law", in Polinsky, A.M., Shavell, S. (eds.), *Handbook of Law and Economics* Vol. 1, North Holland.

Pradiptyo, R. (2007). Does punishment matter? A refinement of the inspection game, *Review of Law and Economics*, 3(2), Article 2, pp. 197–219.

Rabin, M. (1993). Incorporating fairness into game theory and economics, *American Economic Review*, 83, pp. 1281–1308.

Rubinstein, Ariel (1982). Perfect equilibrium in a bargaining model, *Econometrica*, 50(1), pp. 97–109.

Tonry, M. (1997). "Intermediate Sanctions in Sentencing Guidelines", Issues and Practices in Criminal Justice. National Institute of Justice, US Dept. of Justice, http://www.ncjrs.gov/pdffiles/165043.pdf.

Tsebelis, G. (1989). The abuse of probability in political analysis: The Robinson Crusoe Fallacy, *The American Political Science Review*, 83, pp. 77–91.

Tsebelis, G. (1991). The effects of fines on regulated industries: Game theory vs. decision theory, *Journal of Theoretical Politics*, 3, pp. 81–101.

Tsebelis, G. (1993). Penalty and crime: Further theoretical considerations and empirical evidence, *Journal of Theoretical Politics*, 5, pp. 349–374.

US Department of Justice (DOJ) (2003). "Felony Defendants in Large Urban Counties 2000." Washington DC: US Department of Justice.

Weissing, F., Ostrom, E. (1991). Crime and punishment: Further reflections on the counter intuitive results of mixed equilibria games, *Journal of Theoretical Politics*, 3, pp. 343–350.

Endnotes

i. For instance, the maximum fines according to Criminal Code of Indonesia for certain offences may only be in the range of several hundreds rupiah, which is almost neglegible in terms of value. In the Anti-Corruption Act 20/2001, the fines have been adjusted to year 2000 values, and the maximum fine is Rp1 billion or approximately US$100,000.

ii. I am grateful to Eddy Hiarej for providing expert opinion regarding this point.

iii. I am grateful to Eddy OS Hiarej and Hifdzil Alim for suggesting this point.

iv. In the UK, the seriousness of an offence is classified by offence gravity which index is ranging from 1 (the lightest) to 8 (the most serious offence, such as homicide, etc.).

Appendix

Appendix A: Summary of Anti-Corruption Act 2000/2001

Section/Part	Offence types	Minimum Prison (Year)	Minimum And/or	Minimum Finer (million)	Maximum Prison (Year)	Maximum And/or	Maximum Fines (million)	Top
Sec. 5. Parts 1a, 1b	Offering a bribe to Civil Servants or Bureaucrats	1	Or	50	5	Or	250	
Sec. 5. Part 2	Civil Servants or Bureaucrats receive bribery as mentioned in Parts 1a and 1b above.	1	Or	50	5	Or	250	
Sec. 6. Parts 1a, 1b	Offering a bribe to any court staff and expert witnesses to alter their decision in the favor of the individual who offer a bribe.	3	And	150	15	And	750	
Sec. 6. Part 2	Any court staff and expert witnesses who received a bribe as mentioned in part 1a and 1b above.	3	And	150	15	And	750	
Sec. 7. Part 1a	Embezzlement of procurement of government goods and services provision	2	And/or	100	7	And/or	350	
Sec. 8	Fraud and Forgery committed by Bureaucrats for their own benefits.	3	And	150	15	And	750	
Sec. 9	Fraud and forgery committed by Bureaucrats in attempts to destroy and damage administrative evidence which may be used for prosecution.	1	And	50	5	And	250	
Sec. 10a	Damaging and losing any kind of administrative evidence which can be used for prosecution.	2	And	100	7	And	350	

(Continued)

Appendix A: *(Continued)*

Section/Part	Offence types	Minimum			Maximum			Top
		Prison (Year)	And/or	Finer (million)	Prison (Year)	And/or	Fines (million)	
Sec. 11	Civil Servants or Bureaucrats received present or promise due to their position in the government, and the present may hinder them to work professionally.	1	And/or	50	5	And/or	250	
Secs. 12a–12d	Receiving gratification or discount for procurement by Bureaucrats, court staff, expert witnesses who is believed is going to affect to their decisions.	4	And	200	20	And	1000	Live
Secs. 12e–12i	Extortion committed by bureaucrats, court staff.	4	And	200	20	And	1000	Live
Secs. 12b, Parts 1& 2	Any gratification which is suspected as a form of bribery to bureaucrats.	4	And	200	20	And	1000	Live

Chapter 11

Does Governance Reform in a Democratic Transition Country Reduce the Risk of Corruption? Evidence from Indonesia

Budi Setiyono

Faculty of Social and Political Sciences
Diponegoro University, Indonesia

Abstract

Within the last decade, Indonesia has been sympathetically admired by commentators for the smooth running of a democratization process following the end of authoritarian regime under Suharto's administration. So far, along with the alteration of political rules of the game, the democratization process that is taking place has generated significant institutional changes, and brings a fairly major transformation in political landscape. Citizens are enjoying free liberal environment and are receiving the rights of speech and association that is guaranteed by the laws. Regular free and fair elections have been conducted for the third time for electing a president, members of senate (*Dewan Perwakilan Daerah*/DPD) and the people representative assembly (*Dewan Perwakilan Rakyat*/DPR) at both national and local levels. Free media has also been flourishing and plays an important role in scrutinizing governmental and political affairs. As well, power has been significantly distributed both vertically and horizontally: vertically, Indonesia has been carrying out a broad decentralization process where provincial and local governments are receiving a large number of authorities and responsibilities for the provision of public services; horizontally, a number of new democratic institutions (currently there are about 40 Institutions in the form of committees and commissions) have been formed for exercising a different set of power and rotating the wheel of governance. In addition to these, military force has been sterilized from the political arena and no longer engages, at least on formal regulations, in business activities. In sum, as the World Bank (2003: i) maintains, Indonesia has been able to construct basic requirements for a strong functioning democracy.

When it comes to corruption, however, the extraordinary process of governance reform seems to have no effect. Despite the success story of many democratic accomplishments, Indonesia continuously performs poorly in dealing with corruption. In the last 10 years after democratization began, Indonesia still ranked close to the bottom, together with the most corrupt countries of the world, according to Transparency International's Corruption Perceptions Index. The score has never been far away from the score that was achieved during the authoritarian government era.

On the practical context, the appearance of corruption acts could still be easily observed in almost entire governmental buildings, especially in the places where public service is carried out. Street conversations about the way government officials maintain red-tape bureaucratic procedures in order to attract bribery, collusion between government officials and businessmen to capture public resources as in the case of illegal logging, conspiracy of judicial authorities to take illicit profit from court cases, and the way politicians exercise power to grab public budget are still in the daily reports of the Indonesian media. Due to systematic corruption, the quality of public services remains extremely poor. Devolution and decentralization of power has no meaning other than prosperity for the elites and the new power holders. Needlessly to mention that annually the State Auditing Agency keeps finding a huge number of irregularities in almost every government branch. In short, corruption has not only become an endemic in contemporary Indonesian politics, but also, turns into "a new ideology" where everyone seems born corrupt.

This chapter will try to examine these contrasting phenomena by explaining why the governance reform in a new emerging democratic country like Indonesia is not sufficient to curb corruption. While theoretically the implementation of good governance principles could end chronic abuses of power including corruption, evidence shows that this is not an automatic mechanism. Instead, imprudent process of governance reform may create a fertile ground for the spread of corruption.

Keywords: Governance reform, democratic transition, democratization, corruption.

Indonesia suffers from a very poor international reputation regarding corruption, ranking near the bottom alongside the most corrupt countries in the world. It is also perceived as doing worse over time in controlling corruption. Indonesians agree. They liken corruption to a 'disease to combat, denouncing every known case'. While these perceptions may be overly influenced by the new openness of a democratic Indonesia, corruption is high and imposes severe social and economic costs. It also contributes to citizens' loss of trust in governments (World Bank, 2003b: 1).

For the last decade, Indonesia has been sympathetically admired by commentators for its smooth democratization and the reconstruction of governance arrangements following the end of the authoritarian regime. In conjunction with the transformation of the political rules of the game, the governance reform following the democratization process has reformulated formal accountability systems and caused a major transformation in the political landscape. The reform has enabled citizens to enjoy a free liberal environment while fully receiving the rights of speech and association that are guaranteed by law. Regular free and fair elections have been conducted for the third time, electing the President, members of the House of Regional Representatives (*Dewan Perwakilan Daerah*/DPD) and the Parliament (*Dewan Perwakilan Rakyat*/DPR). Media restriction was revoked, enabling them to play an important role in scrutinizing governmental and political affairs. Also, power has been significantly redistributed: a number of new independent institutions (currently there are about 40 semi-governmental institutions) have been formed for exercising different sets of power; also, Indonesia has carried out a broad decentralization process where provincial and district/city governments are receiving a number of responsibilities for the provision of public services. In addition, the military has been removed from the political arena and no longer engages, at least in formal regulations, in business activities. In sum, as the World Bank (2003b) maintains, Indonesia has been able to construct basic institutions for a strong, functioning democracy.

When it comes to the corruption issue, however, the extraordinary process of democratization and governance reform seems to have had no effect. Despite the success story of many reform accomplishments, Indonesia continuously performs poorly in dealing with the problem. After 10 years of exercising governance reform, Indonesia is still ranked close to the bottom of the most corrupt countries in the world, according to Transparency International's CPI (Corruption Perceptions Index). The index score has not been far above the score that was achieved during the authoritarian era.

In the practical context, the appearance of corrupt acts can still be easily observed at almost all government buildings, especially places where any public service is carried out. The story of government officials maintaining red-tape bureaucratic procedures in order to attract bribes, the collusion between government officials and businessmen to capture public resources, the conspiracy of judicial authorities to take illicit profits from court cases, and the way politicians exercise power to grab public budget resources remain constant topics of public conversations and media reports. Owing to systematic corruption, the quality of public services remains extremely poor. Devolution and decentralization of power only benefits the elites and the new power holders. Each year, the State Auditing Agency (BPK) keeps finding a huge number of irregularities in almost every government branch. In short, corruption has not only become endemic in contemporary Indonesian politics, but also, borrowing the words of anti-corruption activist Saldi Isra (*Media Indonesia*, 18/03/2003), it is turning into 'a new ideology' where everyone seems born to be corrupt. Given the fact that the current corruption problem is worse than during Suharto's era, it is not an exaggeration to say that corruption is an imminent and 'a significant threat to a successful political and economic transition for Indonesia' (World Bank, 2003b: 17).

This chapter seeks to describe the process of democratization in Indonesia, and the governance reform agenda following this democratization. The chapter also discusses the persistence of corruption in the new democratic environment. It argues that governance reform has not been able to develop an effective accountability mechanism and, accordingly, is not sufficient to stop corruption; on the contrary, it complicates and diversifies the problem. Similar to authoritarian actors, the new power holders tend to utilize their political discretion as a commodity, one to be sold in exchange for illicit kickbacks.

Indonesia's Path to Democratization

Scholars explain the process of democratization differently. However, as maintained by Hara (2001: 308), they generally argue that the process is divided into four stages: the collapse of a previous authoritarian regime, transition, consolidation, and the maturing of democracy. The process usually begins with the collapse of an authoritarian regime due to strong pressure from the people and possibly the international community. Then it is followed by a transition where the regime is replaced by a more democratic government through free and fair elections. In the next stage, democracy is consolidated when democratic values have been widely accepted as the only way to organize political life in the country. Finally, a mature democracy is achieved when political practice fully conforms to democratic traditions. An ideal situation at this stage requires two reciprocal requirements: on the one hand, all democratic institutions should function according to their mandates and deliver services that meet public demands; on the other hand, citizens should be able and have opportunities to fully participate in any governmental process.

In Indonesia, regime change started with tensions based on broad public criticism in 1995, prominently led by Amien Rais, the chair of *Muhammadiyah*, against the practice of corruption committed by Suharto's circle and his government officials. During this time, along with the growth of an independent press, public criticism was fuelled by the news of corruption scandals and the unscrupulous behavior of Suharto's clique. The public generally had been disgusted by the practice of a monopolistic economy in the hands of an iron triangle: Suharto's family,[i] Chinese tycoons[ii] and military generals.[iii] Amien Rais called for the end of KKN (collusion, corruption, and nepotism) in government administration.

Public despondency also corresponded to the fact that Suharto had been in power for a long period. Suharto took power from a civilian government following a bloody coup in 1965: he was inaugurated as a temporary President in 1966 and then full President in 1967. He maintained an effective authoritarian regime by using three pillars of power: military, bureaucracy, and conglomerates. By manipulating elections, Suharto was repeatedly elected President in 1973, 1978, 1983, 1988, 1993, and 1998. The durability of Suharto's regime was ensured by his remarkable political skill to control subordinates by distributing patronage and manipulating conflict between them (Aspinall, 2005: 26). Holding power for almost 32 years, the public considered that Suharto was too old and incapable of sustaining his presidency. Some people called him *Pak Tua* (Mr. Elder) as he was sixty-six years old when he was re-elected president in March 1998.[iv]

Another precondition for the democratization process was an incident on 27 July 1996. This affair was a physical attack on Megawati Sukarnoputri's Indonesian Democratic Party (*Partai Demokrasi Indonesia*, PDI) office by elements of the PDI with support from the Indonesian army.[v] Following the attack, the resistance of Megawati's supporters created riots in Jakarta and other cities, leading to nationwide action and contributing to the rise of the people power movement to end Suharto's regime. Later on, the supporters of Megawati transformed themselves into a new political party named *Partai Demokrasi Indonesia Perjuangan* (PDIP) and won the first democratic election after the end of Suharto dictatorship.

In mid-1997 strong momentum for commencing democratization emerged due to an economic crisis that broke out in the middle of the year. The crisis, which stimulated the decline of Indonesian currency (Rupiah) from around 2,000 to the US dollar to over 15,000 and caused the rising price of daily basic needs, created conditions for the birth of 'people power' and a call for the resignation of President Suharto. In May 1997, a general election was conducted, followed by the formation of the People's Consultative Assembly (MPR). Despite strong public pressure to abandon Suharto, the MPR re-elected Suharto for another five-year term. Suharto was installed in the presidency on March 1998 and formed a cabinet that consisted of his close circle.[vi] The continuity of economic crisis and nepotism in the cabinet created strong public opposition to the MPR's decision to elect Suharto. Aware that the government was unable to control the deteriorating economy and KKN, people became angry and openly demanded the resignation of Suharto. In early 1998, pioneered by university students, demonstrations started to break out in every major city demanding Suharto step down.[vii]

Pressure from the people forced Suharto to hand-over his power to his deputy, BJ Habibie, on 21 May 1998. The immediate years following the collapse of Soeharto were marked by efforts to unwrap the old regime, including curbing Suharto's KKN, bringing former President Soeharto and his equally corrupt cronies to court, making constitutional amendments, discontinuing the dual-function of the Army and Police, and granting autonomy to regional districts.

Under strong public pressure, Habibie's administration recorded a number of policies that fitted with public demands. He released political prisoners like academic Sri Bintang Pamungkas and labour activist Muchtar Pakpahan. He also ended restrictions on the media by removing regulations that provided authority for the government to license and control the media. Under Habibie's initiatives, Indonesia for the first time carried out what the World Bank (2003a) called a 'big bang' decentralisation process. Habibie also promised to conduct a general election to refresh the authority of government. For this initiative, Habibie's government launched a new regulation that allowed political parties to freely participate in the general election (Hadiwinata, 2003: 79).

The first internationally recognized free and fair elections for the parliament after the Suharto era was held on 7 June 1999 to elect 450 members of DPR.[viii] As mentioned above, Megawati's PDIP won the election by gaining 153 out of 450 seats in parliament. However, because of the indirect electoral system, whereby the MPR selects the president, the winner of the parliamentary election does not necessarily win the presidential seat. The presidency went to Abdurrahman Wahid, more commonly known as Gus Dur, who successfully assembled the votes of parliamentary members from the Golkar and Islamic parties. Megawati was consigned to the position of vice-president. Gus Dur, however, only stayed in power for less than two years. Still stimulated by the anti-corruption spirit, the public was discontented with corruption cases that were allegedly committed during Gus Dur's presidency, which popularly became known as *Bulog-gate* and *Brunei-gate*.[ix] On 29 January 2001, thousands of people conducted a mass demonstration to put pressure on the MPR to expel Gus Dur from the presidential palace. Following strong public pressure, Wahid was then dismissed by the MPR and replaced by Megawati Soekarnoputri on 23 July 2001.

Despite some positive achievements,[x] Megawati's administration was marked by threats of separatism, economic instability, domestic terrorism, and her unimpressive performance. She was repeatedly criticized by commentators for her habit of taking a nap during working hours while Indonesian people were struggling with conflicts and economic deterioration. President Megawati also had close bonds with military generals on many sensitive issues, creating rumors of the possibility of a resurgence of the military force in the political arena. Weakened by her party's disintegration, the popularity of Megawati dropped from her top position during the early days after the fall of Suharto. In October 2004, Indonesia, for the first time, conducted direct general elections to elect a president and parliament members. Megawati was defeated by Susilo Bambang Yudhoyono who became the first president to be elected directly.

Governance Reform Following Democratization

Strengthening the formal accountability system by reducing excessive government control became the central theme for governance reform during the democratic transition process in Indonesia. This is not surprising, because for over 30 years the regime effectively maintained a bureaucracy, military and police force, as well as a legal system that served the ruling elite rather than the people. The regime also did not give much power to regional government, positioning them merely as the agent of the central government. By oppression and manipulation, the government tightly controlled elections and political parties, thus representation in the parliament did not have substantial meaning because there was no real choice at the ballot box (see for example Heryanto, 1996). Combined with ignorance of formal procedures and favoring informal personal relations, excessive government control created the growth of systemic corruption (see King, 2000; Schwarz, 2000).

Governance reform has been undertaken aiming to tackle this disarray. It has brought about a series of fundamental changes in Indonesia's social, political, and economic landscape, which previously was mismanaged by Suharto. With assistance, and occasionally pressure, from donors, international agencies and CSOs, Indonesia's new democratic regimes have undertaken, at least formally, a number of reform programs for practising good governance principles. Anti-corruption, in particular, turns out to be the most important issue for driving the reform. The following is the general description of the reform process to the extent that it relates to corruption eradication.

Constitutional Amendments for a Democratic Framework

In order to install the necessary requirements for the operation of a democratic system and fortify the accountability of the government, the Indonesian constitution has been repeatedly amended by the MPR. Amendments include strengthening the position of the parliament (DPR) by asserting that DPR members shall be elected by general elections,[xi] providing the institution with full legislative powers and the ability to call the government to account[xii] and impeach the president.[xiii] Further in 2000, amendments were made to emphasize the importance of decentralization,[xiv] recognize the importance of human rights,[xv] and make a clear distinction between defense and security forces.[xvi] Finally, amendments also covered a wide range of reforms in the system and institutional relations of governance. They include the modification of presidential and vice-presidential election system,[xvii] reconstruction of the MPR structure,[xviii] and the establishment of 'an independent central bank'.[xix]

The End of the Military's Role in Business and Politics

The long extensive military role in Indonesian politics and business since the 1950s has meant that the military has been implicated strongly in much of the systemic corruption (see Muna, 2002; Crouch, 1986). Under military reform, the engagement of the military in politics and business has now been formally terminated. Although not complete, important steps have been taken to realize this goal. The repositioning of the military has involved removing the customary dual function (as 'political' and 'armed' forces) of Suharto's era. Part of the military reform also includes the reduction of the military's influence in formal politics, by reducing its membership in parliament from 20% to 10% in 1999. All military representation in legislatures was ended in 2004. Additionally, the military (and the police) have been set in a neutral position in elections, abandoning traditional support for Golkar. As well as the reposition, the military also have been forced to open their activities to audit, and are disbanded from business activities. Under law 34/2004, the armed forces were required to surrender all their commercial enterprises to the government within five years (Palmier, 2006: 158). Despite refusals from conservative groups within the armed forces, some measures have been taken to ensure that their businesses be incorporated into the state's own enterprises and government's budget. In order to facilitate the transfer of military business, on 16 April 2008, the government formed a team responsible to carry out the transformation. The team was ordered to conclude the transformation by 16 October 2009 (*Republika*, 28/04/2008).

Privatization and Economic Liberalization

During Suharto's government, State Owned Enterprises (SOEs) were known as 'cashcows' for financing the regime and enriching government officials. By considering that the lessening role of the state in the economy can both improve performance and reduce corruption, Indonesian democratic government, under IMF (International Monetary Fund) policy prescriptions, started to privatize some SOEs in 1999. All the post-1998 presidents shared a common view that privatization was necessary and made numerous announcements about restructuring programmes and plans for privatization. During the first decade of democratization, around 10 to 15 SOEs were lined up for privatization annually. Based on IMF consultation, the government typically undertook privatization in the sectors of telecommunication, mining, cement, air and sea ports, toll road, steel, plantation, fertilizer, surveyor, and pharmaceutical business (Habir, Sebastian, and Williams 2002).

Devolution of Power: The Establishment of Independent Governance Agencies

In order to reduce the concentration of power within the government, one of the most significant reforms was that Indonesia undertook devolution of power through the establishment of independent institutions to exercise governmental functions that previously rested under state authority. Typically, the institutions were formed under regulation, and their members attained their position through selection processes in the executive and legislative body. Members of the institutions are usually representatives of CSOs, professional groups, and sometimes the government. So far, Indonesia has established around 46 transitional and extra-government institutions, which are relatively independent from the government.[xx]

Returning Sovereignty to the People: Citizens' Rights and General Elections

Along with the amendment of its constitution, Indonesia also abolished laws that contravened civil rights and created new laws considered necessary to protect the rights of citizens. The new laws, driven by the spirit of liberalization from state domination, generally express the absolute right of citizens to live without tight government restrictions. This condition stimulated the mushrooming of various organizations, representing all sections of society.

For strengthening the sovereignty of the people, laws on elections have been made to make sure that the people have the right to choose their political leaders. Since 1999 the election system had been administered by a number of different laws. Besides granting the people freedom of association, the regulations[xxi] also provide the opportunity for scrutinizing closely every candidate running for elections. The laws position political parties as the central players in a new political system landscape, and allow the people to freely establish parties to attain political office. These conditions have created the incentive for people to form parties, leading to a flourishing of hundreds of new political parties over the last 10 years.[xxii] The laws also stipulate a direct election system for electing the president and vice president,[xxiii] multimember constituencies for electing DPD members,[xxiv] and the open list system of proportional representation for electing DPR/D members.[xxv] Moreover, these new regulations also enable the execution of relatively free and fair competition among candidates and political parties. The elections are now organized by an autonomous General Election Commission (KPU) that is independent from government intervention.

Regional Decentralization

In the same spirit of implementing democratic principles, as well as to tackle the threat of national disintegration, Indonesia introduced a decentralization policy in 1999.[xxvi] This policy resulted in a massive transfer of power from central to regional government, making Indonesia from 'one of the most centralized systems in the world into one of the most decentralized' (World Bank, 2003a:1). The decentralization regulations (Laws 22/1999, revised by law 32/2004) provide the provinces, districts and cities with new powers previously held by the national government. Regional governments are now responsible for planning, financing and implementing policies in major sectors of social and political life.[xxvii] The regulations also provide the regional councils (DPRD) with more powers to supervise and control the regional administrations.

The Unresolved Problem of Corruption

Despite the achievements in formulating basic democratic institutions and attempts to strengthen the accountability frameworks described above, Indonesia's governance situation is still unable to deal with corruption. As Hornick (2001: 9) maintains, there is much anecdotal evidence indicating that corruption in the post-Suharto era continues to be ubiquitous — despite a formidable array of legislation prohibiting it, and notwithstanding several successful and celebrated prosecutions of corrupt officials. Although a number of reforms have tackled certain parts of the problem of corruption, the failures are evident; many signs indicate that corruption is still widespread, has become systemic, and is ingrained in the power and social structure of the country (Widjojanto, 2006: vii). Overall, accountability systems remain extremely weak, making government officials still relatively 'untouchable'.

In fact, patterns of corruption during the Suharto regime continue during democratic transition. The way power holders sell decrees and legislation to the corporate sector, the way the bureaucrats pursue illicit kickbacks for procurements, and the way judicial officers utilize legal process for bribery are still prevalent (Rais, 2008). This can be seen, for example, in the case of BLBI (*Bantuan Likuiditas Bank Indonesia* — Liquidity

Assistance of Bank Indonesia) that is tainted by systematic corruption practice. According to auditing agencies in Indonesia, the case has created total losses for the state of around Rp138 trillion (World Bank, 2005). The case took place in the last period of Suharto's presidency and has so far not been resolved and even breeds more corruption. Despite some actions being taken, the achievement has been disappointing. Those who are responsible for tackling the case use their authority for personal benefit. Some prosecutors and judges who have handled the BLBI case have been proven several times to have made illicit deals with suspects in the case. They conducted secret meetings and received bribes from suspects to contrive the termination of an investigation or to soften the prosecution.[xxviii]

Public sector services in particular have never retreated from making illegal charges or accepting bribes, creating inefficiency and aggravating the burden for the user of public services.[xxix] Corruption hampers the investors who wish to apply for a business license because it takes a long time and is complicated with various charges. A report of a survey carried out in 2007 by KPPOD, a leading think-tank, notes that many regional governments maintain corrupt, costly, and overly complicated procedures for business licensing (KPPOD, 2007). Not surprisingly, the record of Indonesia's global competitiveness remains poor. According to the *World Competitiveness Yearbook*,[xxx] Indonesia's rankings since 2002–2008 are respectively 47th in 2002, 57th in 2003, in 2004 Indonesia was not included, 60th in 2006, 51st in 2007, and 54th in 2008. These ratings positioned the country on the spot between the second-to fifth-worst of the countries measured. This fact may reflect the poor confidence of international investors to invest in business in Indonesia.

The persistence of corruption in Indonesia is shown in many international surveys, which generally indicate that corruption does not stop following democratization and governance reform. In June 2008, the World Bank Institute marked Indonesia as amongst the worst in developing countries in terms of law enforcement and controlling corruption efforts. The Institute, which combines many individual data sources into six aggregate governance indicators, shows that Indonesia generally still has a poor score in the overall governance indicators and has been doing poorly in handling corruption during the last 12 years (1996–2007). In a similar vein, the Political and Economic Risk Consultancy (PERC)

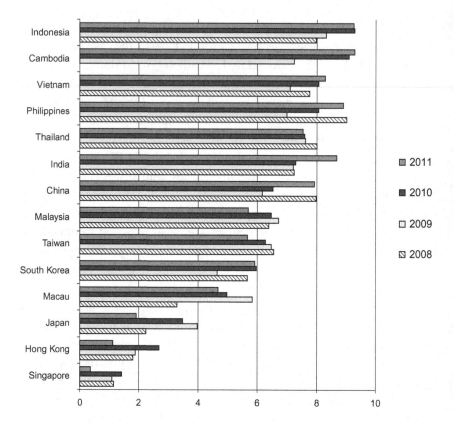

Figure 11.1 PERC's corruption mark in Asian countries (2008–2011)

Source: PERC (2008; 2009; 2010; 2011) (www.asiarisk.com).

Annual Graft Ranking consistently gives Indonesia a poor score on corruption. As Figure 11.1 shows, in 2008–2011 the institution persistently marked Indonesia as one of the most corrupt countries being surveyed. In 2011, the PERC scored Indonesia 9.25 and listed it as the most corrupt country among 14 countries surveyed in Asia. Against the records, the institution comments that 'The absolute scores show corruption in the public and private sectors is still very high' (*Bangkok Post* 09/04/2009) and further remarks that 'the judiciary is one of Indonesia's weakest and most controversial institutions, and many consider the poor enforcement of laws to be the country's number one problem' (AFP, 14/09/2008).

Another business consultant institution, Political Risk Services (PRS), which analyses climate for investment in hundreds of countries, also notes that widespread corruption, bureaucratic obstacles, and inadequate legal protection are the main sources of deterrence for foreign investment and economic growth in Indonesia. PRS further consistently describes that investment climate in Indonesia is undermined by the heavy practice of un-official payments. In 2007, for example, the PRS pointed out that the climate in Indonesia is generally unfriendly for foreign investors, since 'inefficient and corrupt administrative procedures, as well as an arbitrary legal system, frequently hamper international business, adding at least 10% to the cost of doing business' (PRS, 2007: 9).

Similar evidence is also shown by Transparency International's Corruption Perception Index (CPI) survey (see Table 11.1). With the fluctuation of CPI scores ranging between 1.7 at the lowest and 2.6 at the highest on a 10 point scale (with higher numbers indicating lower corruption), Indonesian records show no significant improvement over the last decade. Apart from the conventional types of corruption that took place during Suharto's era, the TI reports that political corruption has become a new trend in Indonesia's democratic governance. According to TI, 'one reason for this trend is the fact that political parties are not allowed to solicit their own funds to the required amount. Ministers and other holders of political office are expected to solicit funds, usually corruptly, to feed their political party's demands' (TI, 2008: 195).

Although the corruption indices reported in these surveys are generally based on subjective rankings by foreign business persons, domestic

Table 11.1 Corruption remains a problem: Indonesia's CPI records

	Authoritarian period				Democratic period									
	1996	1997	1998	1999	2000	2001	2002	2003	2004	2005	2006	2007	2008	2009	2010
Score	2.6	2.7	2.0	1.7	1.7	1.9	1.9	1.9	2.0	2.2	2.4	2.3	2.6	2.8	2.8
Rank	45/ 54	46/ 52	80/ 85	96/ 99	85/ 90	88/ 91	96/ 102	122/ 133	133/ 146	150/ 156	130/ 163	143/ 179	126/ 180	111/ 180	110/ 176

Note: "CPI (Corruption Perception Index) score indicates the degree of public sector corruption as perceived by business people and country analysts, and ranges between 10 (highly clean) and 0 (highly corrupt)".

Source: Annual corruption perceptions surveys of Transparency International (www.transparency.org).

surveys and investigations also articulate a similar picture. A Governance Assessment Survey by Gadjah Mada University in 2007, for example, concluded that illicit capture systematically takes place in governmental offices in all areas of the 10 provinces and 10 districts surveyed (ICW, 2008: 8). Meanwhile, audit investigations undertaken by the State Auditor Agency (BPK) in every semester also revealed that there is a constant misuse of state budgets in most government institutions during the democratic era (*Koran Sindo*, 26/01/2008). During the period of 2003–2008 the BPK has reported 210 cases of misappropriation of money-worth Rp30.18 trillion and US$470 million (*Suara Merdeka*, 13/01/2009).[xxxi]

Evidence of the proliferation of corruption is not only reported by surveys, observations, and investigation reports. There are also testimonies in thousands of Short Message Services (SMS) and letters delivered by ordinary people to President SBY. Since the president launched the postal address of PO BOX 0049 and the telephone line 9949 in 2004 for direct complaints from the people to the government, corruption issues always occupied the top rank of messages delivered to the president in every year (*Rakyat Merdeka*, 23/07/2007).

Although a number of anti-corruption task forces have been established, the poor performance of conventional rule-enforcing agencies such as the police, prosecutors and the courts greatly reduces the prospects for eradication. In fact, during the last four years the rule-enforcing authorities that are charged to uphold law enforcement have been the most corrupt institutions. The Global Corruption Barometer (GCB) of Transparency International revealed that police, parliament, political parties and the courts held the worst records on corruption (see Table 11.2).

This figure is also confirmed by annual reports from the National Ombudsmen Commission. In 2007, for example, 251 (29.7%) out of 846 complaints that the commission received concerned the poor performance of the police agencies, followed by 168 for regional governments, 114 for the court, and 65 for national government departments (*Antara News*, 28/12/2007). Post democratization, judicial officials generally have enjoyed a poor reputation for exploiting the law for self-enrichment. This is shown, for example, by the ongoing bulk of public reporting to 14 Indonesia-wide offices of the Indonesian Legal Aid Agency (LBH) concerning abuse

Table 11.2   The four most corrupt institutions in Indonesia

2005		2006		2007		2008	
Institution	Score/ Rank	Institution	Score/ Rank	Institution	Score/ Rank	Institution	Rank
Political Parties	4.2 (1)	Parliament	4.2 (1)	Police	4.2 (1)	Police	n.a. (1)
Parliament	4.0 (2)	Police	4.2 (2)	Parliament	4.1 (2)	Customs office	n.a. (2)
Police	2.0 (4)	Judiciary	4.2 (3)	Judiciary	4.1 (3)	Immigration	n.a. (3)
Judiciary	3.8 (3)	Political parties	4.1 (4)	Political parties	4.0 (4)	DLLAJR (Transportation authority)	n.a. (4)

Source: ICW (2008: 10) and GCB-TI Indonesia 2005–2008.

committed by law enforcement agencies and the existence of 'court mafia' (KPP, 2008). In a similar vein, a report from the Commission of Prosecutors in 2007 also mentions that the Commission received about 400 incoming reports from the public concerning irregularities and violations related to prosecutors, mostly in the form of extortion (*Suara Merdeka*, 19/10/2008).

A long-serving and reputable anti-corruption fighter, George Aditjondro (2001), maintains that corruption in the democratic transition era is worse than in the era of Suharto, since the uncontrollable disease has spread to numerous groups and actors. Anecdotal evidence shows that during the democratic transition corruption manifested itself in various ways and at all levels of the power structure, from the top levels of power to street-level (ordinary) bureaucrats in the lowest structure of government (Hornick, 2001). In other words, all power holders effectively utilize their authority as a commodity for personal gain. Not surprisingly, former Minister of National Development Planning, Kwik Kian Gie, suggested that in the democracy era an average of up to 40% of the national budget has been embezzled annually (*Banjarmasin Post*, 05/12/2007). In an even more pessimistic view, KPK predicted that the percentage of the budget that is abused may reach 45% of the total APBN (state budget) every year (*Sinar Harapan*, 20/04/2005).

Top officials or high-level executive branches keep extracting illicit payments from SOEs and natural resource exploration activities.[xxxii] The players are high ranking officials including senior bureaucrats, regents/

mayors, governors, heads of national agencies, ministers, and even presidents. Owing to this type of corruption, for example, some companies have the privilege of occupying thousands of hectares of forest and conducting illegal logging without fearing punishment (Rais, 2008: 156–158). In 2008, the public was outraged over the discovery of an irregularity in a gas exploitation contract made under Megawati's administration in 2002. At the time, President Megawati appointed her husband, Taufik Kiemas, to head senior government ministers on a trip to Beijing in December 2002 to hold talks with Chinese Prime Minister Zhu Rongji and negotiate a US$13 billion liquefied natural gas (LNG) contract for Tangguh field. The deal was suspected to be tainted with corruption since the selling price was too low and has caused potential losses to the state of Rp75 trillion. Some commentators believe that the Tangguh gas selling price is only one sixth of the normal selling price, so that the country will be disadvantaged by US$3 billion a year and Rp75 trillion over the 25 year contract (*Kompas*, 02/09/2008).

Political corruption also increased greatly after democratization, since the parliament is now recognized as a major source of power. Lack of funding for political parties, multiple interpretations of legislation, and sudden possession of discretionary power along with the limited capacity of new politicians are cited as the primary explanations for the problem. Political corruption that is reported to involve hundreds of legislative members at national, provincial and local level leads to the public impression that their political parties support the officials involved in the cases (*Suara Merdeka*, 20/12/2007). This is shown, in the TI Global Corruption Barometer survey mentioned in Table 11.2, that consistently put the parliament and political parties among the country's most corrupt institutions. In the period between 2003 and 2006 alone 967 provincial and local parliament members were named as suspects in corruption cases (Hadiz, 2008: 2). National parliament members also seem to wait to be named as suspects of corruption. For example, throughout the first half of 2009 at least five members of the House of Representatives were arrested by KPK on various charges of corruption.[xxxiii] Previously in 2008, there were also several DPR members who were arrested for alleged corruption.[xxxiv]

Meanwhile, petty corruption remains unchanged. Street-level bureaucrats keep taking advantage of their daily jobs by receiving bribes, gratuities and other benefits when providing basic public services and clemency for offences (such as avoiding traffic tickets, false custom clearance, and evading tax).[xxxv] It is still a common practice in Indonesia that people have to pay additional fees for getting services; otherwise they will be in trouble, no matter what their condition. Bureaucrats generally impose private taxation through extortion when people and firms want to be issued with, or to retain, licenses required to undertake particular activities, or if they want to attain services to which the people and firms in question are already entitled, such as protection by the police against violence and intimidation (McLeod, 2003: 8–9). In addition, in most sectors, the system of public procurement still relies on the decisions of bureaucrats who commonly take benefit by attaining kickbacks from government contractors (Hornick, 2001: 14).

To summarize, it is clear that democratization does not necessarily reduce corruption. In fact, as will be described below, due to the decentralization of power and administration, corruption previously concentrated at the central government level has now spread into the regional government level.

The Spread of Corruption to the Regional Government Level

In general theoretical terms, decentralization is considered one of the more effective approaches to tackle corruption. Apart from creating smaller constituencies that more easily facilitate the monitoring of the performance of elected representatives and public officials, decentralization also reduces collective action problems related to political participation for supervising the government (Lederman *et al.*, 2005: 5). Decentralization enables the public to organize small groups of people to undertake dialogue with the government to question and demand service improvement. In this respect, the more decentralized the political system, the stronger are the accountability mechanisms and the lower is corruption (Nas *et al.*, 1986; Rose-Ackerman, 1999). However, when not properly designed, decentralization can also undermine the accountability of government. As supervision from the central government loosens and regional authorities often lack their own checks and balances, regional officials have more space to maneuver for practicing corruption (Fox, 2000: 6).

Once decentralization was undertaken by Indonesia many commentators expressed optimistic expectations concerning its potential to oppose the centralized and corrupt state. It was said that decentralization would create advantages, including narrowing the gap of disparity among regions, the more participatory process of political and social development, and the weakening of vertical authority structures will improve the financing, planning and supervision of social services. Commenting on the early stage of the decentralization process, Alm *et al.* (2001: 86), for example, maintain that:

> The assignment of significant new expenditure responsibilities to provincial and especially to *kota/kabupaten* governments has the potential to achieve the efficiency gains that come when a government's decisions are more responsive to the wishes of its citizens, so that public services are provided in amounts that correspond more closely to the preferences of the individuals in those jurisdictions, rather than at uniform national levels. Other potential gains include greater revenue mobilisation, because citizens may be more willing to pay local taxes to provide local public services and because regional governments may be more familiar with, and so better able to tax, local tax bases.

After several years of implementation, however, the decentralization process in Indonesia suffered from criticism that it only provided more opportunity for local elites to commit corruption. Decentralization did not make significant improvement in accountability and public services; rather, it caused the spread of corruption, increased localism and a 'politics of little emperors' (Aspinall and Fealy, 2003; Hadiz, 2004; McCarthy, 2004). The 'big bang' decentralization caused an 'anarchical' and 'chaotic' institutionalized pattern of corruption during the New Order regime (Webber, 2006: 411). Some Indonesians called the phenomenon *Efek Seratus Suharto*, the '100 Suharto Effect' (Thorburn, 2002: 623). The term describes a trend in regional corruption that multiplied corrupt rulers like Suharto. Governors and district government heads (regents/mayors), who now enjoy tremendous political power within their respective regions, have typically misused their position to enrich themselves, their families, and other close associates; just like Suharto did during his presidency.

Decentralization allows the transfer of significant amounts of revenue to provincial and regional governments. But this has not been accompanied by a corresponding improvement in their financial management capacity, or by increased proper internal and external monitoring/ supervision (DRSP, 2006: 8).[xxxvi] In fact, there is an increasing tendency where oversight bodies at local level tend to abuse their authority, and take illicit benefits from those under their supervision (Dwiyanto, 2002b: 107). As a consequence, as Nordholt (2004: 30) argues, Indonesia's decentralization does not necessarily result in democratization, good governance and the strengthening of civil society at the regional level; instead it allows corruption, collusion and political violence that once belonged to the centralized regime to be now molded into existing patrimonial patterns at the regional level.

The Reform Deficits

While reform programs seem to be achieving impressive progress, the persistence of corruption during democratic transition raises questions about why the new institutional structure of governance does not reduce the problem. One way of examining this question is to understand that the democratic transition process is not always resistant to the influence of the system and the political configuration set up by the previous authoritarian regime. As international experience shows, 'the characteristics of the previous non-democratic regime have profound implications for the transition paths available, and the tasks different countries face when they begin their struggles to develop consolidated democracies' (Linz and Stepan, 1996: 55).[xxxvii]

The persistence of domination of pre-democratic elites occurs partly because democratic transition was not followed by transformation of personnel in the bureaucracy, judiciary and military, or a large-scale redistribution of power in the business sector (Webber, 2006: 410), making an opportunity for the old neo-patrimonial actors to reposition themselves within the new political amphitheatre. Generally speaking, as Robison and

Hadiz (2004) argue, the old power relations in Indonesia have simply reinvented themselves since Suharto's fall rather than being transformed. Indonesia's bureaucracy, in particular, has generally not been too much different to what it was during Suharto's era. The administrative system still tends to emphasize 'rules and compliance' rather than 'incentives and performance' (Cole, 2001: 14). Even if presidents have shown willingness to deal seriously with corruption, because officers in the bureaucracy are still circumscribed by the old traditions, presidential programs will simply be opposed by bureaucrats. In this respect, on one occasion President Megawati complained about the poor performance of Indonesian bureaucracy by calling it a 'waste basket' (*keranjang sampah*), referring to its lethargic performance in responding to public demands (*Kompas*, 11/02/2002). One of her ministers, Kwik Kian Gie, on another occasion, also maintained that the bureaucracy had been contaminated by an acute corrupt mentality under the 32 years of Suharto's government (*Kompas*, 10/06/2000).

In addition, social disorder in Indonesia engineered by Suharto's government persists, hampering the functioning of the democratic mechanism in curbing corruption (Antlöv, 2002: 2; Cole, 2001). On the one hand, for over three decades, citizens were forced to choose between various patrons to channel their interests, and had been subject to the very repressive and unresponsive government. Thus citizens have little to trust the political and judicial system, and have little experience of influencing public policy. On the other hand, the massive accumulation of power and patrimonial governance system has meant that the government has been unaccustomed to the notion of accountability toward society in general. For a long period, government officials have been informally and effectively placed above the law, allowing them to exploit their authority for private benefit. Thus, the old systems, values, and behaviors have survived in the era of new democratic freedom, and are now ever more being put to the service of new political masters (Cole, 2001: 13). Despite decentralization processes, bureaucrats, in particular, have positioned themselves as a strong group with significant support bases via the use of patrimonial practices during the Suharto government. As a consequence, newly established regional and local democratic institutions have been ineffective in promoting responsive and accountable governance.

In other words, the democratic transition in Indonesia has been influenced by the widespread and deep-rooted patrimonial practices that Suharto built 3–4; Robison and Hadiz, 2004). Although the authoritarian regime has changed, the use of personal and particularistic ties still take place as the means by which civilians and elites seek to influence politics. In such circumstances, the governance system fails to operate as it should because state institutions are generally not impartial, are unpredictable, and are in disharmony with the rule of law, while the citizens (as clients) have had to utilize informal connections to obtain services, including bribery.[xxxviii] For example, a national survey carried out by Partnership for Governance Reform Indonesia (PGRI) in 2002 shows that two thirds of its respondents stated that they have been involved in the practice of bribery, not necessarily because they were forced, but because they considered it the only efficient way to attain government services (PGRI, 2002: 22).

The persistence of corruption in Indonesia, however, is not only perpetuated by the inheritance from Suharto's government. It is also a product of incomplete democratic consolidation. As the World Bank (2003b) points out, despite the progress on governance reform discussed above, the accountability mechanism is still characterized by substandard functions on every level (see the summary in Box 1). Moreover, vested interests are too powerful, limiting the state's ability to undertake comprehensive reform in implementing a mechanism of accountability (World Bank, 2003b: vi).

As well, the transitional process, which by nature created social and political instability, allowed informal rules to thrive and provided incentives for corrupt officials and their cronies to retain power without proper monitoring. This situation is even worse due to the co-opting of Indonesia's democracy by criminal networks and drug trafficking. Many leaders of *preman* (semi-criminal) groups, who are relatively uneducated and rely on organized violence, are reported to enter politics where they hijack new political and economic structures (Wilson, 2006; Chadwick, 2006: 72–74). They have succeeded in taking hold of some key positions in the policy-making structure, but are inexperienced and have a very limited capacity to understand and carry out their jobs (World Bank, 2003b: vi).[xxxix] So, while many scholars advocate that the key to combat corruption relies on policymakers developing strategies for addressing the problem, most

Box 1: Accountability Remains Weak: The World Bank Analysis

In 2003, the World Bank analyzed the continuance of the weakness of accountability mechanisms in the governance configuration of Indonesian democratic transition. The Bank summarized that the weaknesses were due to a number of factors, including:

- ineffectual rules enforcing agencies, because they were poorly funded, ill-equipped, and tainted with corruption;
- most politicians and policymakers have a lack in formal experience of government as they are just starting to learn their new job;
- continuations of patterns of behaviors under the New Order regime that fundamentally undermine accountability, not only at central but also, at provincial and district levels;
- strong and fragmented vested interests on state asset redistribution following the financial crisis, making the illicit state capture very difficult to be controlled;
- limitation of the media and civil society to scrutinize the government;
- deficient control of citizens over politicians and service providers;
- poor capacity of politicians in making regulations and keeping agencies in check;
- Non-transparent systems of administration.

Source: World Bank (2003b: vi).

of these new policymakers do not have adequate capacity to develop the strategies. Besides, they do not want such strategies because this would harm their own interests.

Apart from these issues, Suharto's downfall has created the loss of effective government (McLeod, 2003). The governance system that used to be controlled by a single authoritative power has disintegrated. Although the return of authoritarianism is certainly not likely, democratization has created a diversity of groups, leading to conflicting interests and agendas, and eventually eliminating unity in command. The establishment of extra-governmental institutions, which have even less connection to one another, makes coordination among actors more difficult.

The situation is worsened by the fact that the governance reform is taken with the absence of a 'road map', a binding agenda that could lead the reform to a collective destination. After 10 years of reform programs, there is no single blue print for determining the agenda. Rather, the reform programs contain several approaches, which manifest in separate strategy documents produced by government, parliament, bureaucracy, political parties, CSOs, and international development agencies. Each has its own agenda, program and framework for putting the idea of governance reform into practice (UNDP, 2006). These actors not infrequently work independently of each other. Sometimes, the view and keenness for reform is also not uniform across agencies. Stated simply, the absence of a common agenda has created institutional fragmentation, slowing the pace of reform.

Coordination and synchronization of individual agendas have been difficult because of the complexity of power relations. Given the fact that there is no single institution that has a mandate to coordinate the governance reform program, poor coordination in terms of harmonizing authority emerges. The president is no exception. This fragmentation of power has created a situation where key political actors are not necessarily with the presidential circle, making it difficult for presidents to influence key political-governmental agencies (Cole, 2001: 16).

Furthermore, the implementation of reform has been half-hearted due to obstacles that come from elites and political parties pursuing their own interests. Overall, political parties' willingness to realize good governance is only lip service; their genuineness is doubtful as good governance might obstruct their interests (see World Bank, 2007). The attempt to combat corruption is undermined by the nature of political dynamics in the new political system. Given the fact that Indonesian elites are almost defined by the opportunities for beneficial corruption, attempts to tackle the problem will encounter major political upheaval (King, 2008). All presidents, albeit formally articulating the importance of corruption eradication and employing some measures, are unable to escape from the corruption already so pervasive in their immediate circumstances. Taken as a whole, the political arena is tainted by illicit captures promoted by the parties that belong to, and provide political support for the presidents. Sadly, the involvement of political parties in corruption also limits the supervisory role the parliament plays to pressure presidents to work with integrity. A further important factor is that Indonesia's law enforcement agencies are hampered by a number of defective functions, making them unable to work independently to tackle corruption.

Concluding Comments

When democratization started following the fall of Suharto, the notion of governance reform to strengthen formal accountability mechanisms dominated most public forums. Yet the debate rarely pointed to its side-effects. Indeed, governance reform opened many opportunities for people to engage in governmental processes. But they are not necessarily prepared to comply with democratic principles. Thus, while governance reform can produce positive outcomes, it also creates unintended consequences, including the spread of corruption. In the New Order era corruption was committed relatively undercover by a limited number of people. But it is now a more openly and systematically committed practice. As the processes of devolution and decentralization of power deepened, the distribution pattern of corruption was also decentralized. While the initial circle of corruption centered on Suharto's circle, it has now spread to the new power centers in various state institutions and regional governments.

Moreover, the set of governance reforms has created a complex governance landscape, making corruption eradication much more difficult. Despite the domination of elite groups, there is no single element that holds the capacity to retain the power necessary for the operation of effective governance. While the government has tried to initiate several anti-corruption policies, the outcomes were not very effective. If the problem persists, it would be likely that apathy for the democratization process will grow; people may lose their faith in politicians and political parties. If the trend of popular disillusionment continues, the question might be a matter of when, and not if, an authoritarian power structure re-emerges.

References

Aditjondro, G. (2001). 'Political corruption under Megawati Sukarnoputri: From monolithic to multiparty corruption and back to monolithic corruption', paper presented at the International Seminar on the Political Condition in Indonesia: Its Impact on Macro Economic Investment, Griffith University Brisbane, 21 September 2001.

Afadlal (ed.) (2003). *Dinamika Birokrasi Lokal Era Otonomi Daerah,* Jakarta: Pusat Penelitian Politik (P2P) LIPI.

AFP (2008). [Online, accessed 20 July 2009, at http://afp.google.com/article/.

Alm, J., Aten, R., Bahl, R. (2001). 'Can Indonesia decentralize successfully? Plans, problems and prospects', *Bulletin of Indonesian Economic Studies,* 37, pp. 83–102.

Antlöv, H., Ibrahim, R., van Tuijl, P. (2005). 'NGO Governance and Accountability in Indonesia: Challenges in a Newly Democratizing Country', an online paper [accessed 12 February 2009, at http://www.justassociates.org/associates_files/Peter_NGO%20accountability%20in%20Indonesia%20 July%2005%20version.pdf].

Ardiyanto, D. (2002). 'Korupsi di Sektor Pelayanan Publik', in Hamid Basyaib (ed.), *Mencuri Uang Rakyat, 16 Kajian Korupsi di Indonesia (Buku 2),* Jakarta: Yayasan Aksara and PGRI, pp. 87–126.

Asfar, M. (ed.) (2001). *Implementasi Otonomi Daerah (Kasus Jatim, NTT, Kaltim),* Surabaya: CPPS and Pusdeham.

Aspinall, E., Fealy, G. (eds.) (2003). *Local power and politics in Indonesia: Decentralization and democratization (Indonesia Update Series),* Singapore: Institute of Southeast Asian Studies.

Aspinall, E. (2005). *Opposing Suharto: Compromise, Resistance, and Regime Change in Indonesia,* California: Stanford University Press.

Bangkok Post (2009). Indonesia, Thailand: Asia's most corrupt, [Online, accessed 1 November 2009, at http://khmernz.blogspot.com/2009/04/indonesiathailand-asias-most-corrupt.html].

Chadwick, R. (2006). The Quality of Democracy in Indonesia and Russia, Thesis for The Degree of Honour in Asian Studies, The University of Sydney.

Cole, W.S. (2001). 'Roots of Corruption in the Indonesian System of Governance', *Woodrow Wilson International Center For Scholars Report,* Vol. December (100) (Asia Program Special Report), pp. 13–18.

Crouch, H. (1986). *The Army and Politics in Indonesia,* Ithaca: Cornell University Press.

DRSP (Democratic Reform Support Program), (2006; 2008). *Stocktaking on Indonesia's Recent Decentralization Reforms*, Jakarta: USAID.

Dwiyanto, A. (2002b). *Reformasi Tata Pemerintahan dan Otonomi Daerah*, Jakarta: PGRI.

Dwiyanto, A. (ed.) (2005). *Mewujudkan Good Governance Melalui Pelayanan Publik*, Yogyakarta: JICA and UGM Press.

Habir, A.D., Sebastian, E., Williams, L. (2002). *Governance and Privatisation in Indonesia*, Sydney: Research Institute for Asia and the Pacific (RIAP) University of Sydney.

Hadiwinata, B.S. (2003). *The Politics of NGOs in Indonesia, Developing democracy and managing a movement*, London and New York: Routledge Curzon.

Hadiz, V.R. (2004). Decentralization and Democracy in Indonesia: A Critique of Neo-Institutionalist Perspectives, *Development and Change*, 35(4), pp. 697–718.

Hadiz, V.R. (2007). 'The Localization of Power in Southeast Asia', *Democratization*, 14(5), pp. 873–892.

Hadiz, V.R. (2008). Democratisation and Corruption, Paper Presented on the Anti-corruption Public Forum: Approaching Second Conference of State Parties to UNCAC, Bali, 24–26 January 2008.

Hankiss, E. (2002). 'Games of Corruption: East Central Europe, 1945–1999', in Kotkin, S. and Sajo, A (eds.), *Political Corruption in Transition: A Skeptic's Handbook*, Budapest: Central Europe University Press, pp. 243–259.

Hara, A.E. (2001). 'The difficult journey of democratization in Indonesia', *Contemporary Southeast Asia*, 23(2), pp. 307–326.

Heryanto, A. (1996). 'Seakan-akan Pemilu', in Kasim I. (ed.), *Mendemokratisasikan Pemilu*, Jakarta: ELSAM, pp. 79–109.

Hornick, R.N. (2001). 'A Foreign Lawyer's Perspective on Corruption in Indonesia', *Woodrow Wilson International Center For Scholars Report*, Vol. December (100) (Asia Program Special Report), pp. 9–12.

ICW (Indonesia Corruption Watch) (2008). 'Independent Report, Corruption Assessment and Compliance United Nations Convention against Corruption in Indonesian Law', paper presented on Anti-corruption Public Forum of UNCAC on 24–26 January 2008 and Conference of State Party on 28 January–1 February.

King, D. (2000). Corruption in Indonesia: A curable cancer? *Journal of International Affairs*, 53(2), pp. 603–624, 2000.

King, P. (2008). Corruption Ruins Everything: 'Gridlock over Suharto's Legacy in Indonesia', *The Asia-Pacific Journal: Japan Focus*, March 3 [Online, accessed 1 November 2009, at: http://www.japanfocus.org/-Peter-King/2680].

Kompas, 10/06/2000, 'Birokrasi Masih Korup', p. 4.

KPPOD (2007). *Regional Business Climates in Indonesia*, Jakarta: KPPOD.

Kurniawan, L., Puspitosari, H. (2006). *Peta Korupsi di Daerah*, Jakarta: MCW-Yappika.

Lederman, D., Loayza, N.V., Soares, R.R. (2005). 'Accountability and corruption: Political institutions matter', *Economics & Politics*, 17(1), pp. 1–35.

Lynch, A.C. (2005). *How Russia is Not Ruled: Reflections on Russian Political Development*, Cambridge: Cambridge University Press.

Linz, Juan J., Stepan, A. (1996). *Problems of Democratic Transition and Consolidation: Southern Europe, South America, and Post-Communist Europe*, Baltimore: Johns Hopkins University Press.

McCarthy, J. (2004). 'Changing to gray: decentralization and the emergence of volatile socio-legal configurations in Central Kalimantan, Indonesia', *World Development*, 32, pp. 1199–1223.

McLeod, R.H. (2003). 'After Soeharto: Prospects for reform and recovery in Indonesia', *Departmental Working Papers* 2003–10, Canberra: Australian National University, Economics RSPAS.

Moran, J. (2001). 'Democratic transitions and forms of corruption', *Crime, Law and Social Change*, 36(4), pp. 379–93.

Muna, M.R. (2002). 'Money and Uniform: Corruption in The Indonesian Armed Forces', in Holloway, R. (ed.), *Stealing From The People, 16 Studies on Corruption in Indonesia*, Jakarta: Aksara Foundation, pp. 26–35.

Nas, T., Price, A., Weber, C. (1986). 'A policy-oriented theory of corruption', *American Political Science Review*, 80, pp. 107–119.

Palmier, L. (2006). 'Indonesia: Corruption, ethnicity, and the "Pax Americana"', *Asian Affairs*, XXXVII(II) (July), pp. 147–160.

PRS (Political Risk Services) (2007). *Indonesia Country Conditions: Investment Climate*, New York: PRS.

PGRI (Partnership for Governance Reform in Indonesia) (2002). *A National Survey of Corruption in Indonesia,* Jakarta: PGRI.

Rais, M.A. (2008). *Agenda Mendesak Bangsa: Selamatkan Indonesia!*, Yogyakarta: PPSK Press.

Robison, R., Hadiz, V. (2004). *Reorganising Power in Indonesia: The Politics of Oligarchy in an Age of Markets*, London: Routledge Curzon.

Rose-Ackerman, S. (1999). *Corruption and Government: Causes, Consequences, and Reform*, Cambridge: Cambridge University Press.

Rose, R. (1998). *Getting things done in an antimodern society: social capital networks in Russia*. Glasgow: Centre for the Study of Public Policy; University of Strathclyde.

Sender, H. (1996). 'The Suhartos: Bambang's challenge', *Far Eastern Economic Review*, 5 September 1996, pp. 56–57.

Schwarz, A. (2000). *A Nation in Waiting: Indonesia's Search for Stability*, Boulder, CO: Westview Press.

Soesastro, H. (2003). 'Introduction: Indonesia Under Megawati' in Soesastro, H., Smith, A.L., Ling, H.M. (eds.), *Governance in Indonesia*, Singapore: ISEAS, pp. 1–12.

TI (Transparency International) (2008). *Global Corruption Report 2008 Corruption in the Water Sector*, Cambridge: Transparency International. [Online, accessed 18 October 2008, at http://www.ti.org/TICorruptionPerception Index.htm].

Thorburn, C. (2002). Regime Change — Prospects for Community-Based Resource Management in Post-New Order Indonesia Paper Presented at the IASCP Pacific Regional Meeting Brisbane, Australia, 3–4 September 2001.

UNDP (2006). 'Outcome Evaluation Agenda for Governance Reform in Indonesia 2000–2005', unpublished evaluation report paper.

Webber, D. (2006). 'A consolidated patrimonial democracy? Democratization in post-Suharto Indonesia', *Democratization*, 13(3), pp. 396–420.

Widjojanto, B. (ed.) (2006). *Fighting Corruption From Aceh to Papua, 10 Stories of Combating Corruption in Indonesia*, Jakarta: Partnership for Governance Reform Indonesia.

Wilson, I.D. (2006). 'Continuity and change: The changing contours of organized violence in post-new order Indonesia', *Critical Asian Studies*, 38(2), pp. 265–297.

World Bank (2003a). *Decentralizing Indonesia: A regional public expenditure review: Overview report*, Washington, DC: World Bank.

World Bank (2003b). *Combating Corruption In Indonesia Enhancing Accountability For Development*, Jakarta: World Bank Report No. 27246-IND.

World Bank (2005). *A Financial Reform Agenda for Indonesia*, Jakarta: World Bank.

World Bank (2007). *Combating Corruption in a Decentralised Indonesia*, Jakarta: Justice for the Poor World Bank.

Endnotes

   i. Suharto's children in particular, have taken up direct and dominant position in business. Suharto's business empire was estimated to be worth up to US$7 billion: his eldest daughter Siti Hardijanti Rukmana was estimated to control assets of US$2 billion, his second child Bambang Trihatmodjo's business was estimated to reach US$3 billion, Hutomo Mandala Putra was reckoned to have assets worth US$600 million, Sigit Harjojudanto was valued at US$450 million, while the other two Suharto daughters were calculated to be worth US$200 million and US$100 million (Sender, 1996).

ii. Chinese conglomerates maintained close relationships with the Suharto family and top level government officials for mutual trade. They provided cash for the regime and in return received protection for their survival. Some of them acted as mentors for Suharto's children to build their business empires. Throughout Suharto's era, Indonesia's ethnic Chinese, numbering about 3% of the population, dominated the economic sector by holding approximately 70% of the private economy. Although there is no proof on this issue, at the end of the regime 80% of the 50 largest Indonesian conglomerates were Chinese businessmen, who obtained assets of around US$100 billion (King, 2000: 610).

iii. Military generals became engaged in business activities due to the idea of 'extra-budgetary financing' for armed forces whereby Suharto allowed the army to secure their performance by raising funds to supplement funds from the state budget (Crouch, 1986: 274). This condition had enabled them to form a number of foundations that possessed big business companies. Yayasan Kartika Eka Paksi of the Army, Yayasan Dharmaputra of the Kostrad (Army Strategic Command), Yayasan Adhi Upaya of the Air Force, and Yayasan Bhumyamca of the Navy, to name a few, are the prominent foundations that operated Armed Forces businesses during Suharto's era. The military also had privilege to position a number of retired top military commanders on the board of state owned companies. These conditions made it possible for military personnel to broadly abuse their authority for private-individual gain. Most top and even middle-level military commanders possess luxurious properties and have accumulated wealth far beyond their official salary (Muna, 2002: 7).

iv. Iwan Fals, a prominent artist and singer, wrote a famous and popular song entitled *Pak Tua*:
You, who have been old, how are you; People said you just recovered, they said you were sick; Heart, kidney, and rheumatic, little bit mad; be careful Mr. Elder, please have a rest … There is so much wind outside … You, who have generous smile, are touching your tummy; Your fatter body views the sky; The day is just about nightfall, Mr. Elder is

sleepy; Sweet wife is waiting, please have a rest ... There is so much wind outside ... Mr. Elder, enough ... you look tired o ... yeah; Mr. Elder, enough ... we are capable to work o ... yeah; Mr. Elder ... please sleep! (cited in iwanfals.wordpress.com/2006/10/25/pak-tua, translated by the author).

v. The attack correlated to internal conflict between PDI factions, specifically between the groups under Megawati's leadership versus Soerjadi's leadership. At the time, President Suharto disapproved of Megawati as a leader of PDI and preferred Soerjadi instead. Megawati who gained a growing political force was considered by government to threaten the stability of the regime. After several conflicts, a large clash between Soerjadi's and Megawati's supporters broke out in Jakarta on 27 July 1996.

vi. Among others, he appointed his daughter, Siti Hardiyati Rukmana as Minister of Social Welfare, and his close friend, Bob Hasan was appointed as Minister of Industry and Trade.

vii. As usual, the response from the regime was repression by sending troops to the streets. But this only intensified the protests. Nation-wide giant protests against Suharto's government mounted following the 'Trisakti Tragedy' on 12 May 1998, when a number of students from Trisakti University were killed in an a clash between soldiers and the students near their campus. The incident triggered massive riots and public demonstrations in Jakarta and most major cities. Day by day the situation became more out of control. On 14 May, a massive number of students and public occupied the MPR-DPR building, staying on the building site to ensure Suharto would step down. Amien Rais called the public to attend a massive public demonstration on 20 May. On that day, although in Jakarta the action was cancelled due to intimidation from the military, massive student and public demonstrations took place elsewhere, bringing Indonesia to the point of public insurrection.

viii. At this election, there were 141 political parties registered to join the political race, but eventually after verification conducted by the KPU (electoral commission), there were only 48 political parties that could meet the requirements to participate in the election.

ix. *Bulog-gate* refers to some vague transactions involving various government officials who appeared suspiciously corrupt involving the State Logistics Agency in 2000. *Brunei-gate* refers to a donation from the Sultan of Brunei for helping Indonesia encounter economic crisis, which was allegedly accepted by Gus Dur in his private capacity.

x. Under Megawati's administration, for example, Indonesia improved public election mechanisms and began carrying out direct elections for president, members of parliament, governors, as well as heads of district and city. During the Megawati's presidency the KPK (Corruption Eradication Commission), as well as other independent commissions, were formed to deal with the persistent phenomenon of corruption. She was also quite successful in improving economic conditions by stabilising the value of *Rupiah* and maintaining economic growth around 2–3% (Soesastro, 2003: 9–11).

xi. During Suharto's era, 20% of parliamentary seats were available for armed forces representatives who were appointed by the president. By this amendment, the constitution states that Indonesia is a fully democratic country.

xii. Article 20(1) of the amended constitution, for example, mentions that the DPR holds the authority to make laws, which previously rested with the president. The DPR were also entitled with various authorities, including giving consideration and approval for the appointment of ambassadors, military chief commander, and head of the Indonesian police force. In Article 20a, the DPR is given legislative, budgeting, and oversight functions.

xiii. By at least two thirds of a quorum meeting, the DPR could submit a dismissal proposal to the constitutional court if they considered the president violated the law, had been involved in criminal acts, or behaved disgracefully. Within ninety days, the court decides whether the accusation of the DPR against the president is legally acceptable. After receiving the decision of the court, the DPR submits the proposal to the MPR. The MPR will decide the proposal within thirty days. The dismissal decision should be made at a meeting attended by at least three quarters of its members and supported by a minimum of two thirds of members present.

xiv. Decentralisation aims to trim down the strong power of the central government. Article 18 of the new constitution maintains that Indonesia is firstly divided into provinces, secondly subdivided into regency, and finally subdivided into municipalities. Each of these units 'shall administer and manage their own affairs'. This process is accompanied by democratic elections for governor, district head and mayor.

xv. In Chapter Xa, especially Articles 28a–28j of the amended constitution, it is clearly expressed that all Indonesian people have an equal position before the law, have the right to work, and have freedoms to associate, to assemble, and to express opinions.

xvi. Note that previously the military (TNI) and police (POLRI) were managed under ABRI (Indonesian Armed Forces). In Chapter XII, the new constitution stipulates that defense and security affairs are separate domains. The separation, besides aiming to restrict military influence in the political arena, also aims to prevent the abuse of military forces for political and business interests.

xvii. The right to elect the president no longer lies in the hands of MPR, but in the hands of the people through direct election. Article 6a of the amended constitution mentions that the people directly elect the president with the vice-president.

xviii. The MPR is, as regulated by Chapter VIIa, now divided into two chambers: DPD (Regional Representative Council) and DPR (People Representative Council). The members of DPD represent every province, and are elected through a direct election. This is a significant step strengthening democratisation and decentralisation, because unlike old institutions in which some members were appointed by the president, all member of the MPR are now a product of a democratic process.

xix. As mentioned on Articles 23 and 33, it is stated that the creation of an independent central bank is important in order to increase national economy and stabilise the monetary value.

xx. These institutions include, for example, the Corruption Eradication Commission (KPK), the Judicial Commission (KY), the Independent Broadcasting Commission (KPI), the Commission to Audit the Wealth of State Officials (KPKPN), the Centre for Financial Transactions Reporting and Analyses (PPATK), the National Ombudsman Commission (KON), the General Election Commission (KPU), the General Election Supervisory Agency (Bapilu), the Attorney General Commission (KK), the National Police Commission (Kompolnas), the Business Competition Supervision Committee (KPPU), and the like.

xxi. Namely Law 12/2003 (revised by Law 10/2008) on general elections, Law No. 23/2003 on presidential and vice-presidential elections, and Law No. 31/2002 (revised by Law 2/2008) on Political Parties.

xxii. In 1999, there were 141 political parties that intended to participate in the election, but only 48 qualified to participate. In 2004, there were 50 political parties, 24 of them qualified. In 2009, there were 69 political parties and 34 qualified; 18 of the 34 were new political parties that for the first time follows the election.

xxiii. Since 2004, Indonesia has had a direct election for electing the president and vice-president. A party or a coalition of political parties needs to attain at least 3% of the total seats in the DPR to participate in the presidential election, or at least 5% of the total registered voters in the DPR election. Similar to the presidential election, governors, regents or mayors are also elected through direct elections.

xxiv. DPD is a new institution in the Indonesian political landscape, established to accommodate the interests of provinces in the national government. The institution has a number of mandates including submitting draft laws to the DPR in the areas of: regional autonomy; relations between central and provincial/regional governments; formation, separation, and merging of regions; management of natural resources and other economic resources; and the financial balance between centre and provincial/regional governments. The council also has rights for giving advices to the DPR concerning: the formulation of draft budget and expenditure bills; policies on taxes, education, and religion; and the selection of members of the State Audit Agency. The members of DPD are elected through multimember constituency and Single Non Transferable Votes (SNTV) where each province is considered a single electorate region. The participants are individuals, and voters have to vote for one candidate. Numbers of seat for each province are four, determined by the highest votes achieved by the candidates.

xxv. Being considered in a weak position to supervise the government, DPR was reborn as a new institution with major renovations subsequent to democratisation. As discussed previously, the amendment of the Indonesian constitution has reshaped the position and function of the DPR as a full legislative body. The institution, which in the New Order era functioned merely as a rubber stamp, now emerges with a number of new authorities and powers. There is also a significant shift in its membership form. The 550 DPR members are elected through proportional open list system on every electoral boundary that is equivalent with province or sub-province. In this system, every voter elects one party or one candidate from the party list, or both. At the provincial and district level, the members provincial and local parliaments (DPRD) are also elected through a proportional open list system, under which every voter elects one party and one candidate from the electoral party list. At the provincial level, electorate boundaries are formed as equivalent to a district or incorporation of two districts, electing about 35 to 100 parliament members, depending on the population of each province. At the district level, electoral boundaries are formed in parallel with sub-district, for electing about 20 to 45 parliament members, depending on the population of each district.

xxvi. In 1998–1999, independence movements were on the go in Aceh, Papua, Riau, and East Timor. This was followed by the occurrence of other potentially destabilizing events in 2000–2001 when inter-ethnic and inter-religious conflicts broke out under odd circumstances in the Malukus, Papua, Sulawesi, and Kalimantan. The continuing violence and threat of violence underscored the need for stability, and this became a dominant premise in formulating and implementing the decentralisation process.

xxvii. Currently, the general feature of the decentralisation situation under Law 32/2004, which is defined further by GR No. 38/2007, stipulates that regional governments hold authority over all governmental sectors, with the exception of 7 sectors that remain the authority of the centre government: foreign policy; defense; security; judiciary; monetary and fiscal policy; religion; and 'other roles' including policy on macro national development planning and monitoring, fiscal distribution, state administrative system, national economic institutions, human resources, exploration of resources, strategic technology, conservation, and national standardization.

xxviii. In 2008, a scandal involving the team leader of prosecutors probe for BLBI, Urip Tri Gunawan, was revealed by the KPK after his conversation via telephone was tapped. Urip was caught red handed for receiving a bribe of US$60,000 from Artalyta Suryani known as an accomplice of conglomerate Syamsul Nursalim. Following a series of investigations, it was suspected that some senior officials of AGO had been involved in the conspiracy. They included the Deputy Attorney General on Special Crime, Kemas Yahya Rahman, and Deputy Attorney General from the state and civil administration, Untung Udji Santoso (*Kompas*, 15/06/2008; *Suara Merdeka*, 27/09/2008).

xxix. This is not surprising. Despite democratisation, the salaries of civil servants in Indonesia remain low. In a comparative research of bureaucratic corruption in Southeast ASEAN countries, Palmier (1985: 271–272) has identified that low salaries of civil servant as one of the important grounds of, corruption, along with opportunities (which depended on the extent of involvement of civil servants in the administration or control of lucrative activities) and policing (the probability of detection and punishment).

xxx. The WCY was first publicized by the International Institute for Management Development (IMD) in 1989 and has been cited as a respected global reference for ranking and analyzing the competitiveness of industrialized and emerging countries utilizing four factors: Economic Performance, Government Efficiency, Business Efficiency, and Infrastructure.

xxxi. For instance, in the first semester of 2005, BPK discovered that there was a total of Rp4.3 trillion of the budget missing. The number rose in the second semester up to Rp7.8 trillion. In 2006, the trend continued to reach Rp7.9 trillion in the first semester and Rp14.6 trillion in the second semester. In 2007, BPK found 36,009 cases of financial abuse with a sum of potential loss of Rp6,692 trillion in two semesters.

xxxii. Similar to the authoritarian era, State Owned Enterprises (SOEs) in Indonesia are still noted for being an important source of corruption. Owing to the practice of being money machines for the bureaucracy and ruling parties, only a few Indonesian SOEs can be deemed healthy. SOEs generally are subordinated under technical departments and controlled by politicians. Not surprisingly, recruitment is rarely based on ability but often on political lobbying (*Asia Times*, 25/01/2006).

xxxiii. In March, KPK arrested Saleh Djasit (member from Golkar Party) related the case of fire extinguishers procurement when he was serving as Governor of Riau. A month later, KPK also arrested Al-Amin Nur Nasution (member from United Development Party) on allegation of bribery cases in the process of diversion of forest function in Bintan district. A week after the arrest Al-Amin, KPK arrested Hamka Yandhu (Golkar Party) and Anthoni Zeidra Abidin (Golkar Party), who were held concerning the flow of bribery funds from Bank Indonesia. Then KPK arrested Sarjan Tahir (Democratic Party) in May related to the case of diversion of the functions mangrove forests in Banyuasin, South Sumatra. Finally, KPK also arrested Bulyan Royan (Reform Star Party), at the end of June. Bulyan got caught red-handed when he was receiving US$66,000 and €5,500 suspected as bribery from a company that won a patrol boat procurement bidding at the Department of Transportation. He allegedly helped the company to win the tender in the Directorate General of Sea Transportation at the Transportation Ministry earlier this year when he was a member of Commission V DPR for transportation. Disclosure of cases that further exacerbate the face of the DPR does not appear to stop here.

xxxiv. For example at the end of July 2008, KPK arrested Hamka Yandhu for an accusation of receiving bribes from the Bank Indonesia as a kickback for appointing the Bank's board of directors. He then testified that 52 members of the House Commission IX period of 1999–2004, including people who later became ministers like Paskah Suzetta (later became the Minister of National Development and head of Bappenas) and MS Kaban (became the Minister of Forestry), were involved in the scandal.

xxxv. Many surveys on the topics of public service in Indonesia post-democratisation including, for example, Asfar (2001); Ardiyanto (2002); Afadlal (2003); Dwiyanto (2005); and DRSP (2006; 2008) generally point out that all areas of public service delivery such as health services, official documents, mortgages registration, water service, telephone and electricity services, and exit permits are tainted with corruption practices.

xxxvi. Unclear regulations in particular have been blamed for the anarchic process of decentralisation. Since 1999 numerous laws and regulations have been formulated. However, the provision of legal drafting has on the whole not been satisfactory. The description of roles and responsibilities, planning and management, and coordination among institutions vertically and horizontally has not been clear and has frequently created confusion. The decentralisation regulations contain a significant number of complications, including: imprecise language, and inconsistent definitions; contradictions between legal instruments (including with the constitution), and use of lower-level legislation to 'correct' perceived problems in higher legislation; stipulations that fail to regulate; repetition of rather than simple reference to other legislations; too large a reliance on follow-up regulations on key issues; late preparation of implementing regulations; and use of elucidation section to introduce concepts or to regulate (DRSP, 2006: 8). Not surprisingly, this poor legal framework has created ambiguities and led to widespread opportunity for corruption.

xxxvii. In Russia and Eastern European countries, for example, some research reveals that neo-patrimonial practices survive within the framework of a democracy, and the old systems of patron–client relationships have re-invented themselves during democratic transition (see Lynch 2005; Moran 2001). In these countries, democratisation is marked by the difficulty of removing pre-transition elites who continue to exercise significant influence over political and economic power, and resist any reform initiative directed to deprive their privileges (Kryshtanovskaya and White, 2003: 200–222; Hankiss, 2002: 243–259).

xxxviii. Such a situation also takes place in some transitional countries (see for example Rose, 1998; Chadwick, 2006).

xxxix. For example, a survey on the capacity of DPRD members for the period of 1999–2004 conducted in several districts of East Java reveals that as many as 53.3% of the members could not mention five public issues in their district. At the same time, their reason to attain the job was driven by economic motivation to obtain a salary rather than a political motive to represent the people's interest (Kurniawan andd Puspitosari, 2006).

Part 3

Conclusion and Policy Implications

Chapter 12

Conclusion: Good Governance and Sustainable Development

M. A. B. Siddique and R. N. Ghosh

I

Readers of this volume will have noticed that it is divided into three Parts: Part 1 deals with general and theoretical topics, with a bearing on the main theme of the book, viz. "Crime, Corruption and Economic Development"; Part 2 deals with specific case studies, with the primary focus on three countries, viz. Indonesia, India and Bangladesh. Part 3 relates to the present concluding section, in which the two editors try to sum up the contributions of the authors in this volume.

As was stated earlier, the papers included in the volume were previously presented in two international conferences, one held in Perth, Western Australia, in June, 2009, and then, in a follow-up conference, held in India (Kolkata) in December, 2009. The two conferences included papers from a wide range of areas by people with different types of skills and expertise: academics, senior government officials and senior officials from the Police in India. The selected papers included in this volume look at corruption, not only from different angles but also from the varying perspectives of different countries and cultures.

II

After the introductory comments (Chapter 1) made by the two editors, they get involved in Chapter 2 to discuss the meaning of corruption and its various quantitative as well as qualitative measurements which are currently available in the literature. Robin Ghosh and Abu Siddique seek to explain why the current UNDP definition of corruption fails to be inclusive of the various shades of corruption. Limitations include that it only provides a qualitative measure and fails to provide a quantitative measure. Moreover, it does not provide a distinction between "grand" and "petty" corruption. "Petty" corruption is a way of life in many developing countries and has been in existence for centuries. Furthermore, in contrast to the UNDP definition, it is argued that corruption does not have to be associated with "public power, office or authority". The paper then goes on to discuss various quantitative measures of corruption. This paper sparked lively discussions in the Conference. Andrew Williams, an author of another paper included in this volume, raised a very valid issue of the composition of these indices and how their use may lead to fallacious research outcomes. This then led to a lively discussion of the paucity of data in the study of corruption, and the non-standard reporting practices.

In a very interesting paper (Chapter 3), Andrew Williams, discusses how the absence of willingness (or otherwise) of governments to release information of economic and social data can be used as an indicator for the degree of political and institutional transparency. In light of this, Andrew Williams discusses an index (which he has himself developed) that has extensive coverage of countries as well as time and is based on the quantity of reported socio-economic data contained in the World Development Indicators and the International Finance Statistics databases. Using this index, Andrew Williams discusses several case studies that highlight the importance of transparency in economic development.

A final chapter in Part 1, is the paper contributed by Dora Marinova, Vladislav Todorov and Amzad Hossain. In Chapter 4, the three authors ask the question, what is meant by good governance? They argue that in the West, good governance is treated as synonymous with secular democracy. However, they go on to argue that a long-term sustainable development cannot take place without regard to our environment.

Moreover, a country needs to tap the latent spirituality and morality of the people to promote good governance. Finally, the authors note that the present system of Western democracy is far removed from the people's will and should be more 'deliberative' than it is.

III

Part 2 of this volume deals with specific case studies to examine whether, if a region, or a country falls into the trap of crime and corruption, it would face stagnation or decline in its economy.

In a very interesting paper (Chapter 5), Derek Aldcroft examines the extent of corruption in one of the poorest economic performers in the world — the African Continent, especially sub-Saharan Africa. Despite the high hopes of the post-colonization period, many African countries failed to achieve any significant economic growth; and by the end of the 20th century, per capita real incomes had not improved, and in some cases had actually worsened. It is now generally agreed that the main reason for this failure lies in the inability of many African countries to efficiently manage their resources, including manpower; in other words, lack of good governance. The consequences of economic stagnation and decline were extreme, with two-thirds of the population in many African countries living at subsistence or below the absolute poverty line by the turn of the last century. The paper focuses on Africa's weakness in political systems, bureaucracies, administrative organizations and property and legal rights. It is argued that the majority of African counties have failed to achieve economic growth and development because of a deficiency in the social and political structures of these countries.

Abu Siddique's paper "Corruption in Bangladesh: Review and analysis" (Chapter 6) examines the concept and various quantitative measures of corruption. Corruption is understood by the majority to be harmful to a country although the reason why it is, is rarely understood. For this reason, economists have endeavored to determine the causes and consequences of corruption. In light of this, the paper goes into a deeper analysis of the magnitude of corruption in Bangladesh and looks at the effectiveness of the anti-corruption agencies within the country. The paper describes the causes of corruption, with particular emphasis on banking, customs and telecommunications sectors. The consequences of corruption on economic growth are then discussed. Possible remedies for corruption for Bangladesh are also suggested in the paper.

In his provocative paper (Chapter 7), Gautam Chakrabarti, who was then (2009) the Commissioner of Police in Kolkata, discusses the widespread levels of corruption in India since WWII. Pre-WWII corruption in India was generally confined to a limited number of government departments, but with large sums of money being spent during WWII, corruption rapidly spread to all sectors. During the 1960s the Government of India set up anti-corruption agencies, however as the then Commissioner of Police in Kolkata argues that there is a large gap between policy and practice in India. Despite experiencing rapid economic growth in more recent years, India's ranking remains low in the Global Corruption Index. Recently, the Government of India has put in further measures, including the RTI Act 2005 and the WHISTLEBLOWER Resolution. Several recent reports conducted by the government suggest that there are regional variations in the level and impact of corruption. In his paper, Gautam Chakrabarti investigates these variations.

Surajit Kar Purkayastha, presently Commissioner of Police in Kolkata, has contributed the paper in Chapter 8. He attempts to examine the extent of criminal activities in India in the context of the economic progress of the country. Surajit Kar Purkayastha conducts a sample survey with 30 specific questions that relate to corruption. The questionnaire survey covered a cross-section of people. This paper presents and analyses the data obtained from the survey. In particular, the author finds that there seems to be no disagreement among the public about their perception of the role of politicians, about the accountability of the richer sections of the society, and about the inadequate implementation of existing anti-corruption laws, along with an overwhelming concern over the state of corruption in the country. The author uses the survey results along with the study of the Corruption Perception Index to reach conclusions on the extent of corruption within India.

Rimawan Pradiptyo's paper "A Certain Uncertainty: An Assessment of Court Decisions in Tackling Corruption in Indonesia" appears as Chapter 9. In this brilliant and original paper, Pradiptyo assesses court decisions made on cases of corruption in Indonesia. In 1999, the

Anti-Corruption Bill was ratified in Indonesia, and then it was modified in 2001. Rimawan argues that despite a clear legislative guidance on the extent of punishments to be given for each type of corruption, the sentences handed by the judiciary in Indonesia are inconsistent with legislation. Using a regression analysis he finds that the harshness of sentences in Indonesia depends on the occupation of offenders. It is also found that there is a discrepancy in the level of economic losses caused by corruption (US$21.2 billion) and the total financial punishment imposed by courts (US$2.6 billion). The data in Pradiptyo's paper confirms that most incidents of corruption are committed by people earning a medium to high income. The author argues that the total burden of financial punishment should be sufficient to compensate for the social costs of corruption.

In another major paper, dealing with Indonesia (Chapter 10), Budi Setiyono describes the inconsistency between the smooth democratization process, following the end of the authoritarian regime and the extent of corruption within Indonesia. He points to the fact that since the democratization process began, Indonesia's Corruption Perception Index has not improved significantly. As a result of widespread corruption in public offices the quality of public services has become extremely poor in Indonesia. Budi Setiyono, then, goes on to describe the large number of inconsistencies that the State Auditing Agency finds in almost every government office. The paper attempts to explain why reform in a newly emerging democratic country like Indonesia is not enough to decrease the level of corruption. Setinyono argues that when Suharto was removed from office on charges of corruption there were still left hundreds of little Suhartos in Indonesia.

In the final chapter in Part 2 (Chapter 11), Amzad Hossain and Dora Marinova observe the rising degradation of natural resources, water crises, widening gap between the rich and the poor, corruption, crimes and gender issues due to mal-governance in Bangladesh. The paper looks at the need for governance within the cultural and human context of the country to address these unstable situations. The two authors outline several aspects which they believe if improved, can help progress Bangladesh towards achieving better governance in terms of socio-economic and environmental systems. The paper suggests that if the Bangladeshis look to their cultural values the country, they can perhaps achieve good governance. Conference delegates were impressed by the very Confucian ideas offered by the authors of the paper's and agreed that perhaps the best way to eradicate some types of corruption is to return to strict Confucian moral values.

IV

Careful readers will notice that the different papers contained in this volume look at the concepts of crime, corruption and economic growth with differing perspectives. Whether crime and corruption would retard economic growth is an open question. One of the factors that would be apparent is that every individual incident of corruption, whether 'petty' or 'grand', is unique in its nature, despite broad similarities with other incidents. Hence a general policy of anti-corruption that would work universally, is unlikely to be formulated in practice. Each country (and every region) has to work out if a certain type of anti-corruption policy has any relevance to it. What is good for India may not be good for Bangladesh and Indonesia. Even within the same country, it is possible that a single anti-corruption policy might fail to achieve its objectives.

However, in a final analysis, good governance involving an efficient and transparent use and management of resources, together with an honest bureaucracy, would be the only solution to the twin problems of crime and corruption. Such objective may not be achieved through legislation. However, all countries should set up a long-term goal to achieve good governance by way of a transparent and efficient management of the economy and environment. Paradoxically, while it is possible that crime and corruption of a wide ranging nature could inhibit economic development, it might be argued that economic development would itself ensure good governance over a very long-term.

Index

Printed in the United States
By Bookmasters